Instrumental Music Education

ALSO AVAILABLE FROM BLOOMSBURY

Activating Diverse Musical Creativities, edited by Pamela Burnard and Elizabeth Haddon

Narratives of Academics' Personal Journeys in Contested Spaces, edited by Namrata Rao, Anesa Hosein and Ian M. Kinchin

The Racialized Nature of Academic Language, edited by Sultan Turkan and Jamie L. Schissel

Instrumental Music Education

Developing Pedagogies as Instrumental Teachers

**Edited by
Elizabeth Haddon**

BLOOMSBURY ACADEMIC
LONDON • NEW YORK • OXFORD • NEW DELHI • SYDNEY

BLOOMSBURY ACADEMIC

Bloomsbury Publishing Plc, 50 Bedford Square, London, WC1B 3DP, UK
Bloomsbury Publishing Inc, 1359 Broadway, New York, NY 10018, USA
Bloomsbury Publishing Ireland, 29 Earlsfort Terrace, Dublin 2, D02 AY28, Ireland

BLOOMSBURY, BLOOMSBURY ACADEMIC and the Diana logo are trademarks of
Bloomsbury Publishing Plc

First published in Great Britain 2026

Copyright © Elizabeth Haddon, 2026

Elizabeth Haddon and contributors have asserted their right under the Copyright, Designs and
Patents Act, 1988, to be identified as Authors of this work.

For legal purposes the Acknowledgements on p. xvii constitute an extension of this copyright page.

Cover design by Paul Smith
Cover image © alexaldo via Getty Images

This work is published open access subject to a Creative Commons Attribution-NonCommercial-
NoDerivatives 4.0 International licence (CC BY-NC-ND 4.0, https://creativecommons.org/licen
ses/by-nc-nd/4.0/). You may re-use, distribute, and reproduce this work in any medium for non-
commercial purposes, provided you give attribution to the copyright holder and the publisher and
provide a link to the Creative Commons licence.

Bloomsbury Publishing Plc does not have any control over, or responsibility for, any third-party
websites referred to or in this book. All internet addresses given in this book were correct at the
time of going to press. The author and publisher regret any inconvenience caused if addresses
have changed or sites have ceased to exist, but can accept no responsibility for any such changes.

A catalogue record for this book is available from the British Library.

Library of Congress Cataloging-in-Publication Data
Names: Haddon, Elizabeth, 1966– editor
Title: Instrumental music education : developing pedagogies as instrumentalteachers /
edited by Elizabeth Haddon.
Description: [1.]. | London ; New York, NY : Bloomsbury Academic, 2025. |
Includes bibliographical references and index.
Identifiers: LCCN 2025011436 (print) | LCCN 2025011437 (ebook) |
ISBN 9781350408906 hardback | ISBN 9781350408890 paperback |
ISBN 9781350408920 epub | ISBN 9781350408913 pdf
Subjects: LCSH: Instrumental music–Instruction and study | Music–Instruction and study–
Psychological aspects | Music–Instruction and study–Social aspects
Classification: LCC MT170 .I57 2025 (print) | LCC MT170 (ebook) |
DDC 784.071–dc23/eng/20250506
LC record available at https://lccn.loc.gov/2025011436
LC ebook record available at https://lccn.loc.gov/2025011437

ISBN: HB: 978-1-3504-0890-6
PB: 978-1-3504-0889-0
ePDF: 978-1-3504-0891-3
eBook: 978-1-3504-0892-0

Typeset by Newgen KnowledgeWorks Pvt. Ltd., Chennai, India
Printed and bound in Great Britain

For product safety related questions contact productsafety@bloomsbury.com.

To find out more about our authors and books visit www.bloomsbury.com
and sign up for our newsletters.

Contents

List of Figure ix
List of Tables x
List of Contributors xi
Acknowledgements xvii

Introduction Elizabeth Haddon 1

Part I Philosophies and Personas

1 **'Unseen Influences': The Effects of Philosophy and Biases on Approaches to Instrumental Teaching** *Naomi Norton, Richard Powell, James Poole, Federico Pendenza and Sara Norouzi Iranzad* 13

2 **Considering the Effects of the Instrumental Teacher's Personality and Persona on Student–Teacher Relationships** *Marianna Cortesi, Nasim Ansari, Rosemary Lynch, Richard Powell and Jennifer Cohen* 25

3 **Teacher–Performer? Performer–Teacher? How Musical Identity Shapes Teaching and Learning in and Beyond the Lesson** *Caroline Owen and Edwina Smith* 37

Part II Contexts, Roles and Relationships

4 **Avenues for Pedagogical Training in Music Education in China and the UK: Aims, Availability and Implications** *Anca Eskandar and Xinpei Zheng* 51

5 **Cultivating Collaborative Relationships and Positive Working Environments between Instrumental Teachers and School Staff** *Rosemary Lynch and Pete Dale* 65

6 **A Shared Approach? Peripatetic and Classroom Music Teachers' Perspectives on Pedagogy and Professional Relationships** *Hannah Ellis, Caroline Owen, James Poole and Pete Dale* 77

7 **Developing Instrumental Teaching Cross-Culturally: International Preservice Teachers' Pedagogical Understanding with Consideration of Cultural Intelligence** *Xinpei Zheng and Hang Li* 91

8 **Navigating Apprenticeship to Mentorship across Cultures: Adaptive Insights from Chinese Masters Students Working as Instrumental Teachers in China and the UK** *Xin Liu and Elizabeth Haddon* 105

9 **Understanding Subject-Specific Language Challenges for Music Learners with English as an Additional Language (EAL): What Are the Impacts and How Can Teachers Provide Support?** *Hang Li and Xinpei Zheng* 119

Part III Skills-Building

10 **Improvisation: Developing Skills and Confidence as Teachers and Learners** *Alexis Cairns, Nina Kümin and Helen Madden* 135

11 **Music Theory in the Instrumental Music Lesson: Built In or Bolted On?** *Owen Burton and Anca Eskandar* 149

12 **Embodiment in Music Learning and Teaching** *Jennifer Cohen, Caroline Owen, Edwina Smith, Xin Liu and Rosemary Lynch* 163

13 **Hurdles Not Brick Walls: Supporting Students to Overcome Physical and Mental Barriers to Instrumental Practice** *Rosemary Lynch, Marianna Cortesi, Jennifer Cohen and Sara Norouzi Iranzad* 175

Part IV Inclusivity, Support and Resources

14 **Specific Learning Needs: An Exploration of Inclusive and Accessible Approaches** *Kristl Kirk, Bella Powell, Rosemary Lynch, Jennifer Cohen and Pete Dale* 191

15 **Working with Transfer Students: Teachers' Experiences of 'Bridging the Gap'** *Edwina Smith, Polly Sharpe, Elizabeth Haddon and Eleni Perisynaki* 205

16 **Examining a Tradition: Teachers' Views on the Content, Accessibility and Use of Graded Performance Examinations** *Caroline Owen, Rosemary Lynch, Kristl Kirk and Helen Madden* 217

17 **The Language of Tuition Books** *Richard Powell, Elizabeth Haddon, Polly Sharpe, Federico Pendenza and Sara Norouzi Iranzad* 231

18 **Teachers as Creators of Educational Materials for Music Learners** *Federico Pendenza, Elizabeth Haddon, Helen Madden and Marianna Cortesi* 243

19 **Resilience, Autonomy and Well-being in Instrumental Teaching and Learning** *Penny Talbot, Edwina Smith, Rosemary Lynch, Bella Powell and Jennifer Cohen* 255

Index 269

Figure

11.1 *Fun Fair Blues* by Naomi Yandell 156

Tables

9.1 Examples of Translation of Western Musical Terms in Chinese 121
9.2 Key Questions in 'Describing What You Hear' 125

Contributors

Nasim Ansari has been playing the violin since childhood. After high school, she graduated with a BA in music from BIHE (Bahá'í Institute for Higher Education). A desire to learn more about being an effective teacher led her to the UK, where she completed the MA Music Education: Instrumental and Vocal Teaching at the University of York. Nasim has been teaching the violin for eighteen years and delivering aural training for ten years in Iran, and her passion is teaching young people.

Owen Burton gained his PhD in musicology at the University of York, UK, where he then joined the staff as an associate lecturer in 2021, teaching music history and music education. His research interests relate to music theory in education, music analysis and Nordic music. Owen's wider projects have included conducting the Bangor University Community Orchestra, writing performance notes for Trinity College London, as well as producing concert programme notes. He has also led music workshops in primary schools and given public lectures on music as part of the Leeds International Piano Competition. He is an active private instrumental teacher.

Alexis Cairns is a jazz saxophonist, woodwind tutor and postgraduate researcher from Newcastle upon Tyne, UK. She achieved a BA (Hons) in Jazz Studies from Leeds College of Music (now Leeds Conservatoire) in 2006 and an MA in Music Education: Instrumental and Vocal Teaching from the University of York, UK, in 2020. Her PhD research at the University of York focuses on approaches and strategies for teaching jazz improvisation to beginner jazz pupils in the instrumental lesson setting, specifically one-to-one.

Jennifer Cohen is Lecturer in Music Education at the University of York, UK. Active as a professional flautist, one-to-one music teacher, workshop leader and community music project manager, she is particularly interested in the interplay between practice and research. Her specialist areas include embodied music cognition, music and deafness and historically informed performance.

Marianna Cortesi is Associate Lecturer in Music at the University of York, UK. After a BA (Hons) in Piano Performance from the Conservatorio G. B. Martini in Bologna, Italy, she moved to York in 2017 to complete an MA in Music Education: Instrumental and Vocal Teaching, followed by a PhD on 'Constructions and Perceptions of

Competition in a UK Higher Music Education Institution'. As a researcher, Marianna is involved in two collaborative projects at the University of York exploring the relationship between artistic opportunities and well-being awareness, and the experiences of music facilitators leading workshops for refugee communities.

Pete Dale is Lecturer in Music Education at the University of York, UK. He has researched DJ decks in music education for many years and was formerly a head of music in an inner-city secondary school (2003–12). His monographs include *Engaging Students with Music Education: DJ Decks, Urban Music and Child-Centred Learning* (2017). Pete has previously lectured at Manchester Metropolitan University (2013–21) and Oxford Brookes (2012–13). He was PI for the AHRC-funded network CUMIN (Contemporary Urban Music for Inclusion Network) 2022–3 and co-editor of *Inclusion and Healing in Schools and Beyond: Hip Hop, Techno, Grime, and More* (2023).

Hannah Ellis completed her undergraduate degree (music), master's degree (English Church Music) and PhD (investigating the relationship between sacred music and the political landscape during early-seventeenth-century England) at the University of York, UK. During her PhD, Hannah began teaching on the MA Music Education: Instrumental and Vocal Teaching at the University of York and developed a passion for this research field. Hannah is currently an associate lecturer at the University of York and a full-time secondary school music teacher at Northampton School with research interests focusing on the accessibility of music education and the relationships between music teachers within schools.

Anca Eskandar holds bachelor's and master's degrees in music performance and is an experienced music educator with a background of teaching in multiple settings including one-to-one and group instrumental music, music theory and classroom music in Romania, the UAE and the UK. Anca is currently undertaking a PhD in music education at the University of York, UK, where she is a Graduate Teaching Assistant. She is invested in researching aspects of instrumental music and music theory pedagogy and training for instrumental teachers, while also preparing students for ABRSM flute, piano and music theory examinations.

Elizabeth Haddon is Emeritus Reader, School of Arts and Creative Technologies, University of York, UK. She is the author of *Making Music in Britain: Interviews with Those Behind the Notes* (2006) and co-editor with Pamela Burnard of *Activating Diverse Musical Creativities: Teaching and Learning in Higher Music Education* (2015) and *Creative Teaching for Creative Learning in Higher Music Education* (2016). She created and led the MA Music Education: Instrumental and Vocal Teaching at the University of York, and continues to be active as a researcher, educator and consultant.

Kristl Kirk is a piano teacher and member of the British Dyslexia Association music committee. After completing the MA Music Education: Instrumental and Vocal

Teaching at the University of York, UK, her PhD research focused on improving and enhancing music education for students with dyslexia by utilizing a strengths-focused and individualized approach to facilitate students' resilience.

Nina Kümin is a researcher, performer and teacher of historical musical improvisation. After completing her PhD in music performance at the University of York (2023) she held the role of Humanities Research Centre Postdoctoral Research Fellow at the University of York, UK (2023–4). Her research interests focus on improvisation practice and pedagogy, baroque music and the violin. She performs professionally as a solo and orchestral, baroque and modern violinist and works as a youth ensemble director, whole class ensemble tutor, peripatetic music teacher and curriculum music teacher for several primary schools and organizations in York.

Hang Li completed her PhD at the School of Creative Arts and Technologies at the University of York, UK, studying with Dr Elizabeth Haddon. Her research focuses on the language challenges faced by Chinese MA music education students and the targeted support provision from the host programme. With a background and a keen interest in music education and English language teaching, Hang aims to bridge the research gaps of non-native students' language needs in their English-based music education programmes and contribute to the knowledge of support provision in response to the increasingly linguistically diverse music classrooms.

Xin Liu holds a PhD in Music Education from the University of York, supervised by Dr Elizabeth Haddon, and a master's in Music Education: Instrumental and Vocal Teaching from the same institution (2018–19). Her research explores the adaptation of intercultural pedagogies in instrumental teaching. During her doctoral studies, she worked as a graduate teaching assistant and presented at several UK conferences. Alongside her academic work, Xin draws on intercultural experience in her piano teaching, using research-informed approaches to foster an open-minded, individualized, and creative learning environment.

Rosemary Lynch is an oboist, woodwind teacher and PhD student at the University of York, UK. Teaching instrumental lessons in schools and privately, her students range in age from five years to more than eighty years and include those from disadvantaged backgrounds and students with learning disabilities. She performs regularly with university ensembles, local orchestras and musical theatre groups. Propelled by a lifelong fascination with how dominant narratives evolve in musical and social settings, her interdisciplinary PhD project explores oboistic discourse from 1695 to the present day. Rosemary lives in York with her husband, four children and a very opinionated Miniature Schnauzer.

Helen Madden is a lecturer, composer, performer and examiner with a background in jazz improvisation and specialization in saxophone. She has composed exam music for all major UK examination boards and her PhD at the University of York, UK focused on composing large-scale works with educational and community groups. Helen serves as a strategy board member for Barnsley Music Hub and is a member of the Barnsley Youth Choir music team. She is also a director of the community interest company Friends of the Future, which aims to develop collaborative solutions to contemporary social issues, particularly in arts and health.

Sara Norouzi Iranzad was born in Tehran. She holds a Bachelor of Arts in Music from the Bahá'í Institute for Higher Education (BIHE) and a Master of Arts in Music Education: Instrumental and Vocal Teaching from the University of York. In 2010, alongside her husband Erfan Vejdani, she co-founded a music academy (piano school) in Karaj, which focuses exclusively on piano tuition, including music theory and musicianship; this is the subject of a co-authored chapter with Elizabeth Haddon in the forthcoming *Oxford Handbook of Piano Pedagogy*. Currently, she teaches piano and the history of Western Music.

Naomi Norton has a varied portfolio that includes education, research and consultancy. Her primary employment is with the School of Arts and Creative Technologies at the University of York, UK, where she works as Lecturer in Music Education and Musicians' Health and Well-being Coordinator. Naomi is Chair of the ISME Musicians' Health and Wellbeing Special Interest Group (2024–30) and is passionate about enabling musicians to overcome barriers relating to health and well-being and achieve their desired level of proficiency.

Caroline Owen is a clarinettist, teacher, music performance examiner and researcher. She completed undergraduate degrees and performance training in Manchester and Paris and an MA in Music Psychology at the University of York, where her PhD focuses on children's perspectives of their lived experiences with music. Her career has involved teaching woodwind instruments, piano, theory and composition; conducting, examining and educational leadership roles; composition and arranging, freelance performing as a clarinettist and educational concerts as a member of Chamberhouse Winds. Caroline's research interests centre around the biocultural evolution of musicality – the capacity for engaging with, making and appreciating music.

Federico Pendenza AFHEA is Associate Lecturer in Music at the School of Arts and Creative Technologies at the University of York, UK. Holding a BA and MA in Classical Guitar Performance and an MA and PhD in Music Education from the University of York, he combines his expertise as a performer and teacher to understand the intersections of music, well-being, pedagogy and community.

Eleni Perisynaki is a pianist and educator. Following her Degree in Education (BA) and a Conservatoire Diploma in Piano Performance, she studied for an MA and PhD in Music Education (University of York, UK), funded by the Onassis Public Benefit Foundation. Her research interests include music pedagogy, early years and special educational needs and sight-reading. Eleni enjoys creating educational material: she has co-authored the book series *Learning Music* and created the initial two books of a piano sight-reading series, the first to be developed in Greek. She is also an active piano performer with a particular interest in contemporary music.

James Poole is an instrumental teacher with experience in delivering whole-class, small-group and one-to-one music lessons. He is also a PhD student at the University of York, UK, where he is investigating the use of dialogic teaching within instrumental lessons. His research explores the efficacy of dialogic teaching and how teachers might develop their use of this approach. He graduated from the University of York's MA Music Education: Instrumental and Vocal Teaching programme in 2022, and his dissertation (an original research project investigating perceptions of dialogic teaching) was published in *Frontiers in Education* in 2023.

Bella Powell is an associate lecturer in the Department of Music at the University of York, UK, where she teaches in the areas of Music Education and Music and Gender. Her PhD at the University of York (supported by a Sir Jack Lyons Research Scholarship) investigated the informal social prohibition on women violinists in England during the eighteenth and early to mid-nineteenth centuries. Alongside this, Bella has a busy instrumental teaching practice, teaching students of all ages and standards.

Richard Powell is Head of Music at the University of York, UK, where he teaches and researches across areas including music education, musicology and music analysis. After four years leading the MA Music Education: Instrumental and Vocal Teaching (2021–5) he continues to promote and develop the student experience in his new role. Much of his academic writing has focused on the experience of musical time, particularly in relation to contemporary music. In addition to working privately as a violin teacher, and as a freelance performer, he also regularly produces concert programme notes for ensembles and organizations around the UK.

Polly Sharpe read music at Exeter College, Oxford, and completed postgraduate study at the Royal Northern College of Music, Manchester. She is an experienced piano teacher, music examiner for ABRSM (Associated Board of the Royal Schools of Music), piano accompanist and coach. She helped establish a music teachers' group in Cornwall through the ISM (Independent Society of Musicians) to enable members to share teaching ideas and has worked as an associate lecturer on the University of York's MA in Music Education: Instrumental and Vocal Teaching.

Edwina Smith is a member of the staff team delivering the MA Music Education: Instrumental and Vocal Teaching at the University of York, UK. She also performs on modern and historical flutes in a wide range of professional ensembles and has taught these instruments at the University of York since 1997. Edwina has over forty years of flute teaching experience and has a particular interest in facilitating a positive transfer to instrumental lessons at the university level.

Penny Talbot has been a private piano teacher for many years. She has a special interest in musicians' health and well-being and through her work as a student in the MA Music Education: Instrumental and Vocal Teaching at the University of York, UK, she was able to research and enhance her knowledge in these areas. Of particular interest has been the application of mindfulness and relaxation techniques to her teaching and encouraging her students to adopt these practices. Penny is an active member of teaching networks and professional bodies.

Xinpei Zheng is a guzheng teacher and completed her PhD at the University of York, UK, supervised by Dr Elizabeth Haddon. Her research focuses on teachers and learners of traditional Chinese instruments, as well as instrumental pedagogy and practices across cultures. Xinpei has a published article in the *Asia-Pacific Journal for Arts Education* (2023) and has presented peer-reviewed papers at international conferences in the UK, China, Turkey, Germany and Finland, including ISME 2024. She holds the ASFHEA qualification, reflecting her role as a Graduate Teaching Assistant in the MA Music Education programmes at the University of York since 2021.

Acknowledgements

The editor and authors are extremely grateful to the University of York for funding open access for this volume. We would also like to thank the team at Bloomsbury, including Alison Baker, for her original interest in the proposal, Elissa Burns, Ben Piggott and Chloe Marchant as well as the production team and Paul Smith for the cover design – your support has been invaluable. Thanks also to Trinity College London Press for permission to reprint Naomi Yandell's *Fun Fair Blues* in Chapter 11.

Sincere thanks to all within the Music Education community at the University of York – our past and current students and departmental and faculty colleagues who have supported and encouraged our work. In particular, thanks to Richard Powell, Naomi Norton and Caroline Waddington-Jones for supporting the editor's early ideas concerning the creation of this project and to Rachel Cowgill, Martin Suckling and Tom Cantrell for their ongoing enthusiasm and support. We are grateful to Andrea Schiavio for insightful comments on drafts of Chapter 12 and to Caroline Owen for bringing this chapter to conclusion when the early arrival of baby Samuel necessitated Jennifer Cohen's focus on motherhood. Further thanks to authors Caroline Owen and Rosemary Lynch for their enthusiastic work and support across multiple chapters of the book and to Edwina Smith, whose attentiveness to detail and passion for the material have been a constant source of energy and support.

During the writing of these chapters the author teams have experienced many life challenges, of which the most exciting have been the births of our 'music education babies': Esmay, Thea, Ada, Francis, Lara, Samuel and Aidan – you've brought new dimensions to our understanding of music education, and congratulations to your parents for remaining involved in this book despite the challenges of parenthood! Finally, thanks to our families and friends for their ongoing support.

Elizabeth Haddon

Introduction

Elizabeth Haddon

This volume is the creation of a team of contributors, all of whom are working as instrumental or vocal teachers within the UK or other countries and who also hold roles as educators in the contexts of higher music education, school and early years education; some are also PhD researchers, others hold academic positions in the UK and elsewhere. Performing, examining, composing, workshop leading and administrative roles also comprise our portfolio work as musicians. This volume explores issues arising from our instrumental and vocal teaching practice that have global relevance to educators working in diverse contexts. In the following chapters, we investigate dimensions of interaction operating within the areas of instrumental pedagogy (wherever this term is used throughout this book, it includes vocal pedagogy where appropriate), specifically concerning questions stemming from particular challenges or critical incidents, which may relate to educational contexts, cultures, resources and teaching experience. Through this process, we legitimize the concerns of teachers, offering research-informed critical reflection on situations encountered by the collaborating authors that have been challenging, thought-provoking and have necessitated reappraisal of practice, philosophy and purpose.

We invite our readers to find commonalities between considerations of pedagogy and to reflect on these in comparison with pedagogical contexts specific and personal to them. Supporting the empowerment of teachers and their ongoing professional and personal development, we situate our reflective engagement with our practices collaboratively, as teams of co-authors; this provides a unique and transformative perspective. This collaborative process has been made possible through the stimulating involvement of members of the Music Education Forum (MEF) at the University of York, UK, who form the author teams for the chapters in this volume.

Working as an instrumental teacher can often be lonely and challenging, whether operating as a private studio teacher or even within an institution (Burwell, Carey and Bennett 2019). In line with provision for professional development in other countries, the availability of training for instrumental teachers in the UK was for many years almost non-existent, limited to occasional short sessions offered by music examination boards such as the Associated Board of the Royal Schools of Music (ABRSM), with attendance likely to be hampered by accessibility issues, location, relevance, concerns of legitimacy and potentially negative financial implications – factors identified by Conway and Zerman (2004) which are of continuing relevance. While possibilities for professional development have increased, teachers still need to invest time and financial outlay: Boyle (2021: 55) noted that 52 per cent of 333 survey respondents in her research were untrained as instrumental teachers, and 17 per cent of the respondents had not taken any training since they started teaching; their concerns around professional development related to 'quality, relevance, availability and access'. My research examining the experiences of undergraduate university music students who were giving instrumental lessons in their spare time (Haddon 2009) showed that training was an issue for these novice instrumental teachers, who were operating mostly on a system of trialling approaches used by their own former teachers and reflecting on them, without comprehensive, systematic or ongoing support. This propelled my motivation to create the taught MA Music Education: Instrumental and Vocal Teaching at the University of York, which commenced in 2015.

The MA offers the opportunity to explore specific pedagogical topics; in particular, the varied possibilities for the student-teacher relationship, such as, but not limited to, master-apprentice (Burwell 2013) and mentor-friend (Lehmann, Sloboda and Woody 2007) and modes of dialogue supporting a student-centred ethos within lessons (Meissner 2022), as well as the development of teaching strategies to facilitate particular skills including practising, sight-reading and memorization, and other areas such as teacher and learner motivation, musicians' health, creative work and inclusive music making. The MA also requires students to submit videos of their teaching accompanied by written reflection, in addition to essays and other academic writing for assessment. Critical thinking on both theory and practice underpins the programme and makes substantial contributions to students' development; additionally, the varied intake of students from diverse backgrounds and countries and teaching across classical, jazz, popular, folk and traditional music styles offer opportunities for rich exchange and consideration of experience. In supporting our desire to enable students to contribute through discussion with peers and tutors, we created various platforms for engagement: lectures, seminars, tutor groups, academic tutorials and pastoral supervision, utilizing online as well as face-to-face activities. We now have a second MA music education programme focused on 'Group Teaching and Leadership' and a third programme, 'MA Music Education with Performance'; these bring further nuance to our consideration of instrumental pedagogy. Interconnections with other disciplines such as community music, music psychology and music marketing and management are further supported by our staff teaching across diverse programmes including other MA and undergraduate modules.

As our doctoral student numbers also grew, it became clear that comparable structures could support our postgraduate music education researchers: doctoral students can experience a sense of isolation despite being part of an academic community (Perfect 2014); this isolation could exacerbate anxiety and have debilitating effects (Haddon 2019). Moreover, music education doctoral students could find themselves isolated both as instrumental teachers and as researchers; consequently, it was important to create a platform to support the growing community in this area. Therefore, our MEF was established in 2019; the group includes academic staff, PhD students and some alumni from our MA Music Education: Instrumental and Vocal Teaching programme. We are fortunate to have members with cultural heritage and pedagogical experience in countries including China, Cyprus, Greece, Italy, Iran, Romania, Singapore, Sweden, the United Arab Emirates and the UK and across varied instruments and genres; this affords rich, diverse and real-world perspectives in both our weekly meetings and in the contributions to this volume.

Communities of practice are identified by Lave and Wenger (1991) as integral to learning when viewed as a social process. Participation in a community of practice enables novices to construct identities through learning from more experienced others; however, while Lave and Wenger envisaged learners moving towards full participation within a community, for example, as trainees becoming professionals, acknowledgement of the likelihood of blurred boundaries for the MEF community could offer a reappraised view. In the MEF context, every member has potential to operate in different dimensions within diverse communities, many of them overlapping, so to position the members as 'experts' and 'novices' may limit the productivity of communication, if restricted to 'advice' from 'experts' channelled in a unilateral direction to those who may view themselves as relative 'novices'. Furthermore, a community of practice may need careful and sensitive underpinning: 'simply labelling a group of people as a learning community does not guarantee that it will function as one' (Li et al. 2009: n.p.).

In our group, the MEF members hold such diverse experiences across cultures and contexts that no one member could possibly occupy an 'expert' position in relation to them all. This is advantageous to cultivating a community in which every member can offer informative insights, helping us all to create new knowledge every time we meet. The familiarity of the members has grown over time, enabling us to share quite personal and at times painful experiences as teachers and researchers in what is a 'safe' space. In this shared space, within which several members also contribute specific interest in musicians' health and well-being in addition to instrumental teaching expertise, we are perhaps advantaged in bringing to this group an ethos of care and sensitivity which mirrors the deployment of compassionate teaching practices such as those advocated by Hendricks, Smith and Staunch (2014): listening to our students and acknowledging the role of emotions within learning, tailoring our teaching to the individual or needs of the group, avoiding comparison of students with others, using praise and modelling with care and bringing carefully considered experimentation to our teaching in order to support the learner. These values are embedded in our MA Music Education programmes; seeing them operating in the MEF context indicates their assimilation into ways of being and relating to others without any separation from professional practice: they have become fundamental to each individual.

In being open about the deconstruction of elements of our practice as teachers, within this volume we share challenges and critical insights gained in our practice, often sparked by reflecting on demanding situations encountered in our work, which we sought to understand and change for the better. These have involved questions around identity; the conceptualization of self and practice underpinning our actions; our expectations of ourselves and of our students; concerns relating to understandings of instrumental pedagogies across cultures; our ability to support our students' needs in relation to specific skills and to situational changes in the workplace environment affecting modes of teaching and educational opportunities; and consideration of inclusivity, support and resources. The chapters each take as a starting point a concept or critical idea that has arisen in our teaching practice and which has been discussed within the forum sessions. We have addressed these through a collaborative writing process; even in cases where the chapters explore topics that form part of an individual's doctoral thesis, they are strengthened through the insights afforded by a team approach, in which the questions probed by the author team members may prompt further insights and a greater critical perspective, supporting objectivity and openness, informed by relevant scholarship. In preparing this volume we have discussed team writing processes and shared literature on multi-authored writing (e.g. Elbow 1999; Frassl et al. 2018; Yeo and Lewis 2019); this has proved invaluable in establishing structures, approaches, shared understanding and discursive working environments and in supporting energy and motivation during the writing process. The research methodology used in this volume is largely qualitative, valuing our developing understanding of situations from the perspective of those within them, aligning with a 'real-world' approach to research (Robson and McCartan 2016), with the practical aim of facilitating the development of those learning with us, supporting our own development and enhancing the teaching environments and wider contexts that we work within.

In Part I, 'Philosophies and Personas', we consider in Chapter 1 how critical incidents can highlight unseen influences on our teaching, including entrenched cognitive biases or logical fallacies and the basic philosophical assumptions that underpin how we choose to teach and learn; this can lead to fruitful reappraisal of individual philosophies and may affect approaches to teaching instrumental music lessons and understanding of learner responses. The five incidents presented by the authors show aspects of real-world practice that acted as catalysts to interrogate their beliefs, with resultant implications for their actions, mindsets and ongoing orientation to the development of their professional practice. Chapter 2 explores the nuances between the persona and personality of the teacher and potential effects on the learner. The authors consider how teachers may consciously examine the subconscious influences on their approaches and reflect on appraisal of their teaching and longitudinal adaptability, seen in relation to traditions of student-teacher relationship modes and cultural influences. Chapter 3 examines professional identity by discussing identification of teachers-as-performers or performers-as-teachers, whether self-labelled or ascribed by others, considering the influence of teachers on our own learning and identity as well as exploring how a musician's identity may change during the course of their career and in response to circumstances, such as the Covid-19 pandemic. These adaptations may not only affect opportunities and capability to work in certain roles but also may impact teachers' creative resourcefulness and resilience.

Part II explores contexts, roles and relationships. In Chapter 4 we consider pedagogical training for instrumental teachers in the current contexts of music education in the UK and China, both in relation to higher music education and general continuing professional development. As teachers with international backgrounds working in the UK, the authors discuss the implications of context, opportunities and relevant policies across the two countries which may influence pedagogical development. Chapter 5 is the first of two chapters exploring the relationships between school music teachers and instrumental teachers working in school contexts in the UK. In Chapter 5, challenges that can impact the delivery of instrumental tuition in this context are examined; a small-scale qualitative research study reveals four key concerns: flexibility, environment, irregularity of employment and managing relationships. These are underpinned by issues of status and hierarchy of staff within institutions, areas of responsibility, variable institutional policies around the sharing of confidential pupil information and the perceived value of music within the institutional context. Chapter 6 investigates further the positionality and agency of instrumental teachers working in school contexts through a research study exploring peripatetic and UK Key Stages 4–5 classroom teachers' perceptions of their working relationships, pedagogical approaches and the interrelationships of student performance and other musical activities including composing and listening. Insights concerning communication, learner motivation and autonomy and the desire of instrumental teachers to support curriculum learning more broadly highlight the possibilities for further collaboration.

The next group of chapters within Part II recognizes the increasing interest in learning across cultures, illuminating this from the findings of empirical research studies investigating the perspectives of pre-service teachers of Chinese and Western instruments and their understanding of instrumental pedagogy, mirrored by an exploration of music-specific language challenges concerning the specialist subject terminology for learners and teachers working across cultures. Chapter 7 positions learning across cultures in relation to cultural intelligence theory, which underpins an individual's ability to understand and adapt to different cultural environments; the lived experience of the co-authors, former MA and PhD students at the University of York, enables empathic understanding of the challenges for students in negotiating pedagogical cultures. While focusing on the teaching of Chinese traditional instruments, the implications arising from the findings of this research project generate insights not only for those working across cultures but also for those open to widening their practice through working with learners from diverse backgrounds with varied interests and goals. Chapter 8 considers the development of student-teachers' utilization of a range of educational relationship modes in the one-to-one setting, informing pedagogical interactions with particular reference to the imperative of understanding hierarchical relationships and results-driven learning environments frequently experienced by learners in China. Detailing the processes of student-teachers' adaptive understanding, particularly through their development of questioning skills to use within instrumental pedagogy, this chapter also questions what 'student-centred' means across cultures and invites reappraisal of applied values of concepts across cultures. Chapter 9 explores further cross-cultural instrumental teaching challenges with regard to subject-specific language usage, pre-service teachers' engagement with English as an additional language (EAL) and the need for musicians to understand terminology in multiple languages. A case study examining pre-service teachers' acquisition of pedagogical vocabulary and technical and imaginative language used in teaching illustrates subject-specific language challenges and the support structures created within the MA Music Education: Instrumental and Vocal Teaching at the University of York, which leads to insights for any teachers working with EAL students to aid the development of effective teaching strategies.

Part III focuses on skills-building, examining key facets of pedagogical practices to develop teachers' pedagogical approaches. Chapter 10 supports teachers' skills and confidence in working with students on improvisation, exploring strategies within Western classical music, jazz, popular and music genres used within the authors' own teaching and by research participants in a study of experienced jazz educators. Chapter 11 discusses the place and value of music theory, positioning it as a central part of instrumental pedagogy despite revealing inconsistencies in aspects of teaching and formal assessment structures within the UK context that have implications for students' understanding and progression. Through reflection on a musical example taken from the Trinity College London Grade 2 piano examination syllabus, the authors illustrate a holistic as opposed to compartmentalized approach with specific consideration of the importance of connecting theory to sound and to embodied understanding. Chapter 12 explores a recurrent concept through this volume, the idea of bringing internalized concepts to the fore, examining them in relation to academic scholarship and real-life practice in order to make our teaching more productive. Here, the authors investigate embodiment – a type of knowledge only truly known through the body – and consider the role of embodiment in sense-making, musical expression and communication. Examples of insights from the practice of the authors reveal understandings of embodiment in teaching and performance; these underscore the importance of active, exploratory participation in music. Chapter 13 concludes this part, focusing on helping students overcome physical and mental barriers to practising, inviting consideration of factors that include the home environment and geopolitical factors impacting access to resources. In order to support strategy use and self-motivated learners, the authors delineate their approaches, which include gamifying practice, chunking and freestyle playing, and offer the acronym 'LEST' (Listen Empathetically, Strategize Together) as a holistic orientation in supporting learners.

In Part IV we explore inclusivity, support and resources. Chapter 14 discusses inclusive and accessible approaches to teaching, underpinned by the authors' critical reflection on specific examples from their teaching practice as well as relevant literature. After considering barriers and misconceptions, the authors draw on the principles of Universal Design for Learning (CAST 2024) to illustrate a strengths-focused approach involving collaboration and teamwork, organizational, social, emotional and behavioural support, also signposting the potential role of wider organizations such as music hubs in providing relevant pedagogical training. Chapter 15 presents the findings of a research project on teachers' experience of working with transfer students, discovering how teachers can best support students transferring to other teachers or coming to work with them. Given the scarcity of research in this area, the findings make a welcome contribution to our understanding of the relevant issues. Pragmatic appraisals of the benefits and challenges for teachers and students, as well as the strategies used by teachers, are complemented by the acknowledgement of the complexities of teachers' emotional responses in this situation and implications for further support and for training to include this important area. Chapter 16 examines aspects that teachers could take into account when assessing the value and relevance of practical examinations for their students, particularly in light of changes to examination options as a result of the Covid-19 pandemic. The findings of a survey conducted by the authors highlight concerns of accessibility, inclusion, exam formats and components, along with perceptions of commercial brand value, which influence teacher and parental perceptions of status, relevance and quality.

Our final chapters focus on resources and support for learners and teachers. Chapter 17 discusses the pedagogical language used within instrumental tuition books: texts that can have a strong and lasting influence on learners. Through thematic content analysis of material written for drummers, the authors probe aspects including writing tone and style and their possible relationship to learner motivation, agency, trust and self-belief. This leads to consideration of how pedagogical language might connect to stereotypical perceptions of players of specific instruments and therefore to aspects of inclusion and shared experience, as well as to further thoughts on the conscious use of language within teaching resources and within informal and formal pedagogical contexts. Chapter 18 draws on pedagogical reflections from three of the authors to discuss insights supporting teachers who may desire or need to create bespoke material for their students. These reflections reveal approaches to fostering learner engagement and progress within diverse contexts, genres and with students of different ages; nonetheless, further research is warranted to investigate issues such as perceptions of educator-creator legitimacy in the role of creating materials for pedagogical use and the extent to which training equips teachers for this approach. Finally, Chapter 19 explores practical insights fostering student and teacher resilience and well-being, considering learner autonomy and age-related concerns as well as reflecting on the legacies of adaptations made to instrumental teaching during the Covid-19 pandemic and the unexpected continued benefits and successes of online teaching.

We hope that teachers across the world will enjoy reading this book and that it sparks further reflection and conversations with other teachers, classroom teachers, students, parents, carers and any other stakeholders. Within a continually changing global landscape for instrumental pedagogy, we also hope that it will make a contribution to supporting teachers' knowledge and confidence, empowering them through new ideas, concepts and strategies for teaching and resource-building, promoting opportunities and mechanisms for their personal and pedagogical reflection and supporting understanding of the situating of teaching in a wide context including institutional structures, assessment platforms and opportunities for global teaching afforded through the use of video-conferencing technology. This may encourage teachers to undertake research within their own practice to examine critical issues and to propel their further development, and for them to feel empowered and supported through participation in communities of practice, as has been the case for the authors within this volume. We also hope that this book will be of value to educators delivering pedagogical training for instrumental teachers and that it will inform further academic scholarship and research, stimulating and supporting the engagement and development of new learners, teachers and communities across the world.

References

Boyle, K. (2021), *The Instrumental Teacher: Autonomy, Identity and the Portfolio Career in Music*, Abingdon: Routledge.

Burwell, K. (2013), 'Apprenticeship in Music: A Contextual Study for Instrumental Teaching and Learning', *International Journal of Music Education*, 31 (3): 276–91.

Burwell, K., G. Carey and D. Bennett (2019), 'Isolation in Studio Music Teaching: The Secret Garden', *Arts and Humanities in Higher Education*, 18 (4): 372–94.

CAST (2024), 'About Universal Design for Learning'. Available online: https://www.cast.org/impact/universal-design-for-learning-udl (accessed 24 August 2024).

Conway, C. M., and T. E. H. Zerman (2004), 'Perceptions of an Instrumental Music Teacher Regarding Mentoring, Induction, and the First Year of Teaching', *Research Studies in Music Education*, 22 (1): 72–82.

Elbow, P. (1999), 'Using the Collage for Collaborative Writing', *Composition Studies*, 27 (1): 7–14.

Frassl, M. A., D. P. Hamilton, B. A. Denfeld, E. de Eyto, S. E. Hampton, P. S. Keller, S. Sharma, A. S. L. Lewis, G. A. Weyhenmeyer, C. M. O'Reilly, M. E. Lofton and N. Catalán (2018), 'Ten Simple Rules for Collaboratively Writing a Multi-Authored Paper', *PLoS Computational Biology* 14 (11): e1006508. https://doi.org/10.1371/journal.pcbi.1006508.

Haddon, E. (2009), 'Instrumental and Vocal Learning: How Do Music Students Learn to Teach?', *British Journal of Music Education*, 26 (1): 57–70.

Haddon, E. (2019), 'University Music Students: Mental Health and the Academic Supervisor', *Musicology Research Journal*, 6 (1): 159–99. https://www.musichealthandwellbeing.co.uk/publications/elizabethhaddon-universitymusicstudentsmentalhealthandtheacademicsupervisor (accessed 24 August 2024).

Hendricks, K. S., T. D. Smith and J. Staunch (2014), 'Creating Safe Spaces for Music Learning', *Music Educators Journal*, 101 (1): 35–40.

Lave, J., and E. Wenger (1991), *Legitimate Peripheral Participation in Communities of Practice*, Cambridge: Cambridge University Press.

Lehmann, A. C., J. A. Sloboda and R. H. Woody (2007), *Psychology for Musicians: Understanding and Acquiring the Skills*, Oxford: Oxford University Press.

Li, L. C., J. M. Grimshaw, C. Nielsen, M. Judd, P. C. C. Coyte and I. D. Graham (2009), 'Evolution of Wenger's Concept of Community of Practice', *Implementation Science*, 4:11. doi:10.1186/1748-5908-4-11

Meissner, H. (2022), 'Teaching Children and Teenagers Expressive Music Performance', in H. Meissner, R. Timmers and S. E. Pitts (eds), *Sound Teaching: A Research-Informed Approach to Inspiring Confidence, Skill, and Enjoyment in Music Performance*, 37–47, Abingdon: Routledge.

Perfect, M. (2014), 'Studying for a Humanities PhD Can Make You Feel Cut Off from Humanity', *The Guardian*, 8 July. Available online: https://www.theguardian.com/higher-education-network/blog/2014/jul/08/humanities-phd-students-isolation (accessed 24 August 2024).

Robson, C., and K. McCartan (2016), *Real World Research*, 2nd edn, Chichester: John Wiley.

Yeo, M., and M. Lewis (2019), 'Co-Authoring in Action: Practice, Problems and Possibilities', *Iranian Journal of Language Teaching Research*, 7 (3): 109–23. doi:10.30466/ijltr.2019.120739.

Part I

Philosophies and Personas

1

'Unseen Influences': The Effects of Philosophy and Biases on Approaches to Instrumental Teaching

Naomi Norton, Richard Powell, James Poole, Federico Pendenza and Sara Norouzi Iranzad

Introduction

This chapter offers a space for readers to engage with material relating to 'unseen influences' on teaching and learning in instrumental education. The authors are not experts in the study of philosophy. We are music educators who have engaged in what the authors of the *Oxford Handbook of Philosophy in Music Education* call 'philosophical inquiry': that is, 'the systematic and critical examination of beliefs and assumptions', which they describe as unavoidable, messy and designed to help educators with 'making sense of the world and our place in it' (Bowman and Frega 2012: 17). We are using the term 'unseen influences' to refer to thought processes that are likely to affect how we approach teaching but may not have been consciously acknowledged or actively examined: this could include 'philosophies', 'cognitive biases' or 'logical fallacies'. At relevant points in the chapter we have shared a 'critical incident' experienced by each author in which we identify, acknowledge and reflect on an unseen influence on our teaching. These incidents serve as catalysts for consideration of how our practical learning and teaching experiences relate to examples of theoretical writing on this topic, which we have discussed in this chapter. In sharing these incidents we hope to reassure others experiencing such moments that they are not alone and provide support for those wishing to explore reactions to similar incidents in more depth or with reference to literature. We start by introducing key terms and considering why philosophy matters for music educators and how it can be (mis)aligned with pedagogical activities in lessons. This flows into a discussion of the purpose of language and its use by music educators to engage with pupils and an examination of how pre-existing beliefs and habitual behaviours influence teaching. The final section focuses on how consideration of cultural narratives can provide opportunities for music teachers to engage in an ongoing process of 'philosophical inquiry' and 'becoming' throughout their lifetimes and careers.

What Is 'Philosophy' and Why Does It Matter?

We have tried to keep the philosophical jargon included to a minimum, but there are a few terms that are useful to define in order to explain fundamental concepts underlying our reflective investigation. Many readers will have heard the terms 'qualitative' and 'quantitative' and could give examples of these types of information: a common approach is to imagine a set of marbles and describe them quantitatively (e.g. 'there are five marbles that are 5cm in diameter') or qualitatively (e.g. 'the marbles are green with yellow swirls'). Less commonly discussed are the philosophical beliefs that underpin these different types of information: there are differences in terms of what people believe about the nature of 'truth' or 'reality' (referred to as 'ontology' or 'ontological beliefs') and also differences regarding how we can study 'knowledge' (which can be referred to as 'epistemology'). Hinchey (2010) provides definitions of two philosophical extremes (positivism and constructivism) in simple terms with descriptions of what these look like in education. They state that 'positivists conceptualize knowledge as a thing – essentially, as verifiable information born of scientific investigation ... Knowledge is there, waiting for us to find it' (Hinchey 2010: 36). The word 'objective' is often used in relation to this approach, and those who use it will generally conduct experiments 'on' their research participants to generate quantitative data that allows them to find out what causes an outcome or what the effect of an action is: this helps them to get closer to understanding the 'one true' reality. In comparison, for constructivists, '"knowledge" is *constructed* by human beings when they assign meaning to data: it is not simply sitting out in the world waiting for us to find it' (Hinchey 2010: 42, emphasis in original). The word 'subjective' will be used by those espousing this approach, and they will generally conduct studies 'with' their participants to generate qualitative data that allows insights into how people are interpreting and constructing their individual realities. In the first of our critical incidents, 'pragmatism' is introduced as a 'middle-ground' between these two strongly opposing beliefs that enables Naomi to reconcile her approach to teaching different musical concepts. Someone with a 'Pragmatic' philosophy recognizes 'the existence and importance of the natural or physical world as well as the emergent social and psychological world that includes language, culture, human institutions, and subjective thoughts', and as a result they view knowledge as 'both constructed and based on the reality of the world we experience and live in' (Johnson and Onwuegbuzie 2004: 18).

Critical Incident 1: Naomi

In 2021 I realized that the Pragmatic philosophy that shaped my approach to research was also integral to my teaching. The moment of realization came when reading a 2019 interview by Skogstad with Paul A. Kirschner provocatively titled 'Constructivist pedagogy is like a zombie that refuses to die'. I started reading because I was outraged at this statement and continued because I was teaching university music students about overcoming confirmation bias by engaging with contradictory beliefs! As I read, I realized that if someone believes there is one universal reality and the purpose of language is to label that reality, then they will think that the fastest way to teach is to simply tell pupils what they think the 'labels' are. Whereas if someone believes that language creates reality then they need to help pupils learn how to use language rather than just learning existing labels. While reading I found that I had moments of connection with someone with opposing philosophical beliefs. Reflecting on this critical incident helped me to realize that I am a Pragmatic educator as well as researcher: I believe that there are some aspects of music that just 'are' and pupils need to be told (e.g. what we call the notes on an instrument), but there are other aspects that are open to interpretation and should not just be transferred from me to them (e.g. expression). This philosophical belief means that I alter my choice of activity based on what I am teaching and what kind of 'knowledge' I think it is.

The 'ontology' and 'epistemology' that a teacher consciously or unconsciously aligns with affect their 'pedagogy' and chosen teaching activities. Naomi reflects on the purpose of language as being either to label reality (loosely aligned with a positivist philosophy) or to create reality (aligned with constructivism) and the implications when it comes to choosing how to help pupils learn. What might be dismissed as surface labels, unhelpfully abstracted from day-to-day teaching practice, can instead be understood to connect with the pedagogical outlooks that profoundly shape an educator's choices. The following thought provocation provides a useful polarization of approaches to teaching:

Would you, as an educator, conceptualise yourself as a 'banker' who acquires information and deposits it into pupils then subsequently makes withdrawals through testing and provides bank statements (test results) to validate the transfer of currency from teacher to pupil? Or would you seek to provide pupils with experiences that enable them to 'develop their own understanding of the data at hand?' (Hinchey 2010: 42)

Which approach is chosen does not matter and may change from moment to moment. What matters is understanding how to most effectively align pedagogical practices with the relevant philosophical underpinnings: that is, ensuring that educational activities help pupils to work towards the type of 'knowledge' that the teacher would like them to gain. Notable events within teaching practice – whether experienced as teacher, learner or observer – can serve to bring this degree of alignment into focus, potentially opening up new vistas of understanding while also eliciting realizations regarding the limitations of one's existing insight, as Richard explores in his incident.

Critical Incident 2: Richard

Early in my development as an educator, I was assisting a project with secondary school pupils run by the educational team of a professional orchestra. Various elements of what would be presented in a final performance were to be devised during (what I viewed as) the rehearsal period, I assumed within some form of prescribed framework or using ready-prepared materials. Rather, what followed (much to my anxiety) was a series of workshops in which content was developed from scratch; musical ideas were not only contributed but honed by the pupils with the facilitation of the project leader. The material ultimately performed was truly co-authored, resulting in a sense of collective ownership over the creative outcome that I had not previously encountered. My preconceptions of effective pedagogy came under devastating scrutiny. My subconscious inclination towards imposing parameters to ensure a 'safe' product contrasted starkly with the project leader's deferral of performance goals in favour of meaningful creative collaboration; these principles that I ostensibly already prized were affirmed, but in a manner that in fact underscored my shallow interpretation of them. The risk-aversion strategies I frequently enacted in my teaching and performing were evidently at the expense of more democratic approaches. My previous conception of creative collaboration amounted to little more than a token gesture compared with the genuine sharing that had been modelled.

Encounters with distinct educational approaches can invite useful reappraisals (or even prompt necessary crises) in our pedagogical 'journeys'. What Richard was presented with might be viewed as a radical 'deepening' of previously accepted values, but such encounters can sometimes appear oppositional in character with seemingly polarized pedagogies creating a sense of confrontation. Educators may struggle to process and assimilate these experiences in a manner that embraces the nuance and compromise that so often prove crucial in teaching: although an 'either–or' mindset allows for greater ease and efficiency than a 'yes, and' one, such a clear cut approach can lead to oversimplification. This can carry through to the conceptualization and articulation of pedagogical approaches as well as how teachers conceive their identities; educational practitioners and researchers have been accused of a 'dichotomising tendency' where they contrast one idea or strategy with another seemingly different one (see Alexander, 2020: 134). We have already considered 'positivism versus constructivism' but other examples suggested by Alexander include 'pupil-centred versus teacher-centred' and 'instruction versus discovery' or the efficacy of 'monologic versus dialogic discourse' for helping pupils to gain knowledge.

Monologic discourse typically involves the teacher acting as 'the possessor of knowledge' who is responsible for 'telling' pupils what they know and 'questioning them to see if they can remember what they have been told' (Skidmore and Murakami 2016: 8), as in the 'banker' analogy used above. In contrast, Bakhtin writes that 'truth is not born nor is it to be found inside the head of an individual person, it is born between people collectively searching for truth, in the process of their dialogic interaction' ([1929] 1984: 110), suggesting that dialogue is vital in the pursuit of 'truth' or in developing pupils' understanding. Similarly, it has been suggested that dialogue enables 'two parties to build up a shared understanding of the educational activity in hand' and allows pupils to 'bridge the gap between their existing knowledge and the goals of a particular sequence of instruction' (Skidmore and Murakami 2016: 8). James reports on a 'light bulb' moment that inspired him to reflect on his use of language in instrumental lessons and come to the realization that both dialogue and monologue can be useful.

Critical Incident 3: James

In my first instrumental teaching role I taught one-to-one piano lessons in a secondary school. I subconsciously adopted a master-apprentice approach, relying on direct instructional guidance and the transmission of my knowledge to pupils. With little teaching experience, I took this approach largely because it mirrored my own teachers' methods, but I also considered it the most time-efficient way for pupils to learn. I later enrolled on the MA Music Education programme at the University of York where I observed lessons by the teaching team. In one of these lessons (an adult beginner violin lesson) the teacher used open questions and two-way dialogue to facilitate learning and, as a result, the pupil was able to use existing knowledge and experiences to support their learning. This was a 'light bulb' moment as I had not experienced this strategy as a learner or considered using dialogue as a teacher. I began experimenting and found that dialogue improved my relationships with pupils and encouraged them to think independently. To my surprise, some peers enrolled on the MA programme were doubtful of the potential efficacy of dialogue, arguing that it wasted time and was not always appropriate for adult pupils or very young beginners. I found myself attempting to justify an approach that I had only just adopted but my engagement with sceptical peers encouraged me to consider instances when direct instruction may be helpful. I became aware of the merits of both approaches and now operate a 'hybrid' approach, facilitating dialogue at certain moments while still drawing from the master-apprentice style I started teaching with.

Dialogue has been found to be effective when used in instrumental lessons to develop musical expression (Meissner and Timmers 2019); it has also been suggested that dialogue can improve pupils' at-home practice, ability to reflect on their performance, pitch and rhythm (Meissner and Timmers 2020). The applicability of dialogue to such a wide range of topics could indicate that teachers and pupils may benefit from approaching *any* topic through dialogue. This, and the potential that dialogue offers for shared understanding and discovery of 'truth', might lead to the assumption that teachers should always seek to initiate dialogue: this reflects the conclusion that James arrived at during his 'light bulb' moment. However, it may be unrealistic to expect instrumental teachers to use dialogue constantly, especially as it has been reported as time-consuming and potentially confusing for pupils (Poole and Norton 2023). Alexander's dialogic teaching framework (2020) suggests that teachers should use a combination of dialogue *and* monologue and provides a repertoire of 'teaching talk' that encourages teachers to consider options to inform their choices, affording a sense of 'agency' as teachers select an approach that is most appropriate for the topic and pupils (133–40). This reflects James's adoption of a 'hybrid' approach that combines both dialogue and monologue and highlights how teachers who may favour one approach can benefit from adopting strategies that initially feel uncomfortable or conflict (to some extent) with their own 'philosophy'. Alexander states that dichotomies 'force us to take sides and reduce our options' (2020: 134), whereas being open to different strategies and flexible in the choice of approach can allow educators the freedom to use language in a way that is most suitable for the teaching environment(s) that they inhabit.

How Do Pre-Existing Beliefs and Habitual Behaviours Act as Unseen Influences on Teaching?

Cognitive biases and logical fallacies are thought processes that make everyday life possible but result in our decisions during it being fallible and perceptions of it unreliable. In his 2011 book *Thinking, Fast and Slow*, Nobel Prize-winning author Daniel Kahneman states:

> You believe you know what goes on in your mind, which often consists of one conscious thought leading in an orderly way to another. But that is not the only way the mind works, nor indeed is that the typical way. Most impressions and thoughts arise in your conscious experience without your knowing how they got there. (2011: 4)

Kahneman's adoption of the terms 'System 1' and 'System 2' helps to explain how our brains have evolved to enable the unconscious and automatic (but inherently biased and prone-to-error) System 1 to act quickly to make the majority of decisions, with System 2 only activating to engage in voluntary, effortful and considered activity 'when an event is detected that violates the model of the world that System 1 maintains' or 'when a question arises for which System 1 does not offer an answer' (Kahneman 2011: 24). In this model, cognitive biases and logical fallacies form some of the shortcuts that our brains can take to get to decisions quickly (but sometimes inaccurately) – they are the potential biases and errors in System 1 – and there are many of them (e.g. see a list created by The Decision Lab, n.d.). In her critical incident Naomi mentioned that she engaged with a text that she disagreed with as a way of challenging her 'confirmation bias', which is described by Matei and Phillips as the 'tendency to search for, interpret, focus on and recall information in a way that confirms one's preexisting beliefs or hypotheses' (2023: 4). They recognized that 'raising awareness of common misconceptions, biases and fallacies and disputing them via discussions might open the doors to new ideas and collaborations' (Matei and Phillips 2023: 15), with music educators having the responsibility to challenge their own biases and promote critical thinking among pupils. By encouraging open-minded inquiry and actively challenging preconceived notions, educators can cultivate an atmosphere of intellectual curiosity that empowers pupils to navigate the multifaceted dimensions of music education within diverse contexts and environments. Sara's and Federico's experiences serve as compelling examples of the influence of such transformative processes on their approaches to pedagogy.

Critical Incident 4: Sara

> I was born and raised in a country where music lessons are expensive, especially for instruments like the piano that are not common in every house. Lessons with my teachers involved them directing and criticizing because these strategies could result in fast improvements in our learning process and made the limited class time seem more fruitful. However, this environment did not give any chance for discussion: asking questions or commenting during the lesson could have been perceived as

insulting and inappropriate in my culture. A teacher once said to me 'I do not need to hear your opinion because if you knew the right thing you would not be in my room now!', and they stopped me from reasoning about my playing. For ten years, I followed the same teaching style of directing and criticizing and believed that a good teacher is one who knows the answer to all questions and can solve all problems quickly. When I started my MA Music Education programme at the University of York, I became familiar with different approaches such as Socratic questioning and other non-verbal communication models. The practical experience of using these approaches in my teaching made a great change to my philosophy and teaching style. To begin with I thought that questioning made the lesson pace too slow and some pupils would refuse to engage with the conversation. I thought it would not work in my country and may cause pupils and families to complain about the slow progress of music learning. Four years later, I have come to the conclusion that this reception is not permanent and gradually pupils learn to think deeply about their own learning, which results in more effective practising, critical thinking, and the development of vital skills such as problem solving that all save time and help pupils to be independent.

Critical Incident 5: Federico

I started teaching guitar during my studies at a conservatoire in Europe. At that time, I lacked formal pedagogical training and relied heavily on intuition. Upon later reflection, I realized that my teaching was shaped by a combination of my personal experiences as a learner (i.e. how I had been taught) and my natural curiosity for acquiring and extending knowledge. In 2014, I had the opportunity to study abroad through a European Union student exchange programme, and this experience was crucial in bringing to the surface my assumptions about tradition and innovation in teaching and how these informed my teaching beliefs. Once, I had a conversation with one of the professors who had authored a book exploring novel approaches to learning a specific musical skill. They shared that their fortunate circumstance of being brought up in a country where a musical tradition was limited had motivated them to think outside of the box, without the fear of being marginalized because of being an outsider. This moment was a revelation as I immediately realized how the cultural and educational environment in which I had grown up had influenced my views on conventional and appropriate approaches to teaching, as well as the types of resources I had chosen to inform these. Indeed, I noticed that some of the resources I had consulted mainly aligned with my existing beliefs of what constituted, for example, a good musical interpretation. While later on I reflected on the relationship between innovation and effectiveness, I have always kept that conversation in my thoughts, ensuring it served as a constant reminder about challenging my assumptions and remaining receptive to new possibilities.

The potential for pre-existing beliefs and habitual behaviours to impact music teaching is evident in many of the incidents shared in this chapter. James's teaching mirrored that of his own teachers, and Sara adopted strategies that were similar to those of her teachers for ten years. Federico's teaching was shaped by personal experiences as a learner and subconsciously influenced by his perception of 'appropriate' and 'conventional' approaches. This phenomenon has also been documented in research with preservice music teachers (e.g. see Schmidt 2012). Pre-existing beliefs can have a powerful effect on teachers who 'interpret and process their ongoing experiences through their prior beliefs, influencing what they choose to or are able to learn from their experiences in the university program' (Schmidt 2012: 29). This suggests that teaching beliefs and habitual behaviours may be based on entrenched ideas that could be difficult to recognize or adapt. Federico, Sara and James's incidents illustrate how teachers may benefit from challenging these beliefs and investigating whether habitual behaviours are preventing experimentation with different, seemingly opposing, approaches.

Cultural Experiences and 'Becoming'

Studies show how engaging in cultural immersion experiences and self-reflection can assist trainee music teachers in exploring their own cultural identities and facilitating transformative processes, thereby fostering the development of cultural competence, which is a fundamental skill for adapting to culturally evolving teaching environments (McBride and Nicholson 2023; VanDeusen 2019). For example, VanDeusen's participants questioned 'their own assumptions and perceptions about cultural differences in music teaching and learning and began to broaden their understanding of culture's role in education and within a larger sociopolitical context' (2019: 54). While Federico's experience was as a music student rather than as a trainee teacher, his exposure to a different educational and cultural background fostered a transformative process through which he started to question his previously held assumptions. Sara, on the other hand, began to re-evaluate her beliefs about teaching practices through a different lens, finding that cultural narratives could also unlock the potential for transferable emphasis on student autonomy. Despite occurring in two different contexts, these accounts emphasize the role of cultural experiences in developing transformative processes and prompting (re)consideration of existing beliefs, behaviours and practices. However, considering that individuals within the same cultural background bring their own wealth of knowledge and experiences, these narratives also highlight the value of exchange between people holding diverse beliefs shaped by overt or subtle cultural practices and differences, thus contributing to the concept of 'becoming'.

Remaining open to such interchanges is of particular value within the intricate *messiness* of what Szekely describes as 'music education's continued becoming', a mercurial characteristic that emerges in spite of the 'systematizing, ordering, regulating, and boundary-setting' tendencies that teachers intent on ensuring structure in their professional lives might display (2012: 164). Comparison might be drawn with the idealistic desire to 'out-predict the uncertainties that lie ahead' that Allsup senses in some teacher training contexts: 'the notion of the real-world is often floated, the idea of a knowable future into which an early career teacher can be inserted with the right skills to survive' (2015: 15). By contrast, the reflections in this chapter suggest the concept of 'becoming' as a salient one for instrumental teachers in highlighting that we are not 'finished products' and that our philosophy may be constantly evolving. This invitation to a less anchored pedagogical identity might in turn facilitate an approach better suited to musical subject matter, meaning that teachers can, as Szekely puts it, 'actively challenge exclusionary dualisms, learning to play with, between, and across the schisms between old and new, tradition and innovation, style and culture' (2012: 178).

Conclusions and Reflections

The critical incidents reported in this chapter demonstrate that engagement with colleagues, and exposure to distinct approaches, can benefit teachers as they exchange views and develop philosophical beliefs. Indeed, Bowman and Frega – for whom philosophical inquiry is a 'collective responsibility ... that extends to all practitioners' and is not 'reserved for experts with specialised training' (2012: 22) – suggest that such tensions between music educators are 'desirable' (2012: 26). Crucially, this underlines a key message from this chapter: teachers should not feel they need to join a particular philosophical 'camp'. Rather, they might benefit from considering a variety of teaching philosophies and approaches that may (or may not) align with their own teaching beliefs. Openness and flexibility can allow teachers the freedom to adapt to educational contexts with greater effectiveness, enabling a versatility that echoes Dewey's assertion that 'while a habit apart from knowledge supplies us with a single fixed method of attack, knowledge means that selection may be made from a much wider range of habits' (1916: 396).

It is the metacognitive advantages of philosophical inquiry that have proved most potent in our practice: a heightened awareness of self and of connection (or disparity) between pedagogical practice and beliefs. As individual teachers enriched through collective reflection, engagement with the philosophical underpinnings of our educational world views has served to deepen as much as it has to clarify. The 'unseen influences' shaping day-to-day teaching decisions have been, if not fully unveiled, then at least partially understood; what cannot be seen is at least 'sensed' to some degree. The benefits of this have been manifold: opportunities to align teaching approaches with values have arisen, but precedent has also been set for instigation and reception of further experiences – marked or unmarked, immediate or gradual, confrontational or affirmational, sought or unsolicited – that might continue to mould our 'becoming' as educators.

References

Alexander, R. (2020), *A Dialogic Teaching Companion*, Abingdon: Routledge.

Allsup, R. E. (2015), 'Music Teacher Quality and the Problem of Routine Expertise', *Philosophy of Music Education Review*, 23 (1): 5–24.

Bakhtin, M. ([1929] 1984), *Problems of Dostoevsky's Poetics*, trans. and ed. C. Emerson, Manchester: Manchester University Press.

Bowman, W., and A. L. Frega (2012), *The Oxford Handbook of Philosophy in Music Education*, Oxford: Oxford University Press.

Dewey, J. (1916), *Democracy and Education: An Introduction to the Philosophy of Education*, New York: Macmillan.

Hinchey, P. H. (2010), 'Chapter Three: Rethinking What We Know: Positivist and Constructivist Epistemology', *Counterpoints*, 24: 33–55. http://www.jstor.org/stable/42976884.

Johnson, R. B., and A. J. Onwuegbuzie (2004), 'Mixed Methods Research: A Research Paradigm Whose Time Has Come', *Educational Researcher*, 33 (7): 14–26.

Kahneman, D. (2011), *Thinking, Fast and Slow*, London: Penguin Books.

Matei, R., and K. Phillips (2023), 'Critical Thinking in Musicians' Health Education. Findings from Four Workshops with Experts', *Health Promotion International*, 38 (2): 1–19.

McBride, N. R., and G. Nicholson (2023), 'Finding "Otherness" in Music and Pedagogy: A Critical Ontological Analysis of an Immersive International Music Education Exchange Program', *Journal of Music Teacher Education*, 32 (2): 42–56.

Meissner, H., and R. Timmers (2019), 'Teaching Young Musicians Expressive Performance: An Experimental Study', *Music Education Research*, 21 (1): 20–39.

Meissner, H., and R. Timmers (2020), 'Young Musicians' Learning of Expressive Performance: The Importance of Dialogic Teaching and Modelling', *Frontiers in Education*, 5. https://doi.org/10.3389/feduc.2020.00011.

Poole, J., and N. Norton (2023), 'Investigating Perceptions of Dialogic Teaching amongst Trainee Instrumental/Vocal Teachers: An Exploratory Study', *Frontiers in Education*, 8. https://doi.org/10.3389/feduc.2023.1272325.

Schmidt, M. (2012), 'Transition from Student to Teacher: Preservice Teachers' Beliefs and Practices', *Journal of Music Teacher Education*, 23 (1): 27–49. https://doi.org/10.1177/1057083712469111 (original work published 2013).

Skidmore, D., and K. Murakami (2016), 'Dialogic Pedagogy: An Introduction', in D. Skidmore and K. Murakami (eds), *Dialogic Pedagogy: The Importance of Dialogue in Teaching and Learning*, 68–82, Bristol: Multilingual Matters.

Skogstad, I. (2019), 'Constructivist Pedagogy Is Like a Zombie That Refuses to Die: An Interview with Professor Paul A. Kirschner by Isak Skogstad', 3-STAR Learning Experiences: An Evidence-informed Blog for Learning Professionals. Available online: https://3starlearningexperiences.wordpress.com/2019/03/26/constructivist-pedagogy-is-like-a-zombie-that-refuses-to-die/ (accessed 21 August 2024).

Szekely, M. (2012), 'Musical Education: From Identity to Becoming', in W. Bowman and A. L. Frega (eds), *The Oxford Handbook of Philosophy in Music Education*, 163–79, Oxford: Oxford University Press.

The Decision Lab (n.d.), 'Cognitive Biases: A List of the Most Relevant Biases in Behavioral Economics'. Available online: https://thedecisionlab.com/biases (accessed 21 August 2024).

VanDeusen, A. J. (2019), 'A Cultural Immersion Field Experience: Examining Preservice Music Teachers' Beliefs about Cultural Differences in the Music Classroom', *Journal of Music Teacher Education*, 28 (3): 43–57.

2

Considering the Effects of the Instrumental Teacher's Personality and Persona on Student–Teacher Relationships

Marianna Cortesi, Nasim Ansari, Rosemary Lynch, Richard Powell and Jennifer Cohen

Introduction

Consideration of the professional relationships between music teachers and their students could involve the concepts of personality and persona (Shaw 2017). These include factors such as thoughts, temperaments, behaviours and habits; in particular, the ways in which individuals think, behave and feel over time and in different situations relate to their personality (Funder 2012; Roberts and Mroczek 2008). The *Oxford English Dictionary* (2024a) defines personality as 'the quality or collection of qualities which makes a person a distinctive individual; the distinctive personal or individual character of a person'. More outwardly, persona is defined as 'the aspect of a person's character that is displayed to or perceived by others' (Oxford English Dictionary 2024b). This definition aligns with the ancient Greek roots of the word, indicating persona as a mask or a social role (Marshall and Barbour 2015). It also chimes with Jung's psychological interpretation of persona as a way of being in the social world that allows one's 'true' self to be protected from the world: 'The persona (or mask) is the outward face we present to the world. It conceals our real self, and Jung describes it as the "conformity" archetype' (McLeod 2024: 5). While the boundaries between personality and persona might often be blurred, persona concerns how individuals publicly display themselves in different contexts; in this sense, one's persona is certainly influenced by personality traits; this involves mediation between aspects such as public self-consciousness, self-impression, impression management and situational goals (Leary and Allen 2011).

Persona is a concept that bears a direct relevance to music: while musical persona is a developed idea in the context of musicology, performance and composition (Auslander 2006a; Auslander 2006b; Fairchild and Marshall 2019; Robinson and Hatten 2012), the concept of a teaching persona in music education has received less attention from scholarship. The concept of persona may have a negative connotation in some literature, relating to concerns of inauthenticity; for example, Lang (2007) compares two viewpoints towards persona, both of which presume that persona is different from individuals' true selves. Likewise, Marshall and Barbour (2015) claim that in twentieth-century modern literature and poetry, persona has been illustrated as something different from genuineness, referring to the assumed persona of the literary author as opposed to the revealing of their authentic self. Nonetheless, adopting a conscious persona tailored to specific situations and circumstances may be at times appropriate as opposed to a blanket approach of authenticity across all circumstances (Leary and Allen 2011). Accordingly, this presents a stimulus for reflecting on instrumental music teachers' personality, as well as on how personality relates to teachers' use of persona in order to increase our understanding of how the pedagogical environment might be influenced by these aspects; indeed, the authors of this chapter use persona as a flexible tool to expand their perceptions of the impact of teachers' personality within teaching settings.

In light of their individual experiences as instrumental teachers, the five authors of this chapter (referred to as Authors A, B, C, D and E, with the letters assigned to preserve their relative anonymity and not corresponding to the listed order of the authors) reflect on the concepts of personality and persona and on how these interrelate. We agreed to write individual reflections on the role of personality and use of persona in our own teaching experience and shared these documents. Then, authors A and C conducted a thematic analysis of the reflective responses, identifying common themes across our reflections. Varied perspectives are discussed within the critical reflections in this chapter.

Drawing a Line between Personality and Persona

Author B claims: 'I find it really difficult to know where my personality ends and my teaching persona begins.' Author C asks: 'To what extent am I open to recognize aspects of my personality that I don't like? And to what extent do these aspects emerge within my persona?' The relevance of these reflections resides in the high extent to which teachers' personalities influence students' learning as well as their teaching occupation (Wadlington and Wadlington 2011). Regarding their perception of persona, Author B claims that 'my teaching persona is informed by (1) what I think a "good teacher" looks like (influenced by my education, acculturation, previous experiences etc.) and (2) my experiences (built up over time) of what works and what does not work'. Both factors contribute to determining the teacher's responses to different teaching scenarios and learners, while another author outlined the adaptability of their teaching persona:

> When I'm teaching, I think I unconsciously react to the student and make choices of which persona I need to adopt to facilitate the lesson. This can change so suddenly depending on the environment that I am in and the reaction to how the student is presenting themselves in a given lesson. This then leads me to consider how my personality actually helps facilitate my choice of persona. (Author D)

Persona as an Exaggeration of Personality

Other reflections regarded the extent to which persona can be considered as an exaggeration of aspects of one's personality. Author E explains:

> On reflection, I find it difficult to distinguish between my personality and personae in my teaching work. I would view most of the personae I adopt as extensions – exaggerations, even – of particular aspects of my personality, often in contexts where I have recognized (whether consciously or subconsciously) that a particular trait may be useful to emphasize, or that other traits may need to be de-emphasized.

Similarly, Author C noted that 'I am also aligned with the idea that my persona is an extension or exaggeration of my personality. I would probably describe my teaching persona as an attempt to shape my personality traits in a way that I perceive as advantageous for myself and for my students in a given context'. While acknowledging a difference between persona and personality, Author B reflected on how some elements of their persona are not detached from their personality:

> I do think my persona often exaggerates elements of my 'so-called personality' to achieve something particular, for example, a particular energy in the lesson. That said, my persona does not feel separate or distinct from my personality. It still feels authentic. This is perhaps because I am generally quite an empathetic person: being positive, energetic, outgoing, smiley and bubbly is as natural to me as being calm and listening intently.

The role of empathy in establishing a connection with the learner was also implicitly echoed by Author C: 'As part of my teaching persona, I often find myself naturally responding with my body posture and facial expression to (what I perceive as) the feelings and needs of a particular student in a given situation, which helps build a positive rapport with that student.'

Awareness of Persona in Teaching

A further theme that emerged from our reflections is the extent to which we, as instrumental teachers, are conscious of how we use persona in teaching contexts. In this regard, the authors have a specific take on the dimensions of consciousness. Author B claims: 'I think persona is a mixture of conscious and subconscious decisions. While some things might start off as conscious (for example, we might make a very intentional decision to adopt a particular trait into our persona), I feel some of these traits become subconscious over time and with experience.' Providing a practical example of a conscious use of persona in their teaching practice, Author A claimed:

> I think, in general, I do not have a sense of humour most of the time in my daily life. I believe that it is not a part of my personality. Despite not having a great sense of humour, I intentionally or sometimes unintentionally do make my students laugh and crack a joke in order to create a friendly and relaxed atmosphere and be able to easily teach them different concepts. For instance, I find it easier to correct students' posture by exchanging pleasantries, especially in my communications with kids and young people. This persona has been nurtured and strengthened in my teaching.

Author E also described using persona in their teaching practice in a conscious manner: 'There are various ways in which I am aware that I adopt personae more consciously, and more performatively, to meet what I perceive to be the needs of pupils … More generally, recognizing the *kind* of teacher and teaching the pupils either want or are more responsive to allows me to "put on" personae in order to "become" their teacher of preference' (Author E).

These reflections indicate the influences of previous teaching experience, of personality and empathy, and reveal conscious and intentional flexibility in utilizing persona to create pedagogical benefits to the learner. In light of the aforementioned ideas about persona and personality in music teaching settings, it is useful to consider in what ways these concepts are relevant to instrumental teaching. Therefore, in the following sections three aspects will be discussed. Firstly, we reflect on how the teaching environment is affected by culture, specific norms and regulations in a society. We then discuss conscious and subconscious teaching personae and move on to explore the concept of performance and self-presentation in the teaching environment, with particular emphasis on teachers' and students' public selves.

Enculturation

Interpersonal interactions are an important aspect of our lives. We do not live in isolation; we live within societies and continually move in and out of different social contexts, each of which is uniquely constructed with its own set of norms and expectations. A teaching setting is also a social structure with its own set of social practices. Music teachers, like all members of society, are influenced by the specific circumstances of their background and development, so their response to the particular environment they operate in is likely to be impacted by their culture, its inherent structures, expectations, aims and needs. In the last twenty years, this topic has attracted the interest of several scholars. Baker (2006) studied how the experience of music teachers' schooling and their family environment influence their teaching. In a similar vein, Triantafyllaki (2010) discusses how cultural norms within institutions impact the characteristics and personality of music teachers, concluding that ongoing reflection from both individual teachers and music institutions on cultural norms, expectations and values is valuable to develop awareness of how teachers' professional identity is shaped by these factors. Therefore, it is important to remain aware of how student–teacher relationships and, crucially, students' learning, may be influenced by teachers' identity, personality and culture. In the following paragraphs, two authors of this chapter, who have gained teaching experience across various cultures, analyse how their teaching choices and teaching personality are influenced by cultural aspects.

Author A – West Asian Country

Author A grew up in a country in western Asia, where there are no music lessons in state schools, no courses for music education in universities and no systematic training for music teachers. In this country, instrumental pedagogy in Western classical music is mostly shaped by teachers' experience of their individual studies, their work as music teachers and the experiences they have gained from their own education in various music settings. This situation has both positive and negative implications: some teachers may develop initiatives and creativity in their teaching; others may experience disillusionment, which may cause discouragement for students. Also, it is widely believed in this country that high-achieving performers are good teachers, which is not always the case; therefore teachers may not be fully aware of how teacher training could impact their teaching.

Despite the lack of public music education courses in this country, there are widespread private music institutions as well as home classes, offering one-to-one lessons, group teaching and different types of ensembles. However, given the aforementioned situations, music education is addressed much less than it could be: many teachers are not fully aware of educational methods, diversified perspectives on music teaching or different approaches to students' learning. It is likely that the teachers' personal beliefs and thoughts, their families and the prevailing culture will affect their teaching decisions. This may lead some teachers to use a teacher-directed method, expecting students with different abilities to all become competent or even advanced-level performers. However, if a student-centred method was applied through teachers engaging in a more self-reflective teaching environment, greater consideration could be given to a student's individual capabilities, needs, family background, life circumstances and goals.

Author A has experienced these realities. During their studies for a master's degree in Music Education in the UK (2018–19) they increased their awareness of the power of reflection on aspects of their teaching, which had positive effects on their teaching persona. For instance, previously assuming that each student should become an advanced level performer led to Author A feeling incapable of teaching some students 'properly', resulting in often being unnecessarily strict in lessons. This may have stemmed from being a perfectionist, which is part of Author A's personality. Perfectionism had led Author A to expect every student to be a perfect performer, so their pedagogical behaviours and expectations were based on that part of their personality. After their UK training, which helped this teacher develop their teaching persona and understand that each student is unique, they changed their expectations to align more with each individual student's specific circumstances, needs and abilities. Author A had also been unfamiliar with a range of issues regarding students' barriers to learning such as learning difficulties, which can include physical and mental disabilities. Learning about these challenges further developed their teaching persona: impatience changed to being more patient with these specific students, and their tolerance in difficult conditions during lessons developed gradually. Over time, Author A could critically observe different aspects of their personality and develop relative teaching personae consciously for specific situations.

Author C – Southern European Country

Author C is from a Southern European country where they had been raised and educated until their mid-twenties. The author recognizes that their teaching persona originates from a number of experiences undertaken mainly across two different settings: the European country where they grew up and the UK, where they pursued a university master's degree specializing in instrumental teaching (2017–18) and where they have lived ever since.

Author C's first teaching experience took place in a European conservatoire where they were studying piano performance practice; towards the end of their degree, their former instrumental teacher asked them to give piano lessons to some younger students at an earlier stage of their training. At that point, the author had not received any formal training for music teachers and their approach to these lessons was purely imitative as they essentially replicated what their teacher did and said in their lessons. For example, they used similar words to those of their teacher to talk about repertoire, to praise the students and to discuss points for improvement. In addition, the objectives that the author was working on with these students were aligned with the educational culture of that setting (discussed in the next paragraph). By the time the author left their home country, they had accumulated some one-to-one piano teaching experience and had gradually become more confident about teaching. This type of experiential learning has had a long-lasting influence on the author's teaching persona: thanks to it, they developed familiarity with those adaptability skills, which are an essential tool for teachers working with pupils of all ages and across different contexts. In particular, handling unexpected circumstances – such as students forgetting their music or dealing with excessive parental interference – helped the author develop a teaching persona that is resilient and capable to navigate unforeseen educational scenarios.

Undertaking pedagogical training in a UK university enriched Author C's knowledge and further shaped their teaching persona, particularly in relation to the notion of a student-centred approach, which they did not experience in their home country. Specifically, a different understanding of learners' expectations played an important role: in their experience as a teacher and a learner in their home country there was limited consideration for students' goals; students' learning objectives were often predetermined by teachers assuming that students aimed for advanced performance proficiency. Instead, as a postgraduate student in the UK, the author found that discovering and prioritizing students' goals is fundamental when it comes to defining learning objectives. This orientation supports a student-centred approach and a teaching style that is more flexible and adaptable to a diverse range of needs. Awareness and experience of this teaching style had a significant impact on Author C: it shaped their persona into one that is more flexible and responsive to different needs, fostering an approach that values the unique goals of each learner.

Author C noticed how these two different cultural views, which can conflict at times, informed their teaching persona: the alignment of their teaching approach with students' short-term and long-term goals has become an indispensable part of their teaching. On a number of occasions, Author C found themselves reviewing the lesson content, pace and duration in accordance with a pupil's changing needs. On the other hand, Author C still considers an instructive approach to be extremely beneficial in various circumstances and consciously uses it as part of their teaching persona, particularly with beginners: typically when discussing technical challenges, fingering and individual practice, Author C found that direct instructions are effective and more welcomed by beginner students. In conclusion, the experiences of the culture of two different countries influenced many aspects of the author's teaching practice; the blending of cultural experiences has enriched their teaching persona, ultimately enabling a more versatile teaching style.

Conscious and Subconscious Teaching Personae

The domain of instrumental pedagogy offers examples of how our experiences, inclinations, actions, values and choices, as instrumental teachers, may subconsciously influence our teaching persona. Over time, we learn to respond to the unexpected and unpredictable circumstances we encounter. For example, learners might experience challenges with instrumental individual practice; existing literature demonstrates that early career teachers' responses tend to be based on what they experienced as learners (Haddon 2009; Mills and Smith 2003). The nature of this type of response is not entirely intentional, for it is driven by teachers' subjective past experience. If, on the one hand, personal history inevitably influences one's choices, on the other hand, teachers should be cautious about the extent to which their responses are led by it. Indeed, practice strategies that proved useful for teachers when they were learners may not necessarily apply to their pupils. The effectiveness of these strategies depends on a number of factors other than the teachers' past experiences; a flexible, individualized response is likely to be more effective.

Developing a reflective approach to teaching may help teachers gather insights into the extent to which their teaching is subconsciously influenced by factors such as external experiences. Specifically, becoming reflective teachers may help teachers gain a better understanding of how their persona influences their teaching. Reflective practice typically takes the form of learning logs, journal keeping and collaborative discussions among teachers (Conkling 2003). As mentioned at the beginning of this section, our core values and individual inclinations influence our teaching persona and the choices we make in teaching; by engaging in reflective practice, instrumental teachers might be able to unpack potential subconscious connections between their personality, persona and their values and experience. Having a more accurate understanding of the elements that determine the way we present ourselves in teaching contexts through reflection is likely to result in better awareness and, ultimately, better teaching. In this regard, Parkinson (2017) makes an interesting point deriving from their experience as a peripatetic guitar teacher, relating to the tension between enjoyment and learning in music learning, observing that 'privileging one can be to the detriment of the other' (353). This consideration may prompt instrumental teachers to analyse how these two aspects are addressed within their teaching; natural inclinations and personal experiences might subconsciously prompt a teacher to unintentionally prioritize one aspect over another. As Parkinson (2017) reported, deliberate reflection has been a useful tool to develop a more conscious understanding of how the author acted on these two facets within their guitar teaching. Therefore, such awareness of the processes underpinning our teaching persona may result in positive learning outcomes for music students and, ultimately, in better teaching.

Performance and Self-Presentation

Instrumental teachers are often performers and are likely to have had ongoing performance experience throughout their training; therefore, a crossover may frequently exist in their perception and management of teaching as a performance too (see Chapter 3). This led the authors to discuss the importance of recognizing that a performance-led desire to self-present as likeable or socially acceptable does not necessarily align with success in teaching. The word *performer* itself, which applies to all authors of this chapter, denotes that people are engaged in a performance identity, for example, by performing a piece of music in a given context. They present material, and indeed themselves, in a specific way, thus 'perform[ing] an identity in a social realm' (Auslander 2006b: 101), connecting with the idea of 'goals' and 'self-presentation' discussed by Leary and Allen (2011). Conversely, the word *teacher* is seemingly less explicitly associated with performance. Nonetheless, we are acutely aware that when teaching we are presenting a version of ourselves, a teaching persona; indeed, 'you construct your teaching persona through the actions and pedagogical choices you make, based on the kind of learning environment you want to create' (Bowman 2022: 45).

In addition, Leary and Allen (2011) make a useful observation about social interactions, where people 'are interacting not with another person but rather with their own *impressions* of that person' (1191, emphasis in original). In our teaching roles, not only do we make decisions about how to present ourselves, but we also consciously and unconsciously gauge what our students appear to need and how to plan for this and respond appropriately. By doing so, we make assumptions about their personality based solely on the personae they allow us to see: the personae they present. Experiential discussions among the authors highlighted how a learner may self-present differently in various environments, at odds with the expectations we may have received from parents and teachers. For example, some of the authors have experience of learners who display destructive behaviours in a whole class environment yet appear calm and wholly engaged in individual instrumental lessons. Alternatively, students who are withdrawn in whole class settings can be loud, confident and expressive in instrumental lessons. In whatever way the learner chooses to present themselves, we must choose whether to adapt accordingly or to act more in alignment with our own personality traits. This must be weighed up, as either of these approaches may lead to the desired outcome, depending on what this may be: for example, some of the authors note that when a pupil's exam is scheduled, they may need to alter their persona to present a more formal, authoritative disposition as some learners need this to underpin a structured and disciplined environment to thrive in their exam preparation. For some of the authors, this can create a sense of inner tension between ideal and pragmatic personae, which leads to concerns about inauthenticity, in that they feel the need to engage personae types which are more commonly associated with controlling behaviours. However, as conscientiousness is a trait often found among teachers (Spielmann et al. 2022), it is this personality characteristic that comes into play when endeavouring to meet the needs of the learner. If this means employing a persona that may be outside of their comfort zone, the teacher's flexibility means that they can adapt to the challenge and present the most appropriate persona for the needs of the student: reflecting on discomfort, challenges, approaches and outcomes can support ongoing pedagogical and persona adaptations.

Other examples from our teaching include instances where a student-led approach has hindered the learning outcomes of a lesson, particularly where the learner may have behavioural issues which are exacerbated by too much choice. We have observed that the sense of responsibility to take ownership of their choices can overwhelm some students, particularly if they are used to environments where choices are rarely theirs. This can also be true of learners who may have strong perfectionist tendencies, where these traits are often associated with – and arguably endorsed by – the mainstream musical environment. These learners might benefit from carefully managed and specifically segmented lessons, following the same structure over a period of time, supported by the teacher's persona exuding calm authority. Over time, they may feel more secure and confident with the teacher, which then allows them to present themselves differently, potentially feeling able to express other aspects of their personality and grow in confidence. This in turn means the teacher can gradually morph their persona into a less dominant one for this student to support their autonomous learning behaviours.

Lastly, as mentioned earlier, learners – adults and children – can self-present differently over time. Therefore, the authors of this chapter suggest being conscientiously open to fluctuations in the emotional environment during a lesson. This is a vital skill to nurture as a teacher becomes more experienced. In addition, a reflexive approach to teaching is likely to help the teacher to plan self-presentation strategies while also being calmly reactive to the personae with which their students present themselves. The authors hope that in sharing considerations around self-presentation, we have highlighted that there are circumstances in which self-presentation might conflict with the most socially desirable outcome or with culturally expected norms. Through recognizing the importance of engaging in reflective teaching processes, inherent personality traits can consciously be tailored to certain personae in our teaching environments. Such awareness of our own self-presentation promotes positive outcomes for learners and facilitates self-development as teachers.

Conclusion

Teachers' personalities and choices of persona are likely to have an impact on students' lives; therefore, developing an understanding of these aspects could be regarded as a critical step towards becoming a self-reflective teacher. In particular, cultural and individual values, conscious and subconscious behaviours, insights and personal attitudes are at the core of such inner investigation. This chapter, presenting insights and reflections from the authors' own experiences as instrumental teachers, contributes towards the development of further understanding of connections between personality and persona and how these, ultimately, influence the learning environment.

References

Auslander, P. (2006a), 'Musical Personae', *Drama Review*, 50 (1): 100–19.

Auslander, P. (2006b), 'The Performativity of Performance Documentation', *Journal of Performance and Art*, 28 (2): 1–10.

Baker, D. (2006), 'Life Histories of Music Service Teachers: The Past in Inductees' Present', *British Journal of Music Education*, 23 (1): 39–50.

Bowman, J. (2022), *The Music Professor Online*, New York: Oxford University Press.

Conkling, S. W. (2003), 'Uncovering Preservice Music Teachers' Reflective Thinking: Making Sense of Learning to Teach', *Bulletin of the Council for Research in Music Education*, 155: 11–23.

Fairchild, C., and P. D. Marshall (2019), 'Music and Persona: An Introduction', *Persona Studies*, 5 (1): 1–16.

Funder, I. (2012), 'Accurate Personality Judgement', *Current Directions in Psychological Science*, 21 (3): 177–82.

Haddon, E. (2009), 'Instrumental and Vocal Teaching: How Do Music Students Learn to Teach?', *British Journal of Music Education*, 26 (1): 57–70.

Lang, J. M. (2007), 'Crafting a Teaching Persona', *Chronicle of Higher Education*, 6 February. Available online: https://www.chronicle.com/article/crafting-a-teaching-persona/ (accessed 1 August 2024).

Leary, M. R., and A. B. Allen (2011), 'Personality and Persona: Personality Processes in Self-Presentation', *Journal of Personality*, 79 (6): 1191–218.

Marshall, P. D., and K. Barbour (2015), 'Making Intellectual Room for Persona Studies: A New Consciousness and a Shifted Perspective', *Persona Studies*, 1 (1): 1–12.

McLeod, S. (2024), 'Carl Jung's Theory of Personality: Archetypes & Collective Unconscious', *Simply Psychology*, 24 January. Available online: https://www.simplypsychology.org/carl-jung.html (accessed 1 August 2024).

Mills, J., and J. Smith (2003), 'Teachers' Beliefs about Effective Instrumental Teaching in Schools and Higher Education' *British Journal of Music Education*, 20 (1): 5–27.

Oxford English Dictionary (2024a), 'Personality'. Available online: https://www.oed.com/search/dictionary/?scope=Entries&q=personality&tl=true (accessed 1 August 2024).

Oxford English Dictionary (2024b), 'Persona'. Available online: https://www.oed.com/search/dictionary/?scope=Entries&q=persona (accessed 1 August 2024).

Parkinson, T. (2017), 'Mastery, Enjoyment, Tradition and Innovation: A Reflective Practice Model for Instrumental and Vocal Teachers', *International Journal of Music Education*, 34 (3): 352–68.

Roberts, B. W., and D. Mroczek (2008), 'Personality Trait Change in Adulthood', *Current Directions in Psychological Science*, 17 (1): 31–5.

Robinson, J., and S. Hatten (2012), 'Emotions in Music', *Music Theory Spectrum*, 34 (2): 71–106.

Shaw, J. T. (2017), 'Creating Artistry: Pathways to Teacher Growth in a Professional Development Short Course', *Bulletin of the Council for Research in Music Education*, 213: 27–52.

Spielmann, J., H. J. R. Yoon, M. Ayoub, Y. Chen, N. S. Eckland, U. Trautwein, A. Zheng and B. W. Roberts (2022), 'An In-Depth Review of Conscientiousness and Educational Issues', *Educational Psychology Review*, 34: 2745–81.

Triantafyllaki, A. (2010), '"Workplace Landscapes" and the Construction of Performance Teachers' Identity: The Case of Advanced Music Training Institutions in Greece', *British Journal of Music Education*, 27 (2): 185–201.

Wadlington, E., and P. Wadlington (2011), 'Teacher Dispositions: Implications for Teacher Education', *Childhood Education*, 87 (5): 323–6.

3

Teacher–Performer? Performer–Teacher? How Musical Identity Shapes Teaching and Learning in and Beyond the Lesson

Caroline Owen and Edwina Smith

Introduction

The ways in which a teacher may influence their pupils are manifold and complex. Personality, age, educational and musical background, training and our own experience as a learner may all have a bearing on how we behave as a teacher, how we interact with our pupils and on our expectations of, and ambitions for, them. Watson (2006: 510) suggested that 'who we think we are influences what we do': that our sense of identity is fundamental to our behaviour, both socially and professionally. In this chapter we ask how musical identity shapes teaching and learning in and beyond the lesson. But what do we mean by musical identity, and why might it be influential in our teaching?

Musicians' Identities

Our sense of identity is often closely connected to our profession (Mills 2004a). For musicians, like other creative artists, this can be complicated: we may consider ourselves principally performers, teachers, composers, improvisers or conductors, to select but a few specializations, but we may describe ourselves differently depending on the context in which we are working (Bennett and Stanberg 2006). Our sense of identity may be informed by the balance of these roles within our work. Our culture, upbringing and education, and the views of significant others in our lives are also likely to play a fundamental role in our identity formation and influence how we feel about it. Boyle (2021) noted that teaching musicians may prefer to describe themselves as performers or 'musicians' rather than as teachers, even when teaching is their predominant source of income. Could this be driven by a sense that music teaching is a less desirable or valued career than professional performance? Many scholars have written about identity conflict felt by musicians who have turned to teaching when their performing ambitions did not come to fruition, and some have alluded to a hegemonic culture within higher education promoting a view that teaching should only be considered as a fall-back career for 'failed' performers (Freer and Bennett 2012; Shaw 2023). A negative attitude towards teaching as a career option for musicians, then, may be driven by the very institutions established for the purpose of education.

The Potential Impact on Pupils

A key factor in the development of our identity is socialization. According to Froehlich and Smith (2017), primary socialization occurs during our early upbringing through interaction with our family and closest environment. Secondary socialization takes place once we venture into social contexts beyond home such as we encounter among our peers, friends, teachers, other influential adults and social institutions. As musicians, our instrumental or vocal teachers play a significant role in our socialization (Boyle 2021). Much instrumental and vocal tuition is delivered in small groups or one-to-one lessons, offering an intensely focused form of study tailored to students' individual development – one that is likely to become yet more intense for students who choose to pursue performance training in higher education. As teachers, our sense of identity is likely to have been influenced by our own learning experiences, and in turn we are likely to transmit our own view of identity to our pupils; thus, teaching styles and views of identity can be perpetuated through successive generations (Braz Nunes 2021).

The research literature reveals much about musicians' identities, but few writers (e.g. Braz Nunes 2021; Dalladay 2015) have explored the potential impact a teacher's sense of musical identity might have on their pupils. In this chapter, we consider how two poles of musical identity – the extent to which teaching musicians consider themselves primarily 'performers who teach' or 'teachers who perform' – might influence their teaching and their pupils' learning. Throughout, we share the views of colleagues in the University of York Music Education Forum: instrumental and vocal teachers working in a wide variety of education settings whose teaching experience ranges from under five years to over forty.

Comparing Our Colleagues' Lived Experiences with Research Findings

Inspiration for this chapter came from a Music Education Forum discussion around the topic of identity and its potential impact on teaching and learning. In what follows, we delve into a selection of the vast body of literature exploring musical identities and compare findings with the views and experiences of some of our forum colleagues. In an informal survey, we asked them what they felt had influenced their identity from their education to their experience as a teacher; whether they felt any conflict between the balance of their work and their musical identity; how they had perceived their own teachers' identities; and to what extent all these experiences had influenced their own teaching. Their responses, analysed thematically, revealed a range of personal insights and emergent themes regarding musical identity formation and its potential influence on teaching and learning, which we discuss later.

Fourteen colleagues responded anonymously to our survey, variously describing themselves as 'teacher who performs', 'teacher and performer', 'performer who teaches', 'educator and performer' and 'musician'. For some, their identity had changed during the course of a portfolio career, for one it was 'constantly evolving', but for others – perhaps even despite certain challenges – it had remained the same.

Influences on Identity

Our first area of interest was what influences the development of musicians' identities. Musicians, like other artists, typically take on a wide variety of roles within a portfolio career in order to sustain their income (Bennett 2009; López-Íñiguez and Bennett 2020), and the focus and balance of their work may change radically over the course of this career. Bennett (2008: 2) observes that whereas many working people's personal identity is closely connected to their professional identity, musicians engaged in a portfolio career may well form their identity according to their 'aspirations and goals' – described by Mills (2004b: 180) as 'what one feels one is' – rather than according to what they spend the majority of their time doing. Correspondingly, although many of our forum colleagues described a musical identity matching the role that occupied most of their time or contributed the majority of their income, one identified as a teacher despite spending more time performing than teaching, and another as a performer while spending more time and receiving more income through teaching than performing. A change in the balance of work within a portfolio career had led to a shift in identity for some. Bernard (2005: 5) described identities as 'always evolving in response to our experiences and to the social context'.

Identity Conflict and the Search for Balance

Some forum members expressed a sense of identity conflict following forced change in the balance of their musical work owing to illness, injury, performance anxiety, caring duties or financial pressures. In some, this contributed to a feeling that the balance of their work was biased unfavourably towards teaching because a performing career had proved elusive or, conversely, towards performing when they had discovered greater satisfaction and positivity in teaching.

Research literature is awash with accounts of the conflict felt by musicians who aspired to become professional performers but who were obliged to take on non-performing work, such as teaching, when their performing goals were not realized or if performing work failed to provide sufficient income (Baker 2006; Bennett 2008). Pellegrino (2015: 178) produced a comprehensive summary of research exploring 'teacher' and 'performer' identities among working musicians, describing the 'complex duality of music making and teaching', while Bernard (2004: 281) called music making and music teaching 'a dissonant duet'. British music service teachers interviewed by Baker (2006: 42) recalled originally aspiring to become full-time professional performers, 'however unrealistic it appeared in retrospect'. One of our colleagues described leaving college with 'ideal aspirations' of becoming a performer, while others reported feeling trapped, conflicted or resentful at having to spend time away from performing to sustain their income.

Other writers have described 'role conflict' (Boyle 2021: 10), 'tensions' or 'crisis of identity' (Dolloff 2007: 9), and there are moving accounts by authors for whom personal circumstances left them suddenly unable to perform (e.g. Ryan 2010) and for whom adapting to career change has been an uncomfortable, if eventually enlightening, transition. Ryan (2010: 52) describes a personal sense of upheaval at changing her career focus from professional percussionist to education researcher as well as a change in others' attitudes towards her – most hurtfully, peers who made it clear to her they no longer considered her 'serious about percussion'.

The frequent changing of professional hats may also be a cause of identity conflict in musicians (Creech et al. 2008). The challenge of balancing multiple roles is a feature of a portfolio career. Many teaching schedules leave little time for focused personal practice, while a busy performer may lack the time and energy to concentrate on teaching (or teaching 'has to take a back seat', as one colleague mentioned). Trying to keep employers and stakeholders happy while maintaining a high standard of playing can be a source of stress for teaching musicians who may find their loyalties divided: rescheduling lessons to accommodate rehearsals and performances can frustrate pupils and their families, and schools and music hubs may not agree to rescheduling if there is a risk of disrupting planned activities, even though some institutions expect ongoing professional performing experience as a prerequisite for employment. Some musicians may find themselves working far in excess of normal full-time hours in order to maintain identity and presence as both a teacher and a performer. Within our forum, difficulties balancing multiple professional commitments with family and personal life reflected many practical issues cited in the literature (Pellegrino 2009). Several colleagues found that teaching and related commitments left little time to practise and maintain a high enough standard to accept professional performing opportunities. As one put it, 'Long teaching hours and many extra requirements being a contracted member of a music hub [mean] it is quite a challenge to fit in meaningful practice and sometimes feels like I have to "sneak" it in – as though it's a luxury, rather than fundamental to my role.'

Scheib (2006) suggested that being in an environment such as a school – where the 'performer' identity might not be recognized or considered important – can be conflicting particularly for new teachers and recent graduates of institutions that prize the best performers. Conversely, one of our colleagues felt, when working as an instrumental teacher in universities, that they were afforded greater respect once students and staff had seen them perform 'rather than just knowing me as a teacher'.

What Drives a Sense of Identity Conflict?

Why should 'performer' and 'teacher' identities conflict? Freer and Bennett (2012: 265) argued that a sense of conflict might arise if musicians see themselves as either performers or educators but not both. Some scholars have connected identity conflict in musicians to the segregation of performing and teaching studies in higher education (Bennett 2009; Bennett and Stanberg 2006; Huhtanen 2006; Pellegrino 2009). Forum colleagues from a range of countries reported that teaching and performing were treated as separate career paths in the higher education institutions where they studied. Huhtanen (2006) and Bennett and Stanberg (2006), among others, found higher education institutions lacking in adequately preparing student musicians for the realities of a portfolio career.

Boyle (2021) has suggested that a notional hierarchy of musical roles with career soloist at its pinnacle emerges early in life. Many learners admire and aspire to emulate renowned performers. The 'master' performer as a role model prevails throughout our musical training and in our culture of high-profile competitions within classical and popular genres alike. Freer and Bennett (2012: 267) observe that performance is 'the product that is visible to, and valued by, music lovers in the community'.

Isbell (2008) argues that 'performer' identities are reinforced in children and young people who are recognized as able musicians. As one of our colleagues recalled, performing was 'something that I did well from pre-teenage, and so other people regarded me as a performer and I internalized that from an early age, giving me confidence that this was something I was good at, something that was part of my developing identity.' Ballantyne (2005: 5) acknowledged 'musical efficacy' or confidence as a factor influencing identity: the more confident a performer is, the more likely performing is to dominate their identity. Negative performing experiences and performance anxiety may have the opposite effect, encouraging a shift towards a teacher identity as illustrated by a colleague:

> Issues with performance anxiety and self-confidence, [and an] inner critical voice, have always made me shy away from describing myself as a performer first. I am a much more confident teacher where learning from mistakes is not on major display to a room full of people all the time!

Society's view of music teaching as the weaker sibling of a career in professional performance, perpetuated by the derogatory adage 'those who can, do; those who can't, teach', is well documented in the literature (Bennett and Stanberg 2006; Boyle 2020, 2021). One of our colleagues said, 'I always had the perception that for [their former teacher], performing was more valuable than teaching', while another suggested that in their home country, performing was regarded as 'a more respected and more professional activity than teaching'.

According to Baker (2006: 42), among others, the perception that a teaching career is 'second best to being a "real" musician' is fostered through the education system and propelled in Western culture, while Bennett (2008) has alluded to a 'performance bias' intrinsic to music education and practice. This, combined with the low status of teaching as a profession in much of the Western world (Froehlich and Smith 2017) and perhaps fear of its potential challenges, fuels the notion that a musician should only consider teaching if other plans have fallen through. In the words of one forum member, 'I still struggle a lot because there's a part of me that is still tied up to my identity as a performer and the idea that performance is the ultimate, and more rewarding, goal of my professional life as a musician. I unconsciously think that not performing much or not playing at all equals to being a failure', while another commented, 'When I first started teaching [in the 1980s] it was very much the case that teaching was considered to be something that performers did in order to earn money, or because they hadn't "made it" as performers.'

Some authors have suggested that the notion of teaching as a career solution for *those who can't* has been perpetuated in higher education systems that oblige music students to choose between performing or teaching courses, with the more advanced performers often guided towards the former, and those perceived as musically less 'able' towards the latter (Bennett and Stanberg 2006), leading to a stigmatization of teachers as 'failed performer[s]' (Boyle 2021). Such segregation had been experienced by many of our forum members: one recalled a UK conservatoire (during the 1990s) overtly denying performing opportunities to students who had expressed an intention to become teachers.

The Influence of Teachers' Identities on Pupils' Learning Experiences

If a teacher has absorbed a hierarchical view of performing and teaching through their education, is there a danger of conveying this to pupils whose identities are just beginning to take shape? There is certainly evidence for this in our forum members' comments: one recalls, 'At junior conservatoire, I could see that my teachers there prioritized performance over teaching … they were themselves young professionals establishing their own careers and if they were offered performing work on a Saturday, they would take it and send a deputy in to teach.' Bennett (2008: 2) agrees that as role models, teachers may contribute to ensuring that future generations continue to 'conform to a hierarchy of success, aspiring to careers as soloists ahead of careers as orchestral players, teachers, or other arts professionals'.

Reporting on their own teachers' identities, our colleagues described some who were career performers and others who were full-time music service teachers with varying professional performing commitments. There was no apparent correlation between our respondents' own musical identities and those they had perceived in their teachers; however, it is striking that almost all described their teachers with admiration, as individuals highly influential in motivating their musical and professional choices. A great deal of literature describes the profound impact instrumental and vocal teachers may have on pupils, their career choices and their musical identity (e.g. Bennett 2008; Boyle 2021), starkly contradicting the notion that teaching is a less worthwhile profession than performing.

The extent to which our colleagues' attitudes towards teaching and performing had been influenced by their teachers' musical identities is difficult to ascertain, but the balance of their work and their experiences did make an impact. Two mentioned that their teachers regarded teaching and performing as equally important and that they now wanted to instil the same balanced view in their own pupils. Several aspired to emulate aspects of teaching they had admired. Witnessing their teacher's struggle to maintain a performing career but inspired by their 'exceptional' teaching led one to pursue full-time teaching. Certain colleagues, however, felt their own teacher's approach had been so negative – even damaging – that they were determined to teach in a very different way: 'Getting [my pupils] to see the joy and fun in music and value in the emotional outlet it brings is so important and was lacking from my own lessons as an adolescent.' Another described their teacher as a 'performer who taught reluctantly' and recalled not receiving any positive endorsement of their playing ability until their final lesson. Looking back, they felt this had affected their musical identity: 'If I had had more vocal positive encouragement, I think I would have pursued music performance much earlier and self-belief may have been less of a struggle.'

In terms of their teachers' influence on their learning experience, one colleague said they had 'learned more nuance from those who performed more, but these were also sometimes more difficult to learn from'. Another acknowledged that 'a great performer is not necessarily a great teacher and vice-versa'. Triantafyllaki (2010) suggested that a performer who found playing very easy might not explain things as effectively as a player with experience of needing to solve their own and their pupils' problems, while Carey et al. (2013) noted that performers untrained as teachers might lack pedagogical expertise. Nevertheless, several colleagues described career performers who were inspirational teachers.

Whether a teacher's musical identity may influence their teaching style or their pupils' learning or not, it is intuitive to wonder whether teachers who feel that their musical identity is *compromised* by their teaching role might lack the commitment and enthusiasm of those who consider teaching a calling. We might not be surprised if a teacher who resents having to teach fails to inspire their pupils in the most positive way, as articulated by our colleague who described their 'reluctant' teacher.

Changing Attitudes: Towards a 'Blended' Identity

Research is increasingly calling for higher education institutions to prepare musicians for entry into the profession highly trained for a variety of roles, emphasizing teaching skills among those essential to a portfolio career and promoting a blended 'musician' identity. Mark (1998) suggested that education and performance should both form part of undergraduate training for musicians – a view endorsed by many researchers since. Huhtanen (2006) and Bennett and Stanberg (2006) argued that the value of teaching needs to be promoted throughout music education to ensure that graduates taking on teaching roles do not consider themselves 'thwarted performers', as one of our colleagues put it. Others have called for enhanced professional development for musicians teaching in conservatoires with a view to improving pedagogical practice (Carey et al. 2013; Gaunt 2011). Sieger (2016: 88) has highlighted the value of 'practical teaching experiences' for undergraduates following research with students on a joint performing and teaching degree course who reported a blended identity associated with both specialisms. Previously, Mills (2006) and Bennett and Stanberg (2006) had found that students had more positive views of teaching as a career option following teaching placements, as did several of our colleagues following teacher training or professional development.

Conservatoires now offer degree programmes which, thanks to initiatives such as the Innovative Conservatoire (ICON) project (Duffy 2016), present a broader, richer curriculum than was previously offered. In particular, many UK conservatoires and university music departments now offer undergraduate modules and postgraduate courses in music education. In a positive move towards promoting equality between performing and teaching careers, some conservatoires have also introduced courses in which advanced performing and teaching skills are taught as equal components.

Many music graduates are now emerging with pedagogical training, and those who become teachers may transmit correspondingly positive views of teaching to their pupils. Furthermore, if universities and conservatoires produce outstanding performers who are also trained teachers, there may be fewer who experience identity conflict when they take on teaching roles. Recent changes in higher education appear to be having a positive impact on young musicians' perceptions of career success: teachers interviewed by Boyle (2021: 93) identified as musicians 'enjoying high levels of professional autonomy in careers which involve a variety of professional role identities'. Recent conservatoire graduates interviewed by Shaw (2021: 1) 'considered teaching to be both fulfilling and challenging'. Participants interviewed by Sieger (2016) felt that teaching informed their performing and vice versa. Reciprocally, Pellegrino (2009: 50) highlights the importance of music-*making* for music teachers' well-being, as well as allowing them to 'bring meaningful musical experiences with them into their classrooms'.

Huovinen and Frostenson Lööv (2021) argue that versatility is a core feature of a successful musical career, highlighting how multi-instrumentalists' ability to switch their instrumental identities might inspire performers in general to adapt more readily to other aspects of a portfolio musical career. Such adaptability might prove essential in situations of forced change (Bennett and Stanberg 2006), as discovered by many musicians during the Covid-19 pandemic of the early 2020s. Rather than feeling we are relinquishing a 'performer' identity, embracing multiple identities might rather be seen as our superpower.

The Future: Building Sustainable Careers

Bennett (2009: 326) stresses the importance of seeing success 'not as a performance career, but as a sustainable career', in other words, one that is 'driven intrinsically rather than hierarchically' (Freer and Bennett 2012: 269). Several of our colleagues have found themselves seeking balance, increasingly prioritizing well-being as they move through life. Many expressed the desire to convey a healthy attitude regarding this balance to their pupils and reported drawing continual satisfaction from teaching well and seeing their pupils thrive. Many felt their musical identity had changed over time, mostly away from 'performer' towards 'teacher', although one teacher who was able to take on more playing as their caring commitments reduced sensed their 'performer' identity gaining traction as a reflection of this. Others noted gaining a greater sense of their 'musician' identity through teaching: after becoming a teacher in their early thirties, one now felt 'more assured than ever that I am a capable and confident musician'.

Conclusions

An overriding theme of this chapter is the importance within the education world of inspiring musicians to become good educators themselves. Although our survey was informal and concerned only a small number of participants, their responses resonated with many aspects of findings from the past thirty years of research. As initiatives to prepare trainee musicians for the full range of activities they are likely to encounter over the course of a portfolio career become standard practice, we can hope that future empirical research comparing the attitudes of recent graduates with those of older musicians might reveal an increasingly enlightened attitude towards teaching as a profession, motivation to become a 'virtuoso teacher' (Harris 2012) and a wider aspiration to nurture the next generation of 'fellow musickers' (Southcott and de Bruin 2022: 3).

References

Baker, D. (2006), 'Life Histories of Music Service Teachers: The Past in Inductees' Present', *British Journal of Music Education*, 23 (1): 39–50.

Ballantyne, J. (2005), 'Identities of Music Teachers: Implications for Teacher Education', *Teacher Education: Local and Global: Proceedings of the 33rd Annual Australian Teacher Education Association Conference*, 39–44, Australian Association of Teacher Education.

Bennett, D. (2008), 'Portfolio Careers and the Conservatoire', in D. Bennett and M. Hannan (eds), *Inside, Outside, Downside Up: Conservatoire Training and Musicians' Work*, 61–72, Perth: Black Swan Press.

Bennett, D. (2009), 'Academy and the Real World: Developing Realistic Notions of Career in the Performing Arts', *Arts and Humanities in Higher Education*, 8 (3): 309–27.

Bennett, D., and A. Stanberg (2006), 'Musicians as Teachers: Developing a Positive View through Collaborative Learning Partnerships', *International Journal of Music Education*, 26 (3): 219–31.

Bernard, R. (2004), 'A Dissonant Duet: Discussions of Music Making and Music Teaching', *Music Education Research*, 6 (3): 281–98.

Bernard, R. (2005), 'Making Music, Making Selves: A Call for Reframing Music Teacher Education', *Action, Criticism, and Theory for Music Education*, 4 (2).

Boyle, K. (2020), 'Autonomy and the Instrumental Music Teacher: Negotiating Culture in Professional Practice', *Practice*, 2 (1): 50–67.

Boyle, K. (2021), *The Instrumental Music Teacher: Autonomy, Identity and the Portfolio Career in Music*, Abingdon: Routledge.

Braz Nunes, C. (2021), 'How Musical Learning Experiences Have an Impact on Music Educators' Attitudes and Practices', in H. Meissner, R. Timmers and S. Pitts (eds), *Sound Teaching: A Research-Informed Approach to Inspiring Confidence, Skill, and Enjoyment in Music Performance*, 13–23, Abingdon: Routledge.

Carey, G., C. Grant, E. McWilliam and P. Taylor (2013), 'One-to-One Pedagogy: Developing a Protocol for Illuminating the Nature of Teaching in the Conservatoire', *International Journal of Music Education*, 31 (2): 148–59.

Creech, A., I. Papageorgi, C. Duffy, F. Morton, E. Haddon, J. Potter, C. de Bezenac, T. Whyton, E. Himonides and G. Welch (2008), 'From Music Student to Professional: The Process of Transition', *British Journal of Music Education*, 25 (3): 315–31.

Dalladay, C. (2015), 'The Biography of Music Teachers, Their Understanding of Musicality and the Implications for Secondary Music Education', *Research in Teacher Education*, 5 (2): 17–22.

Dolloff, L. (2007), 'All the Things We Are: Balancing Our Multiple Identities in Music Teaching', *Action, Criticism, and Theory for Music Education*, 6 (2): 1–21.

Duffy, C. (2016), 'ICON: Radical Professional Development in the Conservatoire', *Arts and Humanities in Higher Education*, 15 (3–4): 376–85.

Freer, P. K., and D. Bennett (2012), 'Developing Musical and Educational Identities in University Music Students', *Music Education Research*, 14 (3): 265–84.

Froehlich, H., and G. Smith (2017), *Sociology for Music Teachers: Practical Applications*, New York: Routledge.

Gaunt, H. (2011), 'Understanding the One-to-One Relationship in Instrumental/Vocal Tuition in Higher Education: Comparing Student and Teacher Perceptions', *British Journal of Music Education*, 28 (2): 159–79.

Harris, P. (2012), *The Virtuoso Teacher: The Inspirational Guide for Instrumental and Singing Teachers*, London: Faber Music.

Huhtanen, K. (2006), 'Constructing a Conscious Identity in Instrumental Teacher Training', in M. Hannan and D. Bennett (eds), *Proceedings of the 16th International Seminar of the Commission for the Education of the Professional Musician (CEPROM)*, Hanoi National Conservatory of Music, Vietnam, July 10–14. International Society for Music Education (ISME), 1–11. Available online: https://www.isme.org/sites/default/files/documents/proceedings/2006%20CEPROM%20Proceedings.pdf (accessed 5 July 2025).

Huovinen, E., and C. Frostenson Lööv (2021), 'Narratives of Versatility: Approaching Multi-Instrumentalist Music Teacher Identities', *Research Studies in Music Education*, 43 (3): 386–400.

Isbell, D. S. (2008), 'Musicians and Teachers: The Socialization and Occupational Identity of Preservice Music Teachers', *Journal of Research in Music Education*, 56 (2): 162–78.

López-Íñiguez, G., and D. Bennett (2020), 'A Lifespan Perspective on Multi-Professional Musicians: Does Music Education Prepare Classical Musicians for their Careers?', *Music Education Research*, 22 (1): 1–14.

Mark, D. (1998), 'The Music Teacher's Dilemma – Musician or Teacher?', *International Journal of Music Education*, os-32 (1): 3–23.

Mills, J. (2004a), 'Working in Music: Becoming a Performer-Teacher', *Music Education Research*, 6 (3): 245–61.

Mills, J. (2004b), 'Working in Music: The Conservatoire Professor', *British Journal of Music Education*, 21 (2): 179–98.

Mills, J. (2006), 'Performing and Teaching: The Beliefs and Experience of Music Students as Instrumental Teachers', *Psychology of Music*, 34 (3): 372–90.

Pellegrino, K. (2009), 'Connections between Performer and Teacher Identities in Music Teachers: Setting an Agenda for Research', *Journal of Music Teacher Education*, 19 (1): 39–55.

Pellegrino, K. (2015), 'Becoming Music-Making Music Teachers: Connecting Music Making, Identity, Wellbeing, and Teaching for Four Student Teachers', *Research Studies in Music Education*, 37 (2): 175–94.

Ryan, G. (2010), 'Interruptions Reshaped into Transitions: Personal Reflections on the Identity Challenges of Moving to Music Education', *Action, Criticism, and Theory for Music Education*, 9 (2): 48–59.

Scheib, J. (2006), 'Policy Implications for Teacher Retention: Meeting the Needs of the Dual Identities of Arts Educators', *Arts Education Policy Review*, 107 (6): 5–10.

Shaw, L. (2021), 'From Student to Professional: Recent Conservatoire Graduates' Experiences of Instrumental Teaching', *British Journal of Music Education*, 38 (1): 13–30.

Shaw, L. (2023), '"If You're a Teacher, You're a Failed Musician": Exploring Hegemony in a UK Conservatoire', *Research in Teacher Education*, 13 (1): 21–7.

Sieger, C. (2016), 'Undergraduate Double Majors' Perceptions of Performer and Teacher Identity Development', *Journal of Music Teacher Education*, 25 (2): 81–94.

Southcott, J., and L. R. de Bruin (2022), 'Being and Becoming Instrumental Musicians and Teachers: A Post-Qualitative Exploration', *Frontiers in Education*, 7: https://www.frontiersin.org/journals/education/articles/10.3389/feduc.2022.974184.

Triantafyllaki, A. (2010), 'Performance Teachers' Identity and Professional Knowledge in Advanced Music Teaching', *Music Education Research*, 12 (1): 71–87.

Watson, C. (2006), 'Narratives of Practice and the Construction of Identity in Teaching', *Teachers and Teaching: Theory and Practice*, 12 (5): 509–26.

Part II

Contexts, Roles and Relationships

4

Avenues for Pedagogical Training in Music Education in China and the UK: Aims, Availability and Implications

Anca Eskandar and Xinpei Zheng

Introduction

Instrumental teaching is acknowledged as a versatile profession with multiple roles, as defined in the European Association of Conservatoires' report: performer and artistic role model; planner and organizer; communicator and pedagogue; facilitator; reflective practitioner; advocate, networker and collaborator (Polifonia 2010). This requires that a teacher's expertise has to go 'beyond mere knowledge of content [e.g. music] … but should also include knowledge of learners and learning': learners' cognition, motivation, emotion and existing knowledge (Guerriero 2017: 103). However, musicians with performance expertise are often formally untrained in pedagogical aspects (Casas-Mas and López-Íñiguez 2022; Norton, Ginsborg and Greasley 2019). For example, in China, some musicians may have started their teaching careers in private settings without having studied music formally or having received music pedagogical training; their only relevant qualifications are graded performance exam certificates (Lee and Leung 2022). Additionally, a lack of unitization concerning multiple graded examination boards with distinct syllabi focusing on repertoire and technique (without requiring aural or sight-reading tests;

see Haddon 2024) in the Chinese context (Zheng and Haddon 2023) may further challenge the acquisition of skills supporting qualified instrumental teachers. While school music teachers in China are required to pass the National Teacher Certificate Examination from the National Education Examinations Authority (NEEA 2023), there is not yet a parallel teacher certification process for instrumental teachers. Similarly, no minimum teacher training or qualification is required for instrumental teachers in the UK (Boyle 2021); they remain outside of the Qualified Teacher Status (QTS) requirement by the Department for Education (2014) and are left to their own devices in terms of pedagogical training, with no more than the recommendation in the most recent National Plan for Music Education that 'Music Hubs'[1] should support instrumental teachers with their professional development and a 'clear sense of career progression' (Gov.UK 2022: 55). This may warrant concerns from stakeholders about the quality of the teaching (Lee and Leung 2022) and the availability and accessibility of effective musical and pedagogical materials for instrumental teachers.

Formal instrumental teacher education may be offered through bachelor or master's programmes or might be integrated into school-music-teacher education, depending on societal or national recognition of instrumental teacher qualifications (Polifonia 2010). Additional continuing professional development (CPD) opportunities are also available for classroom music and instrumental teachers to enhance their teaching skills and stay updated with pedagogical advancements (Durrant and Laurence 2010). However, those CPD courses are often criticized for being inconsistent, short-term and inadequate, modelled by a 'one-size-fits-all' curriculum (Bautista, Toh and Wong 2018: 196), while lacking regulation and supervision in the Chinese context (Lee and Leung 2022). Contrasting the opportunities for private and freelance instrumental teachers with those employed by educational institutions, Haddon (2016) highlights the challenges, both practical and financial, of accessing relevant CPD. Notably, the study of Norton, Ginsborg and Greasley (2019) involving 496 UK-based instrumental teachers indicates that despite acknowledging the potential benefits of pedagogical training, participants prioritized professional musical skills and performance experiences as more desirable attributes for instrumental teachers.

This chapter examines available pedagogical education and CPD training sources for instrumental teachers in China, which are compared to the current UK context, and provides a concise view of the multifaceted role of being an instrumental teacher in educational environments such as the UK where mechanisms for monitoring and regulating quality of instrumental teaching are inconsistent or non-existent (Boyle 2021; Stakelum 2024), and similarly in China, where the limited research on instrumental teacher education and practices leads to challenges in portraying an accurate picture of instrumental teaching.

Roles of Instrumental and Vocal Teachers

For many years, instrumental teaching has been sustained by the idea of passing knowledge and skill from the professional musician (the teacher) to the learner, deploying the master-apprentice model with a clear focus on demonstration and imitation (Hallam and Bautista 2018; Lee and Leung 2022). Although the master-apprentice model continues to be utilized by many instrumental teachers (Boyle 2021) as a default across cultural contexts for music transmission (Schippers 2009), numerous music educators have moved towards a more student-centred approach, an idea endorsed by the music education community (Coats 2006; Hallam and Bautista 2018; Mills 2007; Scott and Watkins 2012) and underpinned by empirical and neuropsychological research outcomes (see Hallam and Himonides 2022). This approach involves encouraging the student to express their interests and goals towards learning an instrument so that a plan can mutually be agreed upon between learner and teacher (Hallam and Bautista 2018) with the hope that it would lead to creating a positive educational climate and a teacher–student relationship based on reciprocal regard (Snodgrass 2020).

It has also been suggested that instrumental teachers are often seen as mentors and models of professional expertise towards which students aspire if they decide to follow a music career (Boyle 2021). Hallam (1998) believes this to be the case for students who have reached a professional level, whereas younger and more inexperienced students would not necessarily look for a virtuoso in their teacher but more of an empathic figure who would encourage even the smallest sense of achievement. Many of these learners will choose careers unrelated to music; however, some will continue to engage in musical activities and use their accumulated knowledge as amateur music makers (Hallam and Bautista 2018). With this scenario in mind, fostering independence in the performing skills and musical knowledge that students develop on their instrument or voice could be advantageous, regardless of their long-term music aspirations (Scott and Watkins 2012). In a study involving two experienced and well-known instrumental music teaching experts who have systematically worked with undergraduates as well as younger students, Blackwell (2020) supports the idea that one of the most important attributes of an instrumental teacher is to enable independence: for example, avoiding stopping a student in their playing or singing for every small mistake. This would by no means be encouraging imperfect performances but instead would allow looking at deeper issues such as phrasing. In comparing instrumental teachers with different levels of experience, Coats (2006) indicates that while novice teachers are more likely to be preoccupied with *what* repertoire they should teach, experienced teachers place more significance on *how* materials are being taught. This might in turn reveal how the perceived role of an instrumental teacher would change or evolve as teachers gain experience in the profession and could perhaps indicate the necessity of inclusion of relevant elements within instrumental teacher training.

Instrumental teachers who teach holistically may also deliver wider music content pertaining to subjects such as music theory and analysis or music history in their instrumental lessons (as discussed in more detail in subsequent chapters in Part III). The idea that teaching these wider musical concepts can help students progress more swiftly when faced with new repertoire is broadly supported within the music education community (Abrahams 2015; Coats 2006). In a report for the Society for Music Analysis examining 'the gap in music literacy in England', McQueen (2020) concluded that students' 'musical literacy knowledge and skills have declined, including being able to read and write notation' (2020: 2), while a clear picture concerning whether music literacy was still considered important or not in the music education community (by both teachers and students) was impossible to define due to concerns of social justice and inclusivity. However, instrumental teachers were seen as important pillars in supporting ongoing access to music literacy.

Increasingly, universities are making efforts to provide valuable resources for their undergraduate and graduate music students to prepare them for a 'range of transferable skills' (Creech and Gaunt 2018: 152), creative thinking (Haddon and Burnard 2016; Wan 2023) and the varied identities they will be required to assume once they graduate, often in a portfolio career: from performers to composers, producers and teachers (Latukefu and Ginsborg 2019). However, instrumental teachers also need to take on numerous other administrative roles to support their work. In many cases, they are neither trained for these nor remunerated for the time spent to complete these tasks. As shown in a recent report by the UK's Independent Society of Musicians (ISM), such tasks could include but are not limited to creating schedules, writing reports, booking lesson spaces or venues, exam and performance opportunities, advertising for their services, managing payments, creating invoices and contracts, and tax self-assessment reports for self-employment (Underhill 2022), indicating again the demands and versatility of the instrumental teacher role.

In the next sections, we explore avenues for training available to instrumental teachers in China and the UK, while highlighting aspects such as curriculum and teaching viewed as a means to earn an additional income rather than a primary career.

Higher Music Teacher Education

Programme curricula can influence the professional development and identity of music students as teachers (Haning 2020; Yang 2022). However, music students often prioritize their performer identity over the teacher identity due to their performance-oriented music learning experiences and inconsistent pedagogy-oriented curricula in higher music education (Haning 2020). This negatively impacts how those musicians who teach consider the necessity and value of taking a formal teacher training programme (Norton, Ginsborg and Greasley 2019).

In China, it appears that routes into formal music pedagogical education are exclusively available to music students who are enrolled on preservice teacher training programmes in conservatoires or universities (MA Music Programmes Curricula 2021; Yang 2022). According to the MA Music Programmes Curricula (2021), instead of specialist instrumental pedagogy, the priorities in these teacher-training programmes are school music teaching pedagogy and relevant skills (e.g. improvised piano accompaniment for teaching songs from the school music textbooks and accompanying choirs). This may lead to educational exclusion of support for the development of students' instrumental teaching practices outside of their enrolled programme contexts (e.g. working as a part-time instrumental teacher in private settings) and for those who do not consider the role of a school music teacher as their primary career choice (Yang 2022). A significant finding in Yang's (2022) research discloses music students' compromised decision to step into the school music education profession in China because of their initial performer-prioritized identity and the perception of 'being less capable of doing well [in performance]' than peer students (2022: 323). Moreover, a hierarchical perception regarding musician career options is revealed by López-Íñiguez and Bennett (2020), in which famous soloists are seen as the epitome of success. In an attempt to redefine students' views on professional identities and the evaluation of their career orientations, Miller and Baker (2007) suggested that a pedagogy-integrated curriculum with hands-on teaching experiences may facilitate this process. Deployment of career understanding and employability engagement within the curriculum which can help students respond to the current labour market, is also endorsed by López-Íñiguez and Bennett (2021).

In the UK, music undergraduates have often viewed instrumental teaching as a side opportunity for gaining an additional income and not necessarily as a career path (Mills 2007). However, a more pressing issue emerging from Mills's research indicated that these music graduates and undergraduates were inclined to teach in the ways they were taught by their own instrumental teachers (most likely in a master-apprentice style rather than taking a student-centred approach), due to a lack of pedagogical education and the absence of compulsory pedagogical training regulations (Mills 2007), a concern further highlighted by subsequent music educators (Boyle 2021; Scott and Watkins 2012; Stakelum 2024). In contrast, in a study conducted at the Royal Birmingham Conservatoire, Shaw (2021) observed that fourth-year undergraduate music students who took part in a 'further pedagogy' module noted valuable outcomes: potential for higher employability in educational settings and an elevated sense of confidence in their subject knowledge while being able to make use of the pedagogical knowledge gained.

As with a high personalization of a music student's professional profile that demands specialism diversification for gaining knowledge and skills, bridging theory and practice is another challenging aspect within instrumental teacher education programmes (Polifonia 2010). In the UK, master's degree courses for instrumental teaching in conservatoires and universities have included pedagogy-focused modules such as 'Theories of Teaching and Learning' and 'Musicians as Educators' combined with practical components including teaching placements (MMusEd Teaching Musician, Royal College of Music 2024) and 'Enhanced Student-Centred Pedagogy' and one-to-one instrumental assessed lessons strengthened by reflective writing (MA Music Education: Instrumental and Vocal Teaching, University of York 2024). Other instrumental pedagogy-integrated curricula include 'Pedagogic Theories and Practices' combined with '1:1 and Small Group Teaching' (MA Music and Performing Arts Education, University of West London 2024) and 'Instrumental Teaching' (MA Music Education and Performance, Trinity Laban Conservatoire 2025). Despite these options, questions such as 'When and on what grounds should students make a decision regarding their study programmes, including instrumental teacher education?' and 'What responsibilities does the higher music education institution have in providing information and supporting students in making these decisions?', remain worthy of further attention (Polifonia 2010: 16).

Further CPD Avenues and Support

In China, CPD courses for instrumental teachers are provided by international institutions joined in collaborative programmes (e.g. the Tianjin Juilliard School), conservatories or art-related research institutions (e.g. the Chinese National Academy of Arts, CNAA).[2] These courses are mostly offered online, are short-term, and for musicians are concentrated on repertoire learning and performing skills improvement. The related course descriptions may imply inclusion of teaching priorities in specific repertoire (i.e. *what* to be taught precedes *how* to teach it), while the accessible course syllabi do not indicate the amount of pedagogy-related training content involved nor describe any specific areas of pedagogy addressed in the courses. The College of Continuing Education (2024) of the Central Conservatory of Music, Beijing, China, offers training and certificates for freelance instrumental teachers specializing in piano, violin and voice, as well as the Chinese instruments guzheng and guqin, through the learning of specific graded performance examination pieces while also serving as a platform for educators seeking to enhance their professional skills. Similarly, the CNAA (2024) offers a one-week intensive training course for guzheng teachers, emphasizing performance techniques and musical interpretation, though without mentioning any pedagogical content within the course syllabus

(CNAA 2024). Additionally, the Tianjin Juilliard School (2024) offers CPD courses for facilitating music teachers' practical classroom teaching, with only one course component for instrumental pedagogy listed in the course description. These CPD opportunities typically employ a performance and repertoire-based approach, placing minimal emphasis on theories of teaching and learning and specialist pedagogy in the development of teaching skills for instrumental teachers. Notably, while the assessments are based on video-recorded exam-piece performance and an eight- to fifteen-minute teaching session, no assessment criteria are accessible to the prospective trainee instrumental teachers (e.g. CNAA 2024; College of Continuing Education 2024), leading to the opacity of certification criteria.

In the UK, several organizations offer a variety of CPD programmes designed specifically to include relevant information and training for instrumental teachers. In addition to the aforementioned programmes at the University of York, the Royal College of Music, the University of West London and Trinity Laban Conservatoire, according to the Musicians' Union website (MU 2023) qualifications available in the UK include the Postgraduate Certificate (PGCert) in Performance Teaching (2024) from the Guildhall School of Music and Drama, a Postgraduate Certificate in Education (PGCE) in Secondary Music Education with Specialist Instrumental Teaching from Manchester Metropolitan University, delivered in partnership with the Royal Northern College of Music (pathway to Qualified Teacher Status), and the Certificate for Music Educators (CME), involving courses delivered by regional centres validated by Trinity College London and ABRSM in partnership with Arts Council England and Creative and Cultural Skills. From the three qualifications mentioned above, the PGCert from the Guildhall School of Music and Drama mentions specific pedagogical content for instrumental teaching, with modules such as 'Fundamental Principles in Performance Pedagogy' and 'Reflective Practice in Performing Arts Education' (PGCert Performance Teaching (2024), Guildhall School of Music and Drama, PGCert Programme & module specifications & assessment criteria 2024/5). Other routes for instrumental teacher training are offered through teaching diplomas (exam-based qualifications) designed for instrumental teachers from a variety of teaching backgrounds and experiences. These teaching diplomas are offered by Trinity College London, ABRSM, London College of Music Examinations and Rockschool Ltd. (Music Mark 2024). Additionally, an online search revealed a wide variety of other available PGCE options (focusing mostly on classroom teaching) and other short-term CPD courses or workshops for instrumental teachers (fully online or with mixed in-person and online attendance required).

Aside from CPD opportunities, teachers in the UK can benefit from help and support for financial and legal issues through subscription-based memberships with one of the available professional bodies: the Independent Society of Musicians (ISM) and the Musicians' Union (MU). They each offer a variety of membership options (depending on the personal circumstances of the subscriber: student, recent graduate, early career, standard, disabled, affiliated to an institution, retired), and they all include Public Liability Insurance (PLI). Additionally, Music Mark offers membership to any music educators in the UK but without the added benefit of PLI. No comparable offer for a supporting membership (with or without PLI) is available for instrumental teachers in China.

Conclusion

While the versatility of the instrumental teaching profession challenges how musicianship-focused education within the music programme curricula can be balanced against the pedagogical and practical components (Polifonia 2010), the employment-oriented capabilities of music students such as leadership skills, creativity, resilience and cultural awareness (Bennett, Rowley and Schmidt 2018), as well as the mindset of being an autonomous lifelong learner through critical thinking, reflection, strategic learning and self-regulation are considered beneficial to be developed in higher music education (López-Íñiguez and Bennett 2021). Considering challenges within the initial formation and the redefinement of music students' professional identities (Miller and Baker 2007) across their phases of receiving music education, and actions that support their more or less successful experiences concerning identity development taken by individual learners, educators and institutions, may be worth exploring in future research.

It appears that the CPD courses for instrumental teachers in China have been centred around repertoire performance, with teaching experiences shared by teachers from the conservatories in China. However, Opfer and Pedder (2011) reinforced that CPD courses that did not take into account individual trainee teachers' beliefs, practices and contextualized challenges often led to unsatisfactory training results. Additionally, a lack of empirical investigation on both formal instrumental pedagogical education and the CPD courses for instrumental teachers in China leaves the practicability and sustainability of those opportunities unevaluated. Owing to 'the escalating need to provide both evidence-based accounts of its effectiveness, and ways to improve its practice' (Carey and Grant 2015: 19), we believe that further discussion and research on instrumental teacher support and the instrumental teacher community in China will be able to uncover a more accurate understanding of the country's current position in terms of instrumental teachers' views regarding pedagogical training, how much pedagogical knowledge is imparted within the existing training, whether the facilitators of these courses have the necessary pedagogical knowledge and whether the curricula use the master-apprentice model or alternative student-centred approaches.

Contrastingly, there has been an increased interest in investigating the provision of instrumental teaching in the UK, although processes for monitoring and regulating quality of instrumental teaching continue to be inconsistent or non-existent (Boyle 2021; Stakelum 2024). Worryingly, Stakelum (2024) argues that it is due to the lack of regulation and the often isolated character of the profession that teachers still embrace the master-apprentice method as well as having a tendency to follow graded performance examination syllabi as a given curriculum for their teaching. In doing so, they appear to place the performance side of teaching on a superior level compared to other facets of musical learning, potentially diminishing the importance of theoretical knowledge that a student could connect with learning an instrument and thus hindering the process of acquiring independence in practice. The isolation component would be, in Stakelum's view, relatively straightforward to address through the opportunity for open discussion in the wider music education community (by including freelance instrumental teachers' views in the decisions made) and by offering training opportunities to self-employed instrumental teachers who do not benefit from opportunities such as those offered to teachers employed by schools. In taking such steps, UK organizations such as the ISM, MU and Music Mark are making efforts to contribute towards research for the music education sector by including the views and perceptions of instrumental teachers in their investigations (see Savage and Barnard 2019; Underhill 2022).

The training avenues presented in this chapter (for both UK and China contexts) should not be taken as the only opportunities available but more as a starting point towards the refinement of teaching skills and perceptions of instrumental teachers who are seeking to improve their practice or for those who believe progress is possible at any stage in one's career. In addition to researching the Chinese context to explore the orientation and provision of pedagogical training for instrumental teachers, further development may also arise through the potential not only for cross-genre insights into instrumental pedagogy between, for example, Chinese traditional instruments and Western instruments within China but also for cross-cultural development of training provision, involving sharing insights, practices and opportunities across countries.

Notes

1 Music Hubs are local entities which, in partnership with schools, education trusts, local authorities and other local organizations, are counted upon to ensure the provision of music education in all forms (from whole-class music to individual instrumental lessons) in response to the local needs (Gov.UK 2022).
2 A government-funded institution which integrates research, creation, education and cultural heritage preservation: https://www.zgysyjy.org.cn/introduction.html.

References

Abrahams, F. (2015), 'Another Perspective: Teaching Music to Millennial Students', *Music Educators Journal*, 102 (1): 97–100.

Bautista, A., G. Toh and J. Wong (2018), 'Primary School Music Teachers' Professional Development Motivations, Needs, and Preferences: Does Specialization Make a Difference?', *Musicae Scientiae*, 22 (2): 196–223.

Bennett, D., J. Rowley and P. Schmidt, eds (2018), *Leadership and Musician Development in Higher Music Education*, New York: Routledge.

Blackwell, J. (2020), 'Expertise in Applied Studio Teaching: Teachers Working with Multiple Levels of Learners', *International Journal of Music Education*, 38 (2): 283–98.

Boyle, K. (2021), *The Instrumental Music Teacher: Autonomy, Identity and the Portfolio Career in Music*, Abingdon: Routledge.

Carey, G., and C. Grant (2015), 'Teacher and Student Perspectives on One-to-One Pedagogy: Practices and Possibilities', *British Journal of Music Education*, 32 (1): 5–22.

Casas-Mas, A., and G. López-Íñiguez (2022), 'Instrumentalist Teacher Training: Fostering the Change towards Student-Centered Practices in the Twenty-First Century', in J. Pozo, M. Pérez Echeverría, G. López-Íñiguez and J. Torrado (eds), *Learning and Teaching in the Music Studio: A Student-Centred Approach*, 345–67, Singapore: Springer.

Chinese National Academy of Arts (2024), 'Guzheng News – Teachers' Workshop Enrolment Guide'. Available online: https://m.guzheng.cn/news/291895.html (accessed 24 June 2024).

Coats, S. (2006), *Thinking as You Play: Teaching Piano in Individual and Group Lessons*, Bloomington: Indiana University Press.

College of Continuing Education (2024), 'Outstanding Music Teacher Development Courses', *Central Conservatory of Music, China*. Available online: http://cce.ccom.edu.cn/searchcourse/index?subject=&major=&type=196&level= (accessed 24 June 2024).

Creech, A., and H. Gaunt (2018), 'The Changing Face of Individual Instrumental Tuition: Value, Purpose and Potential', in G. McPherson and G. Welch (eds), *Vocal, Instrumental, and Ensemble Learning and Teaching: An Oxford Handbook of Music Education*, Vol. 3, 145–64, Oxford: Oxford University Press.

Department for Education (2024), Qualified Teacher Status (QTS). Available online at: https://www.gov.uk/government/collections/qualified-teacher-status-qts (accessed 5 June 2025).

Durrant, C., and K. Laurence (2010), 'The Initial and Ongoing Education of Music Teachers', in S. Hallam and A. Creech (eds), *Music Education in the 21st Century in the United Kingdom*, 176–91, London: Bedford Way Papers, Institute of Education, University of London.

Gov.UK (2022), 'The Power of Music to Change Lives: A National Plan for Music Education', *HM Government*, June. Available online: https://assets.publishing.service.gov.uk/government/uploads/system/uploads/attachment_data/file/1086619/The_Power_of_Music_to_Change_Lives.pdf (accessed 24 June 2024).

Guerriero, S., ed. (2017), *Pedagogical Knowledge and the Changing Nature of the Teaching Profession*, Paris: OECD.

Haddon, E. (2016), 'Continuing Professional Development for the Musician as Teacher in a University Context', in M. Stakelum (ed.), *Developing the Musician: Contemporary Perspectives on Teaching and Learning*, 191–206, Abingdon: Routledge.

Haddon, E. (2024), 'Negotiating Pedagogical Cultures: Adaptive Challenges Facing Music Education Graduates on Their Return to China', in R. Prokop and R. Reitsamer (eds), *Higher Music Education and Employability in a Neoliberal World*, 159–72, London: Bloomsbury.

Haddon, E., and P. Burnard, eds (2016), *Creative Teaching for Creative Learning in Higher Music Education*, Abingdon: Routledge.

Hallam, S. (1998), *Instrumental Teaching: A Practical Guide to Better Teaching and Learning*, Oxford: Heinemann.

Hallam, S., and A. Bautista (2018), 'Processes of Instrumental Learning: The Development of Musical Expertise', in G. McPherson and G. Welch (eds), *Vocal, Instrumental, and Ensemble Learning and Teaching: An Oxford Handbook of Music Education*, Vol. 3, 108–25, Oxford: Oxford University Press.

Hallam, S., and E. Himonides (2022), *The Power of Music: An Exploration of the Evidence*, Cambridge: Open Book Publishers.

Haning, M. (2020), 'Identity Formation in Music Teacher Education: The Role of the Curriculum', *International Journal of Music Education*, 39 (1): 39–49. https://doi.org/10.1177/0255761420952215 (original work published 2021).

Latukefu, L., and J. Ginsborg (2019), 'Understanding What We Mean by Portfolio Training in Music', *British Journal of Music Education*, 36 (1): 87–102.

Lee, C., and B. W. Leung (2022), 'Instrumental Teaching as "the Noblest and the Most Under-Praised Job": Multiple Case Studies of Three Hong Kong Instrumental Teachers', *Music Education Research*, 24 (1): 42–55.

López-Íñiguez, G., and D. Bennett (2020), 'A Lifespan Perspective on Multi-Professional Musicians: Does Music Education Prepare Classical Musicians for their Careers?', *Music Education Research*, 22 (1): 1–14.

López-Íñiguez, G., and D. Bennett (2021), 'Broadening Student Musicians' Career Horizons: The Importance of Being and Becoming a Learner in Higher Education', *International Journal of Music Education*, 39 (2): 134–50.

MA Music and Performing Arts Education (2024), 'Course Detail & Modules', *University of West London*. Available online: https://www.uwl.ac.uk/course/postgraduate/music-and-performing-arts-education?start=995&option=33 (accessed 24 June 2024).

MA Music Education and Performance (2023), 'Programme Specification', *Trinity Laban Conservatoire of Music and Dance*. Available online: https://www.trinitylaban.ac.uk/courses/ma-music-education-and-performance/ (accessed 12 May 2025).

MA Music Education: Instrumental and Vocal Teaching (2024), 'Course Content', *University of York*. Available online: https://www.york.ac.uk/study/postgraduate-taught/courses/ma-music-education/#course-content (accessed 24 June 2024).

MA Music Programmes Curricula (2021), '全日制专业学位硕士研究生培养方案' [Full-time Masters' Degree Curricula], *Hangzhou Normal University*. Available online: https://yyxy.hznu.edu.cn/upload/resources/file/2022/09/26/7737719.pdf (accessed 24 June 2024).

McQueen, H. (2020), 'Questioning the Gap in Music Literacy in England: Defining a Role for the Society for Music Analysis in Preparing Students for Music Degrees in Higher Education Today', *Society for Music Analysis*. Available online: https://doi.org/10.13140/RG.2.2.12012.74883 (accessed 24 June 2024).

Miller, J., and D. Baker (2007), 'Career Orientation and Pedagogical Training: Conservatoire Undergraduates' Insights', *British Journal of Music Education*, 24 (1): 5–19.

Mills, J. (2007), *Instrumental Teaching*, Oxford: Oxford University Press.

MMusEd Teaching Musician (2024), 'Course Overview', *Royal College of Music*. Available online: https://www.rcm.ac.uk/courses/postgraduate/mmused/ (accessed 15 July 2025).

MU (29 August 2023), 'Qualifications', *Musicians' Union*. Available online: https://musiciansunion.org.uk/working-performing/education-and-teaching/career-development-in-teaching/qualifications (accessed 24 June 2024).

Music Mark (27 March 2024), 'Qualifications in Vocal and Instrumental Teaching', *Music Mark*. Available online: https://www.musicmark.org.uk/resources/qualifications-in-vocal-and-instrumental-teaching/ (accessed 24 June 2024).

NEEA (2023), 'An Introduction to the Examination', *National Education Examinations Authority*. Available online: https://www.neea.edu.cn/html1/folder/16013/2-1.htm (accessed 24 June 2024).

Norton, N., J. Ginsborg and A. Greasley (2019), 'Instrumental and Vocal Teachers in the United Kingdom: Demographic Characteristics, Educational Pathways, and Beliefs about Qualification Requirements', *Music Education Research*, 21 (5): 560–81.

Opfer, V. D., and D. Pedder (2011), 'Conceptualizing Teacher Professional Learning', *Review of Educational Research*, 81 (3): 376–407.

PGCert Performance Teaching (2024), 'Programme & Module Specifications & Assessment Criteria 2023/24', *Guildhall School of Music and Drama*. Available online: https://www.gsmd.ac.uk/study-with-guildhall/pgcert-performance-teaching (accessed 24 June 2024).

Polifonia (2010), 'Tuning Educational Structures in Europe: Reference Points for the Design and Delivery of Degree Programmes in Music', *European Association of Conservatoires (AEC)*. Available online: https://aec-music.eu/userfiles/File/aec-handbook-instrumental-vocal-teacher-education-european-perspectives-en.pdf (accessed 24 June 2024).

Savage, J., and D. Barnard (2019), 'The State of Play: A Review of Music Education in England 2019', *Musicians' Union*. Available online: https://musiciansunion.org.uk/MusiciansUnion/media/resource/Guides%20and%20reports/Education/MU_The-State-of-Play_WEB.pdf?ext=.pdf (accessed 24 June 2024).

Schippers, H. (2009), *Facing the Music: Shaping Music Education from a Global Perspective*, Oxford: Oxford University Press.

Scott, L., and C. Watkins (2012), *From the Stage to the Studio: How Fine Musicians Become Great Teachers*, Oxford: Oxford University Press.

Shaw, L. (2021), 'From Student to Professional: Recent Conservatoire Graduates' Experiences of Instrumental Teaching', *British Journal of Music Education*, 38 (1): 13–30.

Snodgrass, J. (2020), *Teaching Music Theory: New Voices and Approaches*, New York: Oxford University Press.

Stakelum, M. (2024), 'Music Literacy and the Instrumental Teacher', *Music Education Research*, 26 (1): 47–57.

Tianjin Juilliard School (2024), 'Music Teacher Training Topics'. Available online: https://www.tianjinjuilliard.edu.cn/zh-hans/yinlejiaoshipeixunkecheng (accessed 24 June 2024).

Underhill, J. (2022), 'The Case for Change: The Music Education Workforce in 2022', *Independent Society of Musicians*. Available online: https://www.ism.org/images/images/ISM-The-case-of-change-Report_July-2022_Online.pdf (accessed 24 June 2024).

Wan, W. (2023), 'The Importance of Developing Creative Thinking in the Preparation of Music Education Professionals in Universities', *Interactive Learning Environments*, 2 (7): 3686–96.

Yang, Y. (2022), 'Professional Identity Development of Preservice Music Teachers: A Survey Study of Three Chinese Universities', *Research Studies in Music Education*, 44 (2): 313–30.

Zheng, X., and E. Haddon (2023), 'Pedagogical Transformation and Choice-Making: A Longitudinal Study of Chinese Pre-Service Guzheng Teachers in the UK', *Asia-Pacific Journal for Arts Education*, 22 (special issue): 1–33.

5

Cultivating Collaborative Relationships and Positive Working Environments between Instrumental Teachers and School Staff

Rosemary Lynch and Pete Dale

Introduction

Although there are variations according to the size of the institution, schools tend to be places where faces and spaces are familiar. The staff know each other, many having worked there for years and some for decades. The children recognize not only their peers but also teachers, support staff, administrators, lunchtime supervisors and so forth. Children, teachers and other staff feel that they know their place and the space and hopefully feel that they belong. Teacher–student relationships in schools can be a problem (Quin 2016), but at least members of the school community tend to know roughly who is who. However, the instrumental teacher, at least in a UK situation, is often a much less familiar face in the school. Typically, if they are working in schools, instrumental teachers work peripatetically, going from school to school to work with individual learners or pairs, groups of three and sometimes larger groups. They may visit multiple schools each week, commonly working in two different institutions within a single day (Baker 2005). This chapter reflects some practical realities and problems encountered not only by peripatetic instrumental teachers but also by the school-based music teachers who oversee and support their work; it complements the following chapter, which considers further the relationship between the classroom music teacher and the visiting instrumental teacher.

Existing research literature in relation to this topic is very limited. Typically, researchers with an interest in the work of instrumental teachers have wanted to ask what works and what could be better in a pedagogical and practical teaching sense. The question of relationships between the instrumental teachers and the established, in-school music teacher, however, is rarely touched upon, although Hallam (1998) emphasized the importance of frequent exchange of information, good communication with music and other subject teachers and the need for the instrumental teacher to understand the relevant staff roles and procedural aspects of the school. Lennon and Reed (2012) do mention 'roles' of instrumental teachers in their title and suggest that they should 'work with others as part of an educational team', 'deal with organisational, business, financial and legal (including health and safety) issues' concerning instrumental teaching and 'communicate effectively with parents, colleagues, administrators and others involved in music education in institutional and community contexts' (300). However, the article does not dwell on whether those recommendations are always met, nor does it explore what the instrumental teacher might best do should things go awry (e.g. *ineffective* communication with parents). Coulson's (2012) research provides valuable insights into musicians' experiences of networking and navigating the portfolio careers that they routinely occupy. Although her focus is primarily on the participants' work in the performance sector of their careers, her findings demonstrate the precarious nature of musicians' employment, which may resonate with those including teaching as part of a portfolio career.

The extant literature on peripatetic instrumental teaching largely focuses on signposting individual rights (Musicians' Union 2022; Independent Society of Musicians 2024) and accessing legal advice and support (Musicians' Union 2024a). Literature also documents issues in the lifelong careers of instrumental teachers (Baker 2005), as well as thematic analysis of the career development of school classroom music teachers (Chua and Welch 2020), and more recently, issues including casualization of the instrumental teacher workforce, their status and resultant agency (Underhill 2022). What, though, about the everyday issues in the many and varied school environments in which instrumental teachers may work? These may relate to concerns of facilities, timetabling, priorities and institutional needs, potentially impacting teachers' self-view and ability to deliver tuition to the best of their professional capacity within challenging situations and contexts. It is such lacunae that this chapter seeks to begin to redress: there is at least some academic literature available on visiting specialists and school-based teachers in other subjects such as art (Stein 2004), including acknowledgement that tension can arise between the two parties, but a lack of research since Hallam's (1998) two chapters on instrumental teachers and schools.

Methodology

Both authors of this chapter have worked in schools for many years. Rosemary has over ten years of experience as a woodwind teacher in the UK. Pete worked as a class teacher and subsequently Head of Music in a small secondary school in the Northeast of England (2003–12), overseeing the work of around a dozen different instrumental teachers. The authors consider that it *is* possible, in their experience, for positive and collaborative relationships to be achieved between instrumental teachers and school-based staff through care and determination – but this is not guaranteed.

Data collection began by using existing contacts to request interviews with instrumental teachers and school-based teachers. A wider data collection involving more participants would have been useful, but here the authors sought only to offer initial research with a qualitative emphasis. Having secured ethical clearance for the research from the Arts and Humanities Ethics Committee at the University of York, we obtained informed consent from each of the four participants (two instrumental teachers and two school music teachers, working in different parts of the UK). Clearly a sample of four qualitative interviews (each based on the same semi-structured set of questions) is an extremely small sample.[1] Nonetheless, there were several notable commonalities across the four respondents, with the authors' experiences (in their own practice and from talking with colleagues) resonating with these. Overall, with reference to Gillham (2000) the authors have sought to minimize their own points of view, particularly during the interviews: the pre-planned questions were very open in character, and a reasonable level of researcher distance was maintained throughout the interviews, enabling participants to express their views freely. Both authors contributed to interviewing participants and transcribing the data. Thematic coding was subsequently undertaken by Rosemary, with analyses of the coded data completed together.

The Interviewees

Participants were anonymized at the point of data transcription and are referred to here as ST1 and ST2 for the two school-based teachers and IT1 and IT2 for the instrumental teachers. Some brief information about each one is provided below.

IT1 has experience of working peripatetically in both private and public sectors. Their full-time job is for the local music service, which is the main provider for the region of England in which they live. In the past, IT1 has given home tuition as an instrumental teacher, worked as a visiting music teacher at three different independent schools and delivered some classroom teaching at a state school. IT2 reported working in both private and public sectors and (with a little uncertainty) reported also being employed by private schools for what IT2 described as a 'county music service'.[2]

ST1 is a music coordinator, teaching music only and working in the public sector in one primary school. They reported that 'about 160 out of a possible 260' in this school were receiving instrumental or vocal lessons, suggesting that this is possible thanks to 'pupil premium' funding that is allocated to children from underprivileged backgrounds. ST2 is Head of Music and Music Technology and 'Director of Performing Arts' in a state secondary (a 'faith school'). ST2 reported 'strong links' with a nearby private school that, for example, allows recitals to be recorded there.

Findings

Thematic analysis of the four participants' responses revealed four dominant themes: flexibility, environment, irregularity of employment and managing relationships. These are presented further, with some discussion of the implications of the quoted comments in the latter parts of each section.

Flexibility: 'We've always got to bend to whatever circumstances we find'

For IT1 and IT2, this was an overarching theme. IT1 in particular felt that high levels of flexibility were the key to initiating and maintaining positive relationships in schools, as the instrumental teacher was 'always going into someone else's set-up'. The ever-changing circumstances in a school (such as room allocation, timetabling changes and fire alarms going off) made 'constant reappraisals' a necessity. Bringing a sense of humour and being seen to be adaptable and pragmatic were emphasized: 'You have to not mind the odd bit of inconvenience, and you have to keep smiling and nodding and saying "Yep, I'll do whatever I can" even though inside you're going "Oergh!"' Their advice to those beginning their instrumental teaching careers was to 'try and keep an open mind, try and be generous and kind … because they [the regular school staff] will be having lots of stuff going on in their heads that isn't you, they're trying to juggle things'.

IT2 endorsed the need for flexibility 'to an extent', but experience has taught them the value of 'knowing your limits! What you're prepared to be flexible on and what you are not': 'It took me a long time to get to the stage of saying "no, I'm not doing that". I've got no-one else fighting my corner for me.' For IT2, such insistence that their time and expertise should not be taken for granted was indispensable.

While ST1 seemed to express frustration with an instrumental teacher being 'affronted' after being asked to teach in a corridor, ST2 saw the ability of the instrumental teacher to be flexible as one of the most important things instrumental teachers could do to make their department run as smoothly as possible. This correlated with IT1's suggestion that being adaptable in a variety of circumstances made for a far more harmonious workplace and maintained the instrumental teacher's employment security. ST2 gave an example of an instrumental teacher who was considered to be 'set in their ways' and inflexible, refusing to provide lessons on repertoire that was 'out of their comfort zone a little bit', even if it was more desirable for the student. The result seems to have been that this instrumental teacher lost students through a 'transition to someone else'. Since ST2 could not 'employ five different teachers for [a] particular instrument', the instrumental teacher's lack of flexibility and adaptability would seem to have clear employment implications.

Environment: 'The room you end up in, the time that you can go in, the length of time you can stay there, the access to things like pianos, music stands, whiteboards, computers, all of that is completely dependent on the school that you're in'

Each participant had points to make about the teaching environment: the physical space provided for the instrumental teacher to work in, the equipment available, timetabling considerations (which are closely linked to travel considerations for the peripatetic instrumental teacher) and job viability. Safeguarding and health and safety issues were also all part of the conversation around the differing school environments which instrumental teachers must navigate and which heads of department and music coordinators need to manage to accommodate instrumental teaching in their working environment.

Firstly, IT1 and IT2 reported enormous variations in the room(s) that they taught in. Both reported positive experiences in schools where music is seen as an important activity. For example, IT1 teaches in one school where 'they think music is all-important and they've got fairly serious musicians on staff', resulting in teaching in 'a huge classroom which is "the music room"'. However, IT2's remark that 'there's never really the ideal environment for it in some schools, where music's really, like, low down on the list' was supported by IT1's recollections of teaching in some inadequate spaces. The more extreme examples of these included a car park (during Covid-19 restrictions) and even a toilet. IT2 recalled firmly declining to teach in a certain space as the expectation that they could just teach 'in a cupboard' was 'unfair on the parents' (presumably because the parents were paying for the lesson). Such a working environment is decidedly unfair on the instrumental teacher and the learner, with health and safety implications, as well as the possible detrimental effects on mental health and well-being for everyone concerned (Hallam 1998; Manca et al. 2020). This could in turn compromise the motivation for both pupil and teacher to continue with lessons in these settings and have negative effects on perceptions of the value of music (Hallam 1998).

ST1 mentioned that the post-pandemic school environment has seen an increase in behavioural problems, with 'catch up' interventions for students being regarded as necessary: therefore 'all those spaces ... that we used to use for instrumental lessons ... [have] all been taken for breakout rooms for all sorts of chaos', causing 'issues' and 'fights' (see also the 'Managing Relationships' section). Even in a department with increasing uptake for GCSE and A-level music, resulting in greater numbers requiring lessons with instrumental teachers, ST2 described being 'desperately embarrassed' by the 'pitiful' spaces made available to instrumental teachers as the building itself 'was never designed as a school'. Overall, both ST1 and ST2 reported that provision for the work of instrumental teachers was one of many challenges facing their schools. At present, there are systemic issues within educational buildings in the UK (Booth, Walker and Adams 2023), and although this problem is beyond the control of music teachers, it certainly impacts their and the instrumental teachers' work.

Our participants reported experiencing issues related to safeguarding and health and safety. ST1, for example, reported their concern that during the summer months, students were often at physical education lessons in a field across a main road. This caused delays in locating students, and issues of safety when collecting them, impacting the duration of the instrumental lesson: 'Even if everyone's here [in school], you can't find them.' ST1 suggested that this is a common issue across schools.[3] IT2 mentioned teaching in rooms with no external windows, 'which is not so nice if you're spending your whole day there'. They also reported that in certain schools they taught in, the internal doors always contained a glazed panel, whereas this was not necessarily the case in others. This might suggest that safeguarding is not always regarded as a prominent issue in all institutions, with no standardized approach; this can create safeguarding concerns for both the student and the instrumental teacher. In the UK, all instrumental teachers working in schools must have enhanced DBS clearance,[4] but this can never be a fail-safe guarantee of safeguarding. While internal windows are also not infallible, they add a further layer of safeguarding and can thus benefit all parties (the learner, the instrumental teacher and the school).

Another point of note was the lack of clarity over safeguarding rules and requirements. While one school allowed the instrumental teacher access to timetabling, another school saw this as a breach of safeguarding: regarding the logic behind this decision, IT2 asked, 'Is it safeguarding? I don't know – and the teachers don't even know why!' This caused complications as IT2 would either need to find the Head of Music or go to reception to try to locate students who were late for lessons and eroded teaching time to an extent that IT2 felt 'you might as well not bother' holding the lesson. IT2 also voiced frustration that 'it took me a year to get a lanyard to say I was DBS checked', despite requesting this from HR staff on a weekly basis. This corresponded with their perception that 'in some of the state schools, honestly, I'm made to feel like an inconvenience coming in'.

Irregularity of Employment: 'It's kind of informal, isn't it? This whole set-up is not replicated anywhere else'

The nature of instrumental teachers' employment has effectively been casualized in the UK (Underhill 2022). This leads to misunderstandings around expectations, public liability insurance, fee setting and contractual obligations. Boyle and Widdison (2021: 18), for example, report that 'no standard model' exists concerning rates of pay for instrumental teachers. All our participants articulated difficulties arising from this lack of clarity, which impacted all the other themes. As peripatetic teachers, both IT1 and IT2 are employed differently in different schools, which can impact the fees that can be charged. IT2 commented that in one school, they must pay £2 per pupil per term for a room hire charge which the school justifies as necessary for public liability insurance, although IT2 already has this insurance as a self-employed teacher. The same school is reported to have set the rate that IT2 can charge despite IT2's status as, effectively, a self-employed contractor. Anecdotally, the authors would suggest that room hire charges are happening increasingly in UK schools; this is mentioned by Boyle and Widdison (2021) as a consideration for teachers. ST2 considered this a growing tendency, having heard 'horror stories' about room charges. ST1 suggested that there is a perception of instrumental teachers as being 'bottom of the pile' when they find that the room they were expecting to teach in is occupied at their school: since providing instrumental and vocal lessons 'isn't our core function' (despite being 'vital in nice times'), the implication seemed to be that the instrumental teacher must accept such a situation, chiming with Coulson's finding that 'in most cases, musicians will simply accept whatever arrangement comes with the specific piece of work they are doing at the time' (2012: 252). A question remains, however, as to whether they *should* do so.

The crucial question, here, may be: by whom is the instrumental teacher employed? The answer, arguably, is whoever pays the bills, which is usually the parents or carers. However, there is often a disconnect between the parental expectation of paying for in-school delivery of instrumental lessons and the adequacy (or inadequacy) regarding in-school provision of that service: does the former's expectation match the latter's provision? Further research in this area may benefit from exploring whether the image a school seeks to portray – by advertising the availability of music lessons – fits with the lived experience of instrumental teachers when space is insufficient or inadequate. Our findings (particularly the comments from ST1, who coordinates instrumental teachers' room allocations and who pointedly remarked, 'We don't employ the music teachers') suggest that such questions are well worth asking, and the authors hope to conduct broader research in this area going forward.

The 'very tenuous and grey employment area' (ST1) may impact how the instrumental teacher is perceived in a school environment where other activities are also jostling for space and time. The ambiguous status of the instrumental teacher also manifests when information which is deemed 'sensitive' and available only on a 'need to know' basis is not shared with the instrumental teacher. IT2 mentioned that information about Special Educational Needs (SEN), or behavioural issues that may impact their teaching decisions, is routinely not shared with them. Anecdotally, both authors have repeated experience of this issue, which seems widely discussed among instrumental teachers as something that often stalls instrumental learning and sometimes leads to guesswork by the instrumental teacher regarding a student's (possible) SEN status. The findings suggest that the question as to whom the instrumental teacher's employer is (the parents or carers, the school, the music hub or a mixture of these?) leads to some worrying problems regarding what instrumental teachers may or may not know about the learners with whom they work, and the implications for teaching, learning, ongoing learner support and teacher training.

Managing Relationships: 'I try to be a listening ear rather than somebody who needs something'

At their best, relationships between school staff and instrumental teachers can be nurtured and strong bonds formed, leading to 'joint concerts, joint ventures' (IT1) and making 'connections with what [pupils are] learning in class' (IT1) to benefit all parties. However, IT1 remarked that they and their instrumental teacher colleagues are often treated as if 'it's an imposition you being there … it's just something else they've got to sort out'. Instrumental teachers can be made to feel unwelcome on entering the building: 'You'll get an awkward receptionist who'll say "Who are you, why are you here? Well, I don't know if we can accommodate you" even if you're there every week.' IT2 distinguished between how they were treated in secondary state schools in comparison to a private school, although they thought this could be more about the school size and administrative dynamics rather than being specific to the state or private sector. For example, in the smaller private school, 'everybody knows who I am and everyone in the staff room talks to me at lunch, very friendly', whereas 'in most of the state schools I am 100% ignored. They see me as another random body.'

For ST1 and ST2, building rapport with instrumental teachers was key to successful running of the music provision at their schools. As mentioned previously, if instrumental teachers are flexible, it helps the school staff to manage their department more efficiently. ST1 talked about issues in their school where tempers have frayed between two instrumental teachers on account of space limitations and pupil numbers, reporting a view that the high number of instrumental and vocal learners in their school causes 'strife', which might not happen in other schools with fewer learners. ST1 considered this to be the case for many UK teachers, again citing the impact of the Covid-19 pandemic on space for instrumental music lessons, as well as upon relationships between school staff and instrumental teachers (even reporting that in one case this resulted in physical violence). Regarding their high numbers of instrumental and vocal learners, ST1 mentioned that 'everybody loves it, everyone can recognize the absolute importance ... all of our teachers come to our extra events'. However, 'the goodwill that this runs on is quite thinly stretched'. ST1 expressed a disconnect between some instrumental teachers' sense of entitlement in the school setting and the reality of music provision: the instrumental teacher may feel that 'I am coming in and you don't provide me with the space' whereas from the school's perspective, 'we don't charge for the space [unlike some UK schools, as noted above] and we promote ... a free place to work and we provide you with clients ... It's a school and we have to deliver the National Curriculum.'

ST2 saw the management of interdepartmental tension as a key issue that they deal with. This tended to be when timetabling of an instrumental lesson was regarded by another department as detrimental to a student's progress. For ST2, it could become even more difficult when there was 'a clash of interests' within the music department itself (ST2 did not expand upon this point). Like ST1, they found some instrumental teachers 'frustrating and demanding to work with ... huffing and puffing' with 'tunnel vision ... just fighting over their little bit'. Having said that, ST2 emphasized 'very good' and 'excellent' relationships with most of their instrumental teachers, largely due to ST2 being 'diplomatic' and most of their instrumental teachers being flexible and recognizing the need for rotational timetabling. IT2 also mentioned that they sometimes must write notes for secondary school students who worried about being accused of 'bunking off' if they could not prove that they had been to a music lesson. This contrasts sharply with primary school settings where IT1 found it easier to foster good relationships with staff: 'getting to know the staff, getting to know the headteacher but, as importantly, getting to know the class teachers means that they know who you are, and that they know who the person is who's taking the children out [of their lesson]'. Perhaps the rotational nature and larger scale of secondary schools means that this greater trust element is not possible in those school settings.

Discussion and Conclusion

The findings of this small-scale qualitative study are suggestive but non-generalizable. Nonetheless, a larger-scale investigation, including a quantitative dimension, could yield results with impactful benefits for schools across the UK and perhaps beyond. While a huge proportion of the UK's schools benefit from weekly visits from instrumental teachers, the findings suggest that there may be several problems with the potentially ad hoc functioning of this substantial part of our educational landscape. Indeed, some of these problems seem to be worsening; the perceived trend towards schools charging peripatetic instrumental teachers for working space is a matter of concern.[5]

The participants' responses seem to provide a cautionary tale for early career practitioners in particular: managing flexibility levels appears key to successful partnerships between school staff and instrumental teachers. More broadly, an understanding of the fluctuations in a school's day-to-day administration seems important. For the instrumental teacher to view their role as a benign outsider, an 'external friend' (IT1), may be beneficial: 'If you go in really open, it's really likely to come back to you' (IT1). Thus, over time, the instrumental teacher might come to be seen as an insider-of-a-sort, and reciprocal flexibility could be achieved between the instrumental teacher and the school staff. While it is essential for the instrumental teacher to have limits regarding their efforts to be flexible, finding a workable balance in that regard can become easier once the instrumental teacher understands how a particular school environment works. IT1's remark 'no, I'm not doing that' is clearly a firm wording to decline to teach in an inhospitable environment: it is not necessarily an impolite statement, as it is possible to be both firm and polite. It is clear that careful negotiation, a 'balancing act', will be required in many concrete situations if positive relationships are to be maintained.

Therefore, the findings suggest that collaborative and positive working relationships and environments are achievable, particularly where flexibility is practised not only by the instrumental teacher but also among the school staff. A need for instrumental teachers to access consistent and adequate spaces in which to do their work is apparent: working in a room with an internal and external window should be non-negotiable. The employment of instrumental teachers is clearly something of a grey area: the solution to this is not obvious, but the problem seems to be significant (especially for parents or carers who may not realize that they are paying for a provision that, often through no fault on the part of the instrumental teacher, has inadequacies which may impact on the learning of the pupil). Guidance on this topic from material such as the Musicians' Union 'Charter for Visiting Music Teachers' (Musicians' Union 2024b) may support musicians aspiring to understand their legal rights and the responsibilities of the host institution. The management of relationships, meanwhile, would seem to be of pivotal importance: if collaborative relationships between instrumental teachers and school staff are not achieved, a negative impact upon working environments, teacher satisfaction and teacher and student retention looks to be likely. Further research could usefully explore these tensions and identify ways in which positive outcomes can be brought about in order to benefit all stakeholders in this context.

Notes

1. Ofsted did a similarly small qualitative interview study as part of their report exploring the initial successes and failings of the switch to music hubs. Interviewing only three hub leads, they produced a report that still resonates today with some of the issues that schools and instrumental teachers encounter with the model: https://assets.publishing.service.gov.uk/media/5a8039f7ed915d74e622d370/Music_in_schools_what_hubs_must_do.pdf.
2. Until 2012, county music services were the common model in the UK. Since 2012, however, the 'music hub' has become the new model, which is supposed to differ from the preceding model (Ofsted 2013: 23). https://assets.publishing.service.gov.uk/media/5a8039f7ed915d74e622d370/Music_in_schools_what_hubs_must_do.pdf.
3. The authors' experiences in schools support this: in theory, pupils should follow a given timetable and take themselves to an agreed location (e.g. a practice room) each week for their lesson; in practice, pupils may forget to attend, and the instrumental teacher might attempt to locate them so that the lesson can take place. This can pose a security risk to the belongings of the instrumental teacher, as well as a duty beyond the likely terms of their contract.
4. https://crbdirect.org.uk/school-non-teaching-enhanced-dbs-check/.
5. A lively conversation on this topic recently appeared on the UK Music Teachers social media page, demonstrating varying experiences of contributors and highlighting how contentious this issue is.

References

Baker, D. (2005), 'Music Service Teachers' Life Histories in the United Kingdom with Implications for Practice', *International Journal of Music Education*, 23 (3): 263–77.

Booth, R., P. Walker and R. Adams (2023), 'English Schools Told to Close Buildings Made with Crumble Risk Concrete', *The Guardian*, 31 August. Available online: https://www.theguardian.com/education/2023/aug/31/english-schools-told-to-close-buildings-made-with-crumble-risk-concrete (accessed 20 August 2024).

Boyle, K., and D. Widdison (2021), *The Essential Handbook for Musicians Who Teach: A Practical Guide for Instrumental and Singing Teachers*, London: Faber Music.

Chua, S. L., and G. F. Welch (2020), 'A Lifelong Perspective for Growing Music Teacher Identity', *Research Studies in Music Education*, 43 (3): 329–46.

Coulson, S. (2012), 'Collaborating in a Competitive World: Musicians' Working Lives and Understandings of Entrepreneurship', *Work, Employment and Society*, 26 (2): 246–61.

Gillham, B. (2000), *The Research Interview*, London: Continuum.

Hallam, S. (1998), *Instrumental Teaching*, Oxford: Heinemann.

Independent Society of Musicians (2024), 'Membership Benefits', *ISM*. Available online: https://www.ism.org/join-us/benefits/?gad_source=1 (accessed 20 August 2024).

Lennon, M., and G. Reed (2012), 'Instrumental and Vocal Teacher Education: Competences, Roles and Curricula', *Music Education Research*, 14 (3): 285–308. https://doi.org/10.1080/14613808.2012.685462.

Manca, S., V. Cerina, V. Tobia, S. Sacchi and F. Fornara (2020), 'The Effect of School Design on Users' Responses: A Systematic Review (2008–2017)', *Sustainability*, 12 (8): 3453. https://doi.org/10.3390/su12083453.

Musicians' Union (2022), 'Employment Status for Instrumental and Vocal Teachers'. Available online: https://musiciansunion.org.uk/working-performing/education-and-teaching/music-teacher-pay-and-employment/employment-status-for-instrumental-and-vocal-teachers (accessed 20 August 2024).

Musicians' Union (2024a), 'Benefits of MU Membership'. Available online: https://musiciansunion.org.uk/membership-benefits (accessed 20 August 2024).

Musicians' Union (2024b), 'Charter for Visiting Music Teachers'. Available online: https://musiciansunion.org.uk/working-performing/working-with-musicians-and-music/school-visiting-music-teacher-guide/charter-for-visiting-music-teachers (accessed 20 August 2024).

Ofsted (2013), 'Music in Schools: What Hubs Must Do', *Ofsted*. Available online: https://assets.publishing.service.gov.uk/media/5a8039f7ed915d74e622d370/Music_in_schools_what_hubs_must_do.pdf (accessed 16 June 2024).

Quin, D. (2016), 'Longitudinal and Contextual Associations between Teacher–Student Relationships and Student Engagement: A Systematic Review', *Review of Educational Research*, 87 (2): 345–87. https://doi.org/10.3102/0034654316669434.

Stein, D. (2004), 'Wearing Two Hats: The Case of Visiting Artists in the Classroom', *Goodwork Project Report Series*, 29. Available online: https://static1.squarespace.com/static/5c5b569c01232cccdc227b9c/t/5e90bac8ea07bc61b16f17c1/1586543305183/29-Wearing-Two-Hats-5_04.pdf (accessed 20 August 2024).

Underhill, J. (2022), 'The Case for Change: The Music Education Workforce in 2022', *ISM*. Available online: https://www.ism.org/images/images/ISM-The-case-for-change-Report_July-2022_Online.pdf (accessed 20 August 2024).

6

A Shared Approach? Peripatetic and Classroom Music Teachers' Perspectives on Pedagogy and Professional Relationships

Hannah Ellis, Caroline Owen,
James Poole and Pete Dale

Introduction

During students' secondary school music education journeys there are manifold influences on their learning experiences. Whole class music teachers (WCTs) are present throughout a student's school music education, with this input increasing if students select music as an 'options' subject (at UK Key Stages 4 and 5, for school students aged fourteen to eighteen). If a student pursues instrumental lessons, their development is largely also shaped by their peripatetic instrumental teachers. The authors of this chapter are education practitioners who are either currently working or have worked as instrumental teachers and WCTs in schools. The impetus for our research, which complements the focus of Chapter 5, arose from a desire to investigate the differences and similarities in pedagogical approaches between practitioners in these two roles, with both being integral to students' musical growth.

The need for closer collaborations between school and external music education providers has consistently been highlighted, most notably in multiple UK Department for Education reports (Department for Education 2021; 2022; 2023) and by educators such as Derbyshire (2015). Ofsted[1] recommends that instrumental teachers are seen to know 'how to set their teaching into the broader context of students' music learning, including the National Curriculum' (Ofsted 2002: 4). Educational programmes from Musical Futures and Trinity College London have actively encouraged further connections between these roles (Hallam et al. 2009). Teachers can collaboratively create 'models of creative and inherently musical practices which promote the development of different types of musical learning' (Christmas 2016: 6). Instrumental teachers and WCTs could therefore provide practical support in each other's teaching spaces, helping students to develop positive musical identities and pursue instrumental lessons, particularly to provide differentiation for higher-ability students (Lamont 2017; Philpott 2007). A focus on shared pedagogical practices and the transferability between these different teaching roles has consequently arisen (Kokotsaki 2010; Roulston, Legette and Womack 2007; Welch et al. 2011), though strategies for collaborative practice require further investigation.

Some studies have highlighted potential obstacles to the implementation of such recommendations, especially time constraints (Stijnen, Nijs and Van Petegem 2023), feelings of disconnection when instrumental teachers are moving between schools (Baker 2006) and generally declining numbers of music education practitioners (APPG for Music Education 2019). However, practical recommendations to overcome these have rarely been proposed, despite recognition that music teachers are particularly susceptible to feelings of professional isolation (Davidson and Dwyer 2014). The aim of our study is to gain a greater understanding of instrumental teachers' and WCTs' attitudes towards collaborative working and to identify pedagogical approaches that could be developed to counteract existing challenges and improve working relationships.

Methodology

This study received ethical approval from the Arts and Humanities ethics committee at the University of York. An invitation to complete a questionnaire was sent to potential respondents via a network of instrumental teachers and WCTs. The eleven respondents comprised seven who had only worked as instrumental teachers (whose experience included group, one-to-one and whole-class instrumental tuition) and four who had worked as WCTs and instrumental teachers.[2] The focus on instrumental teachers was not a conscious choice; rather it is a reflection of the respondents who engaged with our questionnaire as no respondent selected the 'WCT only' option. The occurrence of all WCTs having experience of working as instrumental teachers is perhaps indicative of career change or of a tendency in some schools for WCTs to take on some instrumental tuition alongside their class teaching. Respondents worked primarily in secondary schools but also in music hubs, universities and private settings. Respondents' teaching experiences ranged from less than a year to over thirty years.

The questionnaire used open questions with some quantitative Likert scales and was split into three sections: basic information about teachers' experiences and educational workplaces; questions on the working relationships between instrumental teachers and WCTs to gather respondents' attitudes regarding existing and potential benefits and limitations of collaborative pedagogical approaches; and respondents' evaluations of their pedagogical approaches and the transferability of these between instrumental teachers and WCTs. The data was collated and analysed thematically; during this process the authors strove to maintain objectivity and parity between respondents' differing opinions. Within the following text, respondent quotations are provided to ensure detailed representation of teachers' voices. A distinction is made between those with experience working only as instrumental teachers and those who have worked as both instrumental teachers and WCTs to explore any differences in attitude between these groups.

Findings

We begin with a discussion of the *professional relationships* that can underpin a shared approach among instrumental teachers and WCTs. We follow this with a discussion of the *pedagogical approaches* that our respondents identified in their responses to our questionnaire and any common techniques or shared approaches that were identified.

Professional Relationships

In this section, findings concerning professional relationships between instrumental teachers and WCTs are approached in two stages: firstly, perceptions of current working relationships are examined; secondly, we offer an analysis of strategies that might strengthen professional relationships.

How Do Instrumental Teachers and WCTs Perceive Their Professional Relationships?

Respondents were asked to indicate how closely they had worked with one another through a ten-point Likert scale, with 1 indicating that they do not work closely and 10 suggesting very close professional relationships. Instrumental teachers gave a mean response of 4 across a range of 1 to 6, while the four instrumental teachers who (have) also work(ed) as WCTs (Instrumental teachers+WCTs) gave a mean response of 6.25 across a range of 5 to 7. Instrumental teachers appear more likely to believe they work less closely with WCTs; one later reported that they felt 'neglected' as a peripatetic teacher working in a school and 'forced to discover information'. This reflects the 'isolation' experienced by instrumental teachers delivering one-to-one lessons in higher education (Burwell 2005: 199) and private studios (Creech 2010), and the disconnect experienced by a small number of instrumental teachers working in schools in Baker's (2006) study. Given that six of the seven instrumental teachers reported that they teach in schools, perceptions of professional relationships may vary owing to different teaching contexts.

Respondents were also asked to report on any observed changes in their professional relationships over the course of their careers; responses reiterate the range of perceptions concerning professional relationships. Some instrumental teachers felt confident in their professional relationships and believed that these had improved; one described relations as 'more positive', and another reported that 'more communication' takes place. In contrast, two instrumental teachers suggested that professional relationships had not changed, with one highlighting WCTs' increased 'stress levels'. This suggests that the many challenges faced by WCTs (Bath et al. 2020; Savage 2021) make it difficult for them to dedicate time to develop professional relationships despite the potential benefits.

The responses of those with experience of working in both roles are also mixed: one teacher with over twenty years' experience as an instrumental teacher as well as WCT experience claimed that there is 'less collaboration' and 'a wider distance these days between what myself as an instrumental teacher is doing and what the class teachers are doing in the department'. Another with experience in both roles reported that the quality of professional relationships 'depends on the school' and described collaborations in their current school as 'sporadic'. They went on to state that they communicate 'when needs arise', again suggesting that classroom music teachers' availability is limited, and they may only be able to communicate when there is a perceived 'need'. The 'sporadic' nature of these relationships is corroborated by an instrumental teacher who reported that they engage with WCTs when they 'bump into them'. Furthermore, the strength of professional relationships may vary not only *between* schools but also *within* them: a teacher with experience in both roles revealed their former responsibility for coordinating instrumental teachers and that this allowed them to sustain 'a stronger working relationship'. This indicates that instrumental teachers may be familiar with the member of staff who coordinates peripatetic teachers but may not enjoy a close relationship with the WCT who teaches their student(s) whole-class music lessons. In short, communication across a team of WCTs and instrumental teachers may be inconsistent.

Respondents were also asked whether instrumental teachers and WCTs discuss KS4 and KS5 students' progress with one another. Six instrumental teachers reported that they communicate with WCTs (one further instrumental teacher did not give a direct answer, instead suggesting how communication might be improved), but only two of the four with experience in both roles indicated that communication takes place between instrumental teachers and WCTs, with one reporting that this depended on the school that they work in and another simply writing 'no'. This could again point to the current challenges faced by WCTs and their limited available time to build and sustain relationships. Respondents were then asked to describe how beneficial these discussions are through a five-point Likert scale in which 5 indicated that discussions were perceived as very beneficial, and 1 suggested that discussions were not beneficial. Interestingly, four of the seven instrumental teachers gave the highest rating (5), while three others rated 4, 3, and 2, respectively. Three teachers with experience of both roles rated discussions with instrumental teachers 5 and one gave 3. Overall, this indicates that both groups of teachers believe that discussions are beneficial, but the range of responses could suggest that the perceived quality and success of this communication is varied.

Finally, respondents were asked to describe the impact of communication between teachers. Responses reveal that discussions benefit teachers *and* students; for example, communication can enable teachers to make practical arrangements for performance assessments. One instrumental teacher reported that both groups of teachers can discuss the 'suitability of repertoire, issues around performance anxiety and recording, timings of performance, etc.' Respondents also emphasized positive outcomes for students such as creating a 'supportive framework', building student confidence and assessing the suitability of repertoire choices. One respondent said: 'The students see you all as working collaboratively in the shared goal of helping them … it shows the student that communication is good and so there's trust which helps the student feel confident too.' Two instrumental teachers and one with experience of both roles suggested that WCTs could communicate the topics or musical works being studied in classroom music lessons so that instrumental teachers might provide additional support to students, highlighting the potential value of close professional relationships for students' learning. Reports of 'sporadic' or inconsistent communication hint that there is sometimes room to strengthen these professional relationships.

How Might Professional Relationships Be Improved?

Teachers were invited to detail factors that might hinder collaboration between instrumental teachers and WCTs. The most frequently cited factor was a lack of time. One instrumental teacher explained that busy timetables can result in a 'shorter visit' in some schools. Another said that they are 'too busy' to communicate with classroom teachers. This suggests that WCTs *and* instrumental teachers are facing time constraints that may make it difficult to sustain communication. One further instrumental teacher reported that they did not have access to enough information concerning KS4 and KS5 performance assessments, underlining the disconnect felt by some instrumental teachers from the schools in which they work. Three with experience of both roles also suggested that a limited amount of available time can make it difficult to communicate, and a fourth mentioned that it was difficult to find 'the time to actively discuss'. One used a simile to describe this problem, writing, 'We are very often "like ships passing in the night" – we simply don't see each other often enough and have very limited time when we do.'

When respondents were asked to detail factors that support productive collaboration, 'regular' communication was the most cited. One instrumental teacher prioritized 'regular meetings', and another suggested 'regular consultations' are needed. One with experience of both roles suggested that 'regular emails' are also effective. Alternatively, a shared online drive or document that could be updated when needed may enable teachers to communicate efficiently and at a time that suits them.

A teacher with experience of both roles called for a 'willingness from both sides to engage and form positive relationships' while another suggested that 'proactive engagement from both sides' would support collaboration. This underlines that both parties need to be committed to developing these professional relationships and that responsibility for communication should not lie with one member of staff. The notions of 'mutual respect', 'clear communication', a 'non-territorial' attitude and 'flexible approach' were also suggested by instrumental teachers as factors that may underscore strong relationships. One instrumental teacher noted the value of sharing important dates and deadlines, pointing to the need for colleagues in both teaching contexts to be able to plan effectively. Finally, respondents suggested that focusing on the needs of their students can unite teachers and support collaboration. One instrumental teacher suggested that both groups of teachers should have 'the best interests of the students at heart' while another indicated that 'a desire to support [students] to the fullest extent' can support professional relationships. Awareness of this shared goal may further motivate teaching staff to continue developing relationships.

Pedagogical Approaches

Despite potentially different training routes and career experiences, respondents shared views and concerns about many aspects of music education, and the pedagogical practices of both instrumental teachers and those with experience of both roles had much in common. A focus on their students' needs was apparent throughout. This section details some of the similarities in the respondents' teaching approaches, which illustrate a common approach to their students' learning despite the disparate nature of their respective professional roles.

Fostering Autonomy

Respondents unanimously felt that students should develop greater autonomy as they get older and that, by KS4 and KS5, students should be making independent decisions about how they study and practise. In instrumental and academic lessons, teachers used a range of strategies to support KS4 and KS5 students to increase their independence. These included encouraging students to select repertoire and consider this within its historical context to frame their interpretations and wider listening to discover new repertoire. Teachers reported using open questions to facilitate student-led discussions on how to approach practice, expressive interpretation and technical challenges. Two instrumental teachers regularly asked students to make their own lesson notes and to take responsibility for planning the structure of their practice sessions, 'as this really seems to help embed it [lesson content]'. Several mentioned the importance of developing students' capacities to adopt reflective cycles: 'a skill that is essential and can be taught by constantly questioning (why? how? what might happen?)'.

Motivation

In terms of motivating students, several teachers set small, attainable goals every lesson to promote students' sense of achievement, and some offered small rewards such as stickers. All respondents emphasized intrinsic over extrinsic motivation, although some with experience of both instrumental and WCT roles noted the effectiveness of rewards as extrinsic motivators to encourage positive behaviour and effort.

Pedagogical strategies used by instrumental teachers to foster intrinsic motivation included encouraging students to 'take ownership' of their playing by choosing repertoire, finding their own strategies to develop technical fluency, and working towards formal and informal performances. It was noted that young children often enjoy playing to their friends, which might motivate some to seek out and learn new repertoire. Several teachers mentioned using open questions to prompt students to make their own decisions about expressive performance to encourage them to develop their own stylistic interpretations, reflecting the perceptions of instrumental teachers in Meissner and Timmers's (2020) research. One teacher spoke of inspiring students by communicating 'my personal love for the subject'. WCTs found that encouraging students to work in pairs or individually on projects or research could foster intrinsic motivation. Many advocated encouraging students to engage with music that they found enjoyable first and foremost.

Some instrumental teachers used concert performances and graded examinations as strategies to build extrinsic motivation, one describing discussing 'future career goals and pathways' with students as effective motivation. Nevertheless, teachers had mixed views about the value of exams, as detailed further.

Performance Exams

Some respondents with experience of both WCT and instrumental teacher roles viewed graded exams as valuable tools to track progress and provide useful formal training for further assessed performances, but not necessarily essential. Mock recitals or other school concert performances were suggested as equally valuable preparation exercises. Several teachers felt that graded performance exams were not essential for students to progress and that some students might suffer undue stress if pushed to take them unwillingly (see also Chapter 16). Teachers nevertheless generally felt that graded music exams held some importance during preparations for KS4 and KS5 assessed performances. It was considered that any occasion to perform could be helpful and that students with more performing experience often fared better in KS4 and KS5 recitals. One teacher stated that they had 'seen several [students] get A [currently a 7-8 grade in England and Wales] at GCSE when they have no [performance] grade qualifications, although perhaps not A* [equivalent 8-9]'.

Listening, Analysing and Composing

All respondents said that they sought to develop their students' listening, analysing and composing skills, with some teachers working on these skills very frequently. Several instrumental teachers mentioned the value of discussing analysis and composition curriculum requirements with class teachers:

> I often want to do more work on analysis, listening and composition, but am limited by the amount of time I have to cover all the multitude of different areas I'd like to work on ... if I knew what was being worked on in class lessons each week it would be much easier to reinforce that in individual lessons, or prepare for that in what we do so that it could then be reinforced in group lessons.

The chapter authors have observed (from working as instrumental teachers) that students taking KS4 and KS5 music qualifications often demonstrate more sophisticated understandings of musical form and structure, aural analysis skills and wider repertoire awareness in their instrumental lessons than those not taking these courses. This presumably indicates that WCTs are giving valuable support in these areas. It was clear from the questionnaire responses that teachers in both groups wanted to understand more about their colleagues' work to help them better support students, although awareness of the value of such collaborations was balanced by a general agreement that finding time to meet was often difficult.

Individual or Group Tuition

Respondents had mixed views on the relative merits and drawbacks of both individual and group tuition, although most recognized the value of individual tuition for focused work on instrument-specific aspects of learning. Most saw advantages to both learning contexts, recognizing that group lessons might support peer learning and scope to work on ensemble music and group improvising. However, some felt that only individual lessons offered students adequate teacher attention and focus:

> The time constraints when you have a group lesson can be really limiting. It can work well but sometimes the group dynamic can be a nightmare and individuals suffer. They are in groups in class all the time so for some of them, they really thrive when they get 1:1 time and they get to make decisions around what they like to play.

One instrumental teacher and one teacher with experience of both instrumental and WCT roles felt that group learning was preferable for beginners or younger students who might be encouraged by being with their friends. Others expressed concern about teaching mixed-ability groups: '[Students] very rarely progress at the same pace so someone is always left behind' and some students' behaviour can be 'a distraction (for both me and the [learners])'. Several instrumental teachers and those with experience of both roles suggested that senior students could benefit from a mixture of group learning (to share ideas and perform to each other) and individual tuition (to focus on personal learning needs): 'One should not exist without the other, individual teaching is required to master technical skills, group work is important to teach musicality and often has a greater contribution to developing listening skills.' In classrooms, those with experience of both instrumental and WCT roles valued group work for activities such as analysing set works and one-to-one time during composition tasks.

A Shared Approach: Our Students' Musical Prosperity

Our findings highlight that, despite their different working contexts, instrumental teachers and WCTs have many views and approaches in common, their students' musical development and flourishing being paramount. Pressures on time notwithstanding, the value of communication between instrumental teachers and WCTs was a common thread, several teachers mentioning the need to 'gain an understanding of each other's work'.

In terms of involving instrumental teachers in WCTs' lessons, one WCT reported having no contact with instrumental teachers; however, another mentioned two instrumental teacher colleagues who had been particularly helpful finding appropriate repertoire. WCTs mentioned having very little class time to dedicate to performance, highlighting a context in which instrumental teachers could offer help to provide 'opportunities for performance, masterclasses, confidence building'. Two WCTs said they often seek to develop students' performance skills, while others said this happened occasionally. Suggestions made by instrumental teachers regarding specific ways in which WCTs could further support instrumental students generally focused on communicating current topics or themes being studied or specific requirements for school exams. It was acknowledged that class music teachers were very likely already encouraging wider listening, singing, composing and discussing music for all students. One instrumental teacher suggested that instrumental teachers and WCTs could collaboratively produce an 'end-of-term project for the students to perform', which might 'make the visiting staff [instrumental teachers] feel more connected with the music department/school'. While WCTs may be grateful for this type of instrumental teacher support, budgetary concerns could of course arise here.

The consensus emerging from our survey is that all colleagues should be aware of students' current projects and learning needs. In addition to the benefits for students when their teachers work together, such collaborations can foster stronger ties between school-based and visiting colleagues, allowing visiting teachers to become more integrated into teaching teams. If instrumental teachers and WCTs can speak to each other and develop their professional relationships (although this might be timetable-dependent or even daunting for instrumental teachers as visitors to the school), such actions would benefit those people we are all trying to support – our students.

Conclusion

This chapter offers evidence of shared attitudinal and pedagogical approaches between instrumental teachers and WCTs that support musical learning in schools. The findings of this small-scale study indicate that beneficial outcomes include support for appropriate student repertoire choices; stronger relationships between teachers, their colleagues, and students; shared knowledge between instrumental teachers and WCTs regarding the needs of their students; and supportive approaches towards performance opportunities such as end-of-term concerts. When instrumental teachers and WCTs are working together well, students benefit. Autonomy, agency and effectiveness during self-study and practice sessions were highlighted as important motivational factors for all students of all ages. Pedagogical approaches to ensure such autonomy and independence are therefore recommended from the outset of students' lessons in both classroom settings and instrumental teaching contexts.

Within the range of pedagogical approaches discussed here, it is clear that instrumental teachers and WCTs can work in highly complementary ways to identify common threads between their lessons. Regarding instrumental teacher and WCT relationships, the dominant finding seems to be that time pressures bring huge challenges. Crucially, respondents outlined that professional relationships require input from both parties and that teachers are likely to be united through the shared goal of supporting student achievement. The desire expressed by our respondents to keep in regular communication with their school-based or visiting colleagues indicates an awareness of the importance of collaboration for students' learning and development. Perhaps a more holistic approach to timetabling than the typical arrangement where only '[student] contact hours' are counted in a (peripatetic) teacher's contract might afford all groups the time, space and motivation to organize regular meetings or to chat informally. The respondents' comments suggest that this would be of benefit to all parties, most importantly, to students.

Further research beyond the UK might investigate whether similar relationships and issues exist in other countries where instrumental learning takes place in schools, as compared with those in which it takes place outside school entirely (such as France). Future research could also explore some of the timetabling limitations identified by our respondents with a view to finding ways to facilitate more regular communication between school-based and visiting teachers. Research into peripatetic teachers' perceptions of their place as visiting teachers might be informative in this regard. Exploring whether communication systems are more or less effective in larger or smaller schools could also be a valuable future research topic; the potential efficacy of shared online drives (used by staff to update one another on student progress at key moments) could be evaluated, for example. Research could also determine how widespread the issues identified in this chapter are among a larger sample of instrumental teachers who work in schools.

Notes

1 Ofsted is the UK Office for Standards in Education, Children's Services and Skills.
2 Joint instrumental teacher and WCTs' responses referenced teaching KS4 and KS5 students' instrumental lessons, but not all made explicit references to teaching whole-class KS4 and KS5 groups.

References

APPG for Music Education (2019), *Music Education: State of the Nation*, London: All-Party Parliamentary Group for Music Education, University of Sussex, Incorporated Society of Musicians. Available online: https://www.ism.org/images/images/State-of-the-Nation-Music-Education-WEB.pdf (accessed 2 August 2024).

Baker, D. (2006), 'Life Histories of Music Service Teachers: The Past in Inductees' Present', *British Journal of Music Education*, 23 (1): 39–50.

Bath, N., A. Daubney, D. Mackrill and G. Spruce (2020), 'The Declining Place of Music Education in Schools in England', *Children and Society*, 34 (5): 443–57.

Burwell, K. (2005), 'A Degree of Independence: Teachers' Approaches to Instrumental Tuition in a University College', *British Journal of Music Education*, 22 (3): 199–215.

Christmas, F. (2016), 'Knowledge in Education – Working Collaboratively to Provide a Rich Music Education', *ISME Commission on Music Policy: Culture, Education, and Mass Media*, 75. Available online: https://www.isme.org/sites/default/files/documents/2016%20ISME%20Commission%20on%20Music%20Policy%20Proceedings.pdf#page=75 (accessed 3 August 2024).

Creech, A. (2010), 'The Music Studio', in S. Hallam and A. Creech (eds), *Music Education in the 21st Century in the United Kingdom: Achievements, Analysis and Aspirations*, 295–313, London: Institute of Education.

Davidson, J., and R. Dwyer (2014), 'The Role of Professional Learning in Reducing Isolation Experienced by Classroom Music Teachers', *Australian Journal of Music Education*, 1: 38–51.

Department for Education (2021), *Model Music Curriculum: Key Stages 1 to 3: Non-Statutory Guidance for the National Curriculum in England*, March. Available online: https://assets.publishing.service.gov.uk/media/6061f833d3bf7f5ce1060a90/Model_Music_Curriculum_Full.pdf (accessed 2 August 2024).

Department for Education (2022), *The Power of Music to Change Lives: A National Plan for Music Education*, June. Available online: https://www.gov.uk/government/publications/the-power-of-music-to-change-lives-a-national-plan-for-music-education (accessed 2 August 2024).

Department for Education (2023), *Striking the Right Note: The Music Subject Report*, September. Available online: https://www.gov.uk/government/publications/subject-report-series-music/striking-the-right-note-the-music-subject-report (accessed 2 August 2024).

Derbyshire, S. (2015), *Musical Routes: A Landscape for Music Education*, London: Royal Philharmonic Society. Available online: https://www.musicmark.org.uk/wp-content/uploads/MUSICAL-ROUTES-report-Sarah-Derbyshire-Royal-Philharmonic-Society.pdf (accessed 2 August 2024).

Hallam, S., A. Creech, C. Sandford, T. Rinta and K. Shave (2009), *Survey of Musical Futures: A Report from Institute of Education, London: University of London, for the Paul Hamlyn Foundation*. Available online: https://discovery.ucl.ac.uk/id/eprint/1507448/ (accessed 2 August 2024).

Kokotsaki, D. (2010), 'Musical Involvement Outside School: How Important Is It for Student-Teachers in Secondary Education?', *British Journal of Music Education*, 27 (2): 151–70.

Lamont, A. (2017), 'Musical Identity, Interest, and Involvement', in R. MacDonald, D. J. Hargreaves and D. Miell (eds), *Handbook of Musical Identities*, 176–96, Oxford: Oxford University Press.

Meissner, H., and R. Timmers (2020), 'Young Musicians' Learning of Expressive Performance: The Importance of Dialogic Teaching and Modelling', *Frontiers in*

Education, 5. Available online: https://doi.org/10.3389/feduc.2020.00011 (accessed 2 August 2024).

Ofsted (2002), *Local Education Authority Music Services Survey of Good Practice: A Report from the Office of Her Majesty's Chief Inspector of Schools (HMI 458)*, London: Office for Standards in Education. Available online: https://dera.ioe.ac.uk/id/eprint/10206/7/lea_music_good_practice_Redacted.pdf (accessed 2 August 2024).

Philpott, C. (2007), 'Musical Learning and Musical Development', in C. Philpott and G. Spruce (eds), *Learning to Teach Music in the Secondary School*, 2nd edn, 102–14, Abingdon: Routledge.

Roulston, K., R. Legette and S. T. Womack (2007), 'Beginning Music Teachers' Perceptions of the Transition from University to Teaching in Schools', *Music Education Research*, 7 (1): 59–82.

Savage, J. (2021), 'Teaching Music in England Today', *International Journal of Music Education*, 39 (4): 464–76.

Stijnen, J., L. Nijs and P. Van Petegem (2023), 'Instrument Teachers' Practices, Beliefs, and Barriers Regarding Musical Creativity: Exploring the Creative Process of Interpretation', *International Journal of Music Education*, 42 (3): 425–41.

Welch, G., R. Purves, D. Hargreaves and N. Marshall (2011), 'Early Career Challenges in Secondary School Music Teaching', *British Educational Research Journal*, 37 (2): 285–315.

7

Developing Instrumental Teaching Cross-Culturally: International Preservice Teachers' Pedagogical Understanding with Consideration of Cultural Intelligence

Xinpei Zheng and Hang Li

Introduction

This chapter presents a nuanced understanding of cross-cultural psychological and pedagogical transformation in one-to-one instrumental teaching practices, embodied in the perceptions of student-teachers from China who teach Chinese traditional instruments while simultaneously receiving instrumental pedagogical training at a UK university. Tensions between their retained home-culture identities and their reinvigorated pedagogical values influenced by the host educational culture are coupled with individual differences in cross-cultural pedagogical reception and delivery. This qualitative study is facilitated by the theoretical framework of cultural intelligence (CQ) introduced by Earley and Ang (2003) and developed by Ang and

Van Dyne (2015): a micro-level interpretation of cognition (existing knowledge), metacognition (self-understanding), motivation (self-determination) and behaviour (actions) of individuals engaging with culturally diverse environments (specific to those Chinese student-teachers in the UK in this current study). The individual-dependent nature of CQ supports the complexity of international students' cross-cultural adaptation, emphasizing the diversity and individuality of those students from the same cultural background. Moving beyond Ford's (2020) suggestion of unfolding culturally specific knowledge to break down cultural stereotypes and assimilationist attitudes in Western higher education (HE), cross-cultural psychological knowledge would benefit the comprehension of interrelationships between culturally contextualized mindsets and behaviours (Berry et al. 2011) of individual international students. Revealed by those student-teachers learning to teach outside of their home context, their psychological and pedagogical dynamics across cultures may be of educational value to illuminate relevant concerns for instrumental (preservice) teachers, teacher educators and programme curriculum design within culturally diverse contexts.

Propelled by the ever-increasing marketization and consumerization within China of the values of overseas study (Li 2022), Chinese students constitute a large proportion of international students at conservatories and music departments within Western HE (Ford 2021); this includes those who particularly work with Chinese traditional instruments, embarking on UK MA instrumental teacher training (Zheng and Haddon 2023). As reported by Bamber et al. (2019) and The Quality Assurance Agency for Higher Education (QAA 2020), compact one-year UK master-level programmes aspire towards postgraduate students' independence and adaptability. However, Barnes, Macleod and Huttly (2018) and Haddon (2019) state that Asian students new to the UK academic environment are challenged by these expectations due to pedagogical-culture differences and a lack of readiness concerning academic skills and language (see Chapter 9 on subject-specific language challenges). Notwithstanding the academic aspect, within instrumental teacher training, international preservice teachers may also be challenged by differences in instrumental pedagogy across cultures, underpinned by expectations such as results-oriented hierarchical authority in one culture (Haddon 2019, 2024) and personal enjoyment and psychological well-being which may be emphasized in another (Meissner, Timmers and Pitts 2021). While teacher education communicates subject-specific pedagogical skills and facilitates 'a shift in thinking from past experiences as students to the perspectives of teachers' (Couchenour and Chrisman 2016: 1072), teachers' transition of pedagogical identities in cross-cultural settings 'dynamically encompasses multiple perspectives': their past experiences as learners and teachers, professional pathways, new pedagogical inspirations and home sociocultural values (Luguetti et al. 2019: 864). Additionally, synergistic negotiations between qualifications, teacher role socialization and value internalization impact teacher belief and agency (Tucker and Powell 2021).

Instrumental Pedagogical Expectations across Cultures

Considering cultural differences in defining instrumental learning attainment and perhaps, 'more fundamentally, being musical' (Ford 2021: 184), values prioritized in the teaching of Chinese traditional instruments can be distinct from instrumental pedagogy developed within the UK context. In China, Chow-Morris (2010) recognizes that Chinese-instrument teachers own a well-respected authority in performances, and students historically preserve 'the nuances of the music, especially its rhythm and phrasing, from the teacher' by imitation (Yung 1987: 85) due to the retained traditional repertoire, notation systems, literary roots and aesthetic beliefs (Yung 2010): 'aural traditions where musical knowledge and repertoire are primarily embodied in living musicians' in Asian cultures (Schippers 2009: 68). This reproduction of inherited interpretations from the teacher including how to semi-improvise with the music (e.g. adding ornaments) authenticates the pupil's playing (Chow-Morris 2010) – a historically constructed authenticity in music education; however, questions such as how personal-meaning-making authenticity (Koops 2010) could be approached by learners are worthy of investigation. While robust control of teacher-centred preservation-focused pedagogy in the teaching of Chinese instruments appears to be assumed by cultural continuity ideologies, Zheng and Haddon (2023) highlight the paucity of empirical research on Chinese-instrument lessons in current China HE, private and school settings that may rationalize the underlying mechanism of the pedagogy. This appears to be dissimilar from research-informed student-centred instrumental pedagogy in the West that promotes neuropsychological implications (Creech, Hodges and Hallam 2021) such as learner autonomy, pupil-personalized interpretations (Meissner, Timmers and Pitts 2021) and learner self-regulation (Concina 2019).

Cross-Cultural Pedagogical Challenges and Adaptable CQ

When these dissimilarities in pedagogical expectations encounter each other through international education communications, challenges relating to cross-cultural pedagogical reception and delivery may emerge. For instance, Bremner (2021) identifies differences in conceptualizing pedagogical theories such as student- or learner-centred education between Western and Asian contexts leading to potential pedagogical misinterpretations; further research indicates collisions between adapting to student-centred pedagogy and the retained Chinese expectations concerning exam results (Haddon 2024), teacher-driven efficiency and adherence to inherited practices (Zheng and Haddon 2023). Notably, Zhu and O'Sullivan (2022: 280) acknowledge Chinese students' metacognitive adaptation in 'thinking about how to learn and how to perform [behave]' due to the juxtaposition of unfamiliar pedagogical methods and language challenges in UK HE, yet some students' appearance of adaptive quietness is preconceived as passive learning; within international study contexts, Wu (2015) emphasizes the evolving cognition, motivation and learning behaviours of Chinese students alongside their psychological and behavioural adjustment.

This aligns with the four adaptable CQ aspects (i.e. cognition, metacognition, motivation and behaviour) of individuals that contribute to their cross-cultural psychological and performance outcomes (Hong et al. 2021; Leung, Ang and Tan 2014). Empirical evidence has identified a positive correlation between international students' motivation and their cross-cultural happiness and self-efficacy (Peng, Van Dyne and Oh 2015), while cross-cultural collaborative behaviours are influenced by international students' metacognitive adjustment and action-taking (Chua, Morris and Mor 2012). While metacognitive processes help individuals be aware of cultural differences and be flexible with the existing cultural knowledge they possess (ibid.), motivations play a key role in determining whether an individual directs their efforts – and to what extent – to engage with culturally diverse contexts and other individuals (Leung, Ang and Tan 2014; Yang 2023). These findings provide an account of how the overarching four areas underscore the cross-cultural experiences of individuals and, in turn, can practically inform organizers, leaders and individual members who participate and interact in international environments (Ang, Van Dyne and Rockstuhl 2015). Despite a wide range of research on international students and their CQ adaptations, understanding the cross-cultural pedagogical learning of international instrumental preservice teachers (specializing in Chinese instruments in this current study) through the underlying CQ aspects is lacking. This chapter highlights nuances within cross-cultural psychological and pedagogical developments of a sample of Chinese-instrument student-teachers in the UK, embodying individual cultural sensitivity, adaptability, identity and value dynamics.

Research Methodology

This study was part of the first author's doctoral research project comparing pedagogical practices of Chinese-instrument pre- and in-service teachers in both China and the UK. Chinese students teaching Chinese traditional instruments enrolled in the MA Music Education in Instrumental and Vocal Teaching at the University of York, UK, were invited to participate in a case study, an approach to gaining in-depth understandings of a specific context, illuminating professional practices and community actions (Simons 2014). This research utilized an interpretive paradigm, grounded in a 'subjectivist, interactionist, socially constructed ontology', and acknowledges an epistemology that values diverse realities (Cohen, Manion and Morrison 2018: 175). From this standpoint, the authors' backgrounds should be noted: both of us were former student-teachers on this programme, teaching guzheng and piano, respectively, during our UK MA study. We continued our explorations within cross-cultural music education as PhD candidates and during three years working as graduate teaching assistants on the MA programme we have had the opportunity to experience and support the cultural and pedagogical adaptation and challenges of other student-teachers from China.

Ethical approval for the first author's research was given by the Arts and Humanities Ethics Committee, University of York. Within the study, semi-structured interviews in Mandarin were conducted with sixteen Chinese-instrument student-teachers (defined as ST1, ST2, ST3 etc. where quotations are presented); after participants' validation of their transcripts the first author translated the Mandarin transcripts into English. The participants were aged twenty-two to twenty-seven and had learned a Chinese instrument from eight to fifteen years in China, including guzheng (n = 11), erhu (n = 2), dizi (n = 1), pipa (n = 1) and yangqin (n = 1). They had teaching experiences of their Chinese instruments from less than a year to eight years in Chinese school and private music studio settings before the MA and gave instrumental lessons online or in-person with beginner to advanced Chinese-instrument pupils one-to-one in English during the MA, alongside writing commentaries on their videoed lessons submitted as part of the programme assessments.

The interview questions were designed to explore the CQ four aspects in an open-ended manner, asking about interviewees' awareness and feelings of differences in instrumental pedagogical cultures, their experiences and strategies in cross-cultural learning and adaptation, mindset and behavioural adjustments and challenges encountered during their MA study. No rationale for the CQ theory was explained to the participants in advance of the interviews to maintain spontaneity, 'interconnectedness and internal coherence' of responses (Cohen, Manion and Morrison 2018: 662). The data analysis followed the steps of thematic analysis (Braun and Clarke 2006) using MAXQDA for the coding and thematizing process. Findings concern instrumental pedagogical dissimilarities between China and the UK, cross-cultural pedagogical learning and challenges concerning pedagogical implementation in Chinese-instrument lessons, learning independence and adapting to the UK music academic context.

Findings

Pedagogical Differences between Instrumental Lessons in China and the UK

After observing how the UK MA tutors delivered one-to-one piano, violin and flute lessons to different ages of pupils, most of the student-teachers compared these lessons during their interviews to their previously received Chinese-instrument lessons in China. These UK teachers' prioritization of their pupils' self-efficacy and independence was considered different from the Chinese-instrument teachers' emphasis on hard practice and progress. The student-teachers identified encouraging and relaxing learning environments established by the UK teachers with their pupils by caring about the pupils' feelings, using praise and open-ended questioning and less teacher-dominance: 'the pupil can choose what they want to learn' (ST7)[1]; 'the [MA] flute teacher encouraged the pupil to describe how they felt [about the music] instead of the teacher's talking' (ST16); 'the questions [asked by the teacher] were inspiring … their teaching was creative' (ST10). As described by ST3, ST12 and ST15, contrastingly, their guzheng and erhu teachers in China often used verbal instructions such as 'You "should" or "shouldn't" or "can't"' or 'Your interpretation is incorrect, follow me' (ST9).

'Strict', 'straightforward' and 'serious' were the most frequent words used by the student-teachers when describing their previous Chinese-instrument teachers and their learning atmosphere in China. For example, ST14 identified a deficit-focused way of teaching adopted by their yangqin teacher, who 'only saw problems and mistakes I made in playing and never praised [what I did well]'. While fast learning progress, enhanced technical skills and 'avoid[ing] misdirected attempts in playing the music by myself' (ST6) were acknowledged as benefits from their received teacher-led lessons in China, little autonomy and more anxiety were also revealed: 'My personal interpretation was never good enough for my teacher … they always corrected things in their way' (ST4); 'My teacher required me to practise making zero mistake by repeatedly playing the piece three times without a break – it's like a reassurance of perfect performance' (ST14); 'I experienced stage anxiety, but my teacher attributed that to "not practising hard enough so you got nervous"' (ST16). Apart from the negative impression of making mistakes, it appears that the Chinese-instrument teachers prioritized their deployment of authority and high expectations as compared to the learners' feelings and agency, whereas the opposite was advocated by the UK instrumental-teacher MA tutors, who gave their lessons in a pupil-autonomy-prioritizing manner.

Cross-Cultural Pedagogical Learning and Understanding

Many student-teachers in the interviews used the words 'student-centred, student-oriented' and 'systematic' to describe their cross-cultural pedagogical learning on the MA, but they revealed that within their experience, student-centred pedagogy was not yet effectively understood in the Chinese music teaching context: 'Student-centred teaching for music teachers in China was like a slogan, they always say, "being student-centred" but they don't really know what it means' (ST10). Similarly, ST2 stated that 'I knew the student-centred concept when I was in China but didn't understand how it worked. Teachers also didn't explain it clearly', while the MA helped to 'provide the definition and theories' (ST12) and 'sorted out the [student-centred] related concepts I came across in China' (ST2).

Student-teachers expressed their appreciation for writing lesson commentaries that helped their pedagogical adaptation and reflection as teachers, whereby they were able to 'recall and re-consider the effect of the strategies used' by themselves in the lessons (ST8) and 'not take personal impression [as the teacher on the pupil] for granted' (ST12). While using academic sources to inform reflective writing was considered an unfamiliar practice by the student-teachers due to their previous experience with music programme curricula or syllabi in Chinese HE, this practice benefited their awareness of other available and 'more creative' (ST10) teaching strategies, their use of teaching materials: 'I used to think my pupil was too lazy to practise the piece I gave, but now I realized I didn't ask whether the pupil was interested in learning the piece' (ST3); verbal communication: 'I purposefully used more encouraging words. I can see the pupil became more active' (ST5); and pupils' well-being: 'I now understood there can be varied reasons behind the pupil's behaviour, and their feelings are important to check' (ST15). This may indicate a lack of research-informed self-evaluation practices within music teacher education in China; furthermore, the absence of 'learn[ing] from research' warrants critical attention concerning the supervision of instrumental teachers' qualifications and (continuing) professional development (Lee and Leung 2022: 52).

Challenges in Cross-Cultural Pedagogical Practice and Learning

While the pedagogical differences between the Chinese and UK contexts reinvigorated the student-teachers' routinized teaching procedure (which they recognized as being similar to the teacher-centred styles of teaching influenced by their former Chinese-instrument teachers) and motivated them to learn more about pupil-centred instrumental pedagogy on the MA, the actual pedagogical adjustment and implementation in teaching Chinese instruments were considered challenging by the student-teachers. In the MA, imitating how the UK instrumental teachers used open-ended questions was the first step made by many student-teachers in their assessed lessons. However, as articulated by ST1,

> although I imitated to ask the question as the [MA] teacher did, asking [my pupil], 'What do you think could be done with this phrase?', I couldn't help telling them how they should play if they didn't know the answer. After I received my [lesson feedback] report, I realized I was still instilling my idea into my pupil's mind rather than cultivating their own thinking.

Teaching by telling instead of inspiring the pupil to find answers independently was commonly self-disclosed by the student-teachers; not surprisingly, their pupil's over-reliance on the teacher's directives and demonstration in learning was evident, as indicated by three participants. While the student-teachers acknowledged the advantages of prompting the pupil's active communication and independent thinking during lessons, they also expressed concerns about the time constraints in their assessed and future lessons, the slowed-down pace of teaching and the delivery of the preserved features and interpretations of Chinese music concerning the traditional repertoire featured by Chinese literary categorizations in music (e.g. ST8, '文曲 Wénqǔ' [civil] and '武曲 Wǔqǔ' [martial] in pipa repertoire), regional characteristics (e.g. ST11, 'Northern and Southern musical styles') and distinct regional-technical applications (e.g. ST9, '[dizi] tonguing techniques in the South are "颤 Chàn, 叠 Dié, 赠 Zèng, 打 Dǎ" while in the North they are "花 Huā, 滑 Huá, 剁 Duò, 吐 Tǔ"'). As stated by ST14, 'Though I learned many teaching approaches on the MA, I still don't know how to teach those traditional elements in a pupil-engaged way and what to do when my pupil doesn't want to follow [the traditions].' ST9 illustrated that

> learning traditional repertoire is fundamental for dizi and other Chinese-instrument learners, though there's hardly any space for the pupil to interpret the traditional music themselves, as learners need to imitate how the teacher breathed, phrased, and used the tonguing, otherwise the music wouldn't sound right.

Additionally, ST14 mentioned that 'it's irresponsible if I knew there's a [regional] stylistic problem [in the pupil's playing] but didn't correct them'. This appears to show the Chinese-instrument teachers and learners' understanding of the interrelationship between the music, the historically inherited and authentic performance and the music culture continuity that may impact their ongoing pedagogical choices (e.g. falling in line with the teacher-dominated teaching) and may limit personalized and creative interpretations.

The challenge of building up their own learning independence during the MA study was also mentioned by the student-teachers: while they appreciated how the MA teaching staff established a mentor–friend relationship with them and encouraged them to try varied ideas in teaching and academic writing, it appears that some student-teachers still preferred receiving straightforward answers from the MA tutors to 'know specifically how I should teach' (ST14) and to 'avoid misunderstanding what the tutor wanted me to do' (ST15). ST12 explained that the educational environment in China led by the teachers' and parents' regulation of 'what you should do at every stage' hindered the development of independence and self-regulation capabilities.

Moreover, adapting to the Western postgraduate academic environment using a second language was another challenge: 'I thought English was my strength when I was in China, but it's not enough for this [MA] literature-based learning and academic writing that meets Western [academic] standards' (ST4); 'I could have got higher marks [in MA assessments] if my English could be better' (ST7). The distinct academic criteria within music programmes in China and UK HE were revealed: 'Evidence from the literature is always needed for what I wrote [on the MA], but this wasn't mentioned by my teacher when I wrote my [undergraduate] dissertation [in China]' (ST12); additionally, students expressed the confusion of using culture-specific instrumental terminologies in English such as 'specify[ing] the playing positions on pipa' (ST8) and '[dizi] tonguing' (ST9). While these issues are not exclusive to Chinese-instrument students studying in English-speaking countries, they indicate the need for 'alternate paradigms' in music scholarly and linguistic communities across cultures that help communication and understanding (Stock 2023: 505).

Discussion

By means of the CQ theory-informed lenses exploring cross-cultural pedagogical learning, it appears that the cognition, metacognition, motivation and behaviour of those Chinese-instrument student-teachers interact with pedagogical-culture differences between China and the UK. The UK instrumental teacher training helped those student-teachers' comprehension of student-centred pedagogy in the UK educational context and their conscious awareness of different criteria or learning objectives within instrumental education and music academic environments across cultures. As indicated by the student-teachers, definitions and theories of student-centred teaching were necessary to understand their teaching practice, whereas the conceptualization of this approach in the Chinese music teaching context remained ambiguous. Embodied in a collective (instead of individual) student-centredness and 'unified knowledge acquisition' by following the teacher, Zhang, Leung and Yang (2023: 283) recognize the culturally localized pedagogical practice of student-centred education in school music teaching in China with inadequate opportunities provided for students to think independently and creatively.

The findings present distinct pedagogical priorities and philosophies within music instrumental education in China and the UK, where the cultural continuity-oriented teacher-led Chinese-instrument teaching differs from the empirically supported instrumental pedagogy which promotes learner autonomy. This culture-centred music education appears to be featured in values education in China, where teachers' identity, agency and practices are permeated with the politically formed significance of the relationship between music teaching and the transmission of cultural and societal moral values and responsibilities (Ho 2018). Emphasis on learner empowerment, self-regulation and well-being in the UK instrumental teacher training appears to provide alternative pedagogical possibilities in teaching Chinese instruments; this motivated the UK Chinese-instrument student-teachers' cross-cultural pedagogical learning towards learner-centredness. However, embedded in the Chinese sociocultural expectations (also see Haddon 2024) and the teacher-led and external-regulated learning environment in China, tensions could arise from how these Chinese-instrument student-teachers cope with the preserved Chinese music traditions while also enabling pupils' learning engagement and personalized and creative practices underpinned by pupils' understanding and preference of the music. To illuminate this, research on effective practices in culture-specific instrumental teaching contexts is suggested, unfolding and building upon potential contextual and pedagogical constraints (e.g. as identified by Luguetti et al. 2019; Zheng and Haddon 2023).

Challenges perceived by the student-teachers emerged in their pedagogical implementations that foster pupil-active lesson participation and in their adaption to literature-based academic learning and independent learning with less teacher dominance. However, it appears that some student-teachers retained their pre-formed cognition of needing the so-called correct answers and external recognition of their teaching from authority (e.g. the MA tutors). This may concern the convergent thinking of many Chinese students, a socioculturally shaped mindset believing in a single standardized solution to a question yet lacking critical and creative thinking (Wan 2023; Wang 2019). Despite these challenges, the student-teachers exhibited their metacognitive and behavioural adjustment in their reflective practices by self-evaluation and adopting alternative strategies they learned in the MA. Nevertheless, their awareness of the importance of English proficiency in the UK masters course and a lack of relevant academic training or support (e.g. literature-informed academic writing) in Chinese educational contexts may result in their frustration as international students. Moreover, considering the challenge of distinguishing 'advanced training in scholarly English from deep inculcation into the values and norms of an anglophone-dominated academy', to avoid colonial knowledge assimilation (Stock 2023: 500), international HE programmes could consider further the advocating and supporting of linguistic pluralism in music teaching concerning culture-specific instruments, their playing techniques and use of musical terminologies, supporting students to gain greater educational value from cross-cultural pedagogical opportunities.

Conclusion

This chapter offers insights into the dynamic interplay between culture, pedagogy and individual experiences in instrumental music teacher education across cultures to inform ongoing educational practices, and highlights the significance of understanding the interrelationships between culturally contextualized mindsets and behaviours in educational settings. Guided by the framework of CQ, this study explores how the cognitive, metacognitive, motivational and behavioural aspects of those Chinese-instrument student-teachers interact with cultural and pedagogical differences between China and the UK. Despite encountering challenges in implementing student-centred pedagogy and adjusting to independent learning, the student-teachers demonstrated metacognitive and behavioural adaption through reflective practices. Moving forward, further research and instrumental pedagogical practices are warranted to address the multifaceted challenges faced by international instrumental teachers and learners and to inform the development of effective pedagogical strategies to meet the needs of music students from diverse cultural backgrounds.

Notes

1 ST = the quoted student-teacher.

References

Ang, S., and L. Van Dyne (2015), *Handbook of Cultural Intelligence: Theory, Measurement, and Applications*, New York: Routledge.

Ang, S., L. Van Dyne and T. Rockstuhl (2015), 'Cultural Intelligence: Origins, Conceptualization, Evolution, and Methodological Diversity', in M. J. Gelfand, C. Chiu and Y. Hong (eds), *Handbook of Advances in Culture Psychology*, 273–323, Oxford: Oxford University Press.

Bamber, V., C. J. Choudhary, J. Hislop and J. Lane (2019), 'Postgraduate Taught Students and Preparedness for Master's Level Study: Polishing the Facets of the Master's Diamond', *Journal of Further and Higher Education*, 43 (2): 236–50.

Barnes, T. A., G. Macleod and S. Huttly (2018), 'National Survey of PGT Programme Directors and Administrators', *The UK Council for Graduate Education*. Available online: https://ukcge.ac.uk/assets/resources/29-National-Survey-of-PGT-Directors-and-Administrators-2018.pdf (accessed 23 June 2024).

Berry, J., Y. Poortinga, S. Breugelmans, A. Chasiotis and D. Sam (2011), *Cross-Cultural Psychology: Research and Applications*, 3rd edn, Cambridge: Cambridge University Press.

Braun, V., and V. Clarke (2006), 'Using Thematic Analysis in Psychology', *Qualitative Research in Psychology*, 3 (2): 77–101.

Bremner, N. (2021), 'The Multiple Meanings of "Student-Centred" or "Learner-Centred" Education, and the Case for a More Flexible Approach to Defining It', *Comparative Education*, 57 (2): 159–86.

Chow-Morris, K. (2010), 'Going with the Flow: Embracing the "Tao" of China's "Jiangnan Sizhu"', *Asian Music*, 41 (2): 59–87.

Chua, R. Y., M. W. Morris and S. Mor (2012), 'Collaborating across Cultures: Cultural Metacognition and Affect-Based Trust in Creative Collaboration', *Organizational Behavior and Human Decision Processes*, 118 (2): 116–31.

Cohen, L., L. Manion and K. Morrison (2018), *Research Methods in Education*, 8th edn, New York: Routledge.

Concina, E. (2019), 'The Role of Metacognitive Skills in Music Learning and Performing: Theoretical Features and Educational Implications', *Frontiers in Psychology*, 10: 1583.

Couchenour, D., and J. K. Chrisman, eds (2016), *The SAGE Encyclopedia of Contemporary Early Childhood Education*, Los Angeles: Sage.

Creech, A., D. A. Hodges and S. Hallam, eds (2021), *Routledge International Handbook of Music Psychology in Education and the Community*, New York: Routledge.

Earley, P., and S. Ang (2003), *Cultural Intelligence: Individual Interactions across Cultures*, California: Stanford University Press.

Ford, B. (2020), 'Can Culturally Specific Perspectives to Teaching Western Classical Music Benefit International Students? A Call to Re-Examine "What the Teacher Does"', *Frontiers in Education*, 5: 113.

Ford, B. (2021), 'From a Different Place to a Third Space: Rethinking International Student Pedagogy in the Western Conservatoire', in A. Kallio, H. Westerlund, S. Karlsen, K. Marsh and E. Sæther (eds), *The Politics of Diversity in Music Education*, 177–89, New York: Springer.

Haddon, E. (2019), 'Perspectives of Chinese Students on Studying MA Music Programmes in a UK University', *ORFEU*, 4 (2): 30–58.

Haddon, E. (2024), 'Negotiating Pedagogical Cultures: Adaptive Challenges Facing Music Education Graduates on Their Return to China', in R. Prokop and R. Reitsamer (eds), *Higher Music Education and Employability in a Neoliberal World*, 159–72, London: Bloomsbury.

Ho, W. C. (2018), *Culture, Music Education, and the Chinese Dream in Mainland China*, New York: Springer.

Hong, J. Y., H. Ko, L. Mesicek and M. Song (2021), 'Cultural Intelligence as Education Contents: Exploring the Pedagogical Aspects of Effective Functioning in Higher Education', *Concurrency and Computation: Practice and Experience*, 33 (2): e5489.

Koops, L. H. (2010), '"Can't We Just Change the Words?" The Role of Authenticity in Culturally Informed Music Education', *Music Educators Journal*, 97 (1): 23–28.

Lee, C., and B. W. Leung (2022), 'Instrumental Teaching as "the Noblest and the Most Under-Praised Job": Multiple Case Studies of Three Hong Kong Instrumental Teachers', *Music Education Research*, 24 (1): 42–55.

Leung, K., S. Ang and M. L. Tan (2014), 'Intercultural Competence', *The Annual Review of Organizational Psychology and Organizational Behavior*, 1 (1): 489–519.

Li, J. (2022), *Shaping Education Policy Discourse: Insights from Internationalization of Education Development in China*, New York: Springer.

Luguetti, C., R. Aranda, O. Nuñez Enriquez and K. L. Oliver (2019), 'Developing Teachers' Pedagogical Identities through a Community of Practice: Learning to Sustain the Use of a Student-Centered Inquiry as Curriculum Approach', *Sport, Education and Society*, 24 (8): 855–66.

Meissner, H., R. Timmers and S. E. Pitts, eds (2021), *Sound Teaching: A Research-Informed Approach to Inspiring Confidence, Skill, and Enjoyment in Music Performance*, Abingdon: Routledge.

Peng, A. C., L. Van Dyne and K. Oh (2015), 'The Influence of Motivational Cultural Intelligence on Cultural Effectiveness Based on Study Abroad: The Moderating Role of Participant's Cultural Identity', *Journal of Management Education*, 39 (5): 572–96.

Quality Assurance Agency for Higher Education (QAA) (2020), 'Master's Degree Characteristics Statement'. Available online: https://www.qaa.ac.uk/docs/qaa/quality-code/master's-degree-characteristics-statement.pdf?sfvrsn=86c5ca81_22 (accessed 23 June 2024).

Schippers, H. (2009), *Facing the Music: Shaping Music Education from a Global Perspective*, Oxford: Oxford University Press.

Simons, H. (2014), 'Case Study Research: In-Depth Understanding in Context', in P. Leavy (ed.), *The Oxford Handbook of Qualitative Research*, 455–70, Oxford: Oxford University Press.

Stock, J. P. (2023), 'Conclusion: New Directions in Chinese Music Research', in Y. Hui and J. P. Stock (eds), *The Oxford Handbook of Music in China and the Chinese Diaspora*, 491–510, Oxford: Oxford University Press.

Tucker, O. G., and S. R. Powell (2021), 'Values, Agency, and Identity in a Music Teacher Education Program', *Journal of Music Teacher Education*, 31 (1): 23–38.

Wan, W. (2023), 'The Importance of Developing Creative Thinking in the Preparation of Music Education Professionals in Universities', *Interactive Learning Environments*, 32 (7): 3686–96. https://doi.org/10.1080/10494820.2023.2188400.

Wang, F. (2019), *Chinese Cultural Psychology: A New Look (中国文化心理学新论)*, Shanghai: Shanghai Educational Publishing House.

Wu, Q. (2015), 'Re-Examining the "Chinese Learner": A Case Study of Mainland Chinese Students' Learning Experiences at British Universities', *Higher Education*, 70: 753–66.

Yang, C. (2023), 'Motivational Cultural Intelligence and Well-Being in Cross-Cultural Workplaces: A Study of Migrant Workers in Taiwan', *Employee Relations*, 45 (3): 743–61.

Yung, B. (1987), 'Historical Interdependency of Music: A Case Study of the Chinese Seven-String Zither', *Journal of the American Musicological Society*, 40 (1): 82–91.

Yung, B. (2010), 'Tsar Teh-yun at Age 100: A Life of Qin Music, Poetry, and Calligraphy', in H. Rees (ed.), *Lives in Chinese Music*, 65–90, Illinois: University of Illinois Press.

Zhang, L.-X., B. Leung and Y. Yang (2023), 'From Theory to Practice: Student-Centered Pedagogical Implementation in Primary Music Demonstration Lessons in Guangdong, China', *International Journal of Music Education*, 41 (2): 271–87.

Zheng, X., and E. Haddon (2023), 'Pedagogical Transformation and Choice-Making: A Longitudinal Study of Chinese Pre-Service Guzheng Teachers in the UK', *Asia-Pacific Journal for Arts Education*, 22: 1–33.

Zhu, H., and H. O'Sullivan (2022), 'Shhhh! Chinese Students Are Studying Quietly in the UK', *Innovations in Education and Teaching International*, 59 (3): 275–84.

8

Navigating Apprenticeship to Mentorship across Cultures: Adaptive Insights from Chinese Masters Students Working as Instrumental Teachers in China and the UK

Xin Liu and Elizabeth Haddon

Introduction

Diversifying one's teaching approach in order to encourage the development of pupils' agency is particularly relevant to those who, either individually or culturally, have become habituated to an apprentice-style student-teacher relationship (Jorgensen 2008). Varied teacher-student relationship types include master-apprentice (Jørgensen 2000) and mentor-friend (Lehmann, Sloboda and Woody 2007), and many nuances within these frameworks of interpersonal relationships will operate, with potential transitions between these for learners at all levels (Gaunt 2017).

As musical diversity is influenced by cultural diversity and students can have a wide range of musical preferences and interests, it has been recommended that music educators diversify their pedagogical approaches and relationships (Gaunt 2017). However, knowledge of practical ways of achieving these within intercultural instrumental teaching appears to be underdeveloped. In China, examination-oriented, memorization-based and passive learning attitudes are framed by the construct of apprenticeship in which apprentice music learners pay great respect to their masters as a 'moral guide' in instrumental lessons (Yeh 2001: 37). Liu (2022) and Haddon (2024) also identify a habitual preference for hierarchical relationships among Chinese master's students who studied in a UK music education programme, as well as the teaching differences and adaptive challenges they face in implementing pedagogical approaches advocated by the programme. Exploring the adaptive and transitional perspectives of student-teachers on this programme could support understanding of how these relationships can be adapted practically or transitioned interculturally.

This chapter explores how transitional processes concerning apprenticeship and mentorship perceived by Chinese student-teachers in relation to their MA Music Education programme influence their teaching; the findings might inform others working with international students through utilizing varied student-teacher relationships. Issues that emerged in negotiating the desire of these MA student-teachers to move towards using a mentor-friend mode alongside the practical and emotional demands of their pupils are discussed; these are of relevance to educators in the UK, China and elsewhere across the world.

Transition between Apprenticeship and Mentor-Friend Teaching Modes

Education goes beyond merely transmitting knowledge; it also embodies a dynamic exchange of information across diverse cultural backgrounds (Qi 2024). In traditional apprenticeships, characterized by direct transmission of knowledge, apprentices focus on refining their skills by mirroring their master's demonstration and problem-solving techniques (Gaunt 2017). However, this process may seem restrictive to the development of students' creativity and knowledge construction if they merely passively receive knowledge (Qi 2024). Recognizing the growing emphasis on personal agency in higher music education, mentoring relationships characterized by student-centred facilitation involve shared values, respect and expectations (Gaunt 2017). This relationship, marked by open dialogue, collaboration and empowerment, is perceived to expand possibilities for fostering students' active engagement, independence and creativity (McWilliam 2009).

Music education studies show the possibility of fluidity between the apprenticeship and mentoring relationships by breaking down barriers between the distinctive roles of educators and students, recognizing and empowering students as active agents in their learning process rather passive recipients of knowledge (Creech and Gaunt 2012). This requires a decrease in domination for masters and a shift from top-down instructions to a more student-centred, interactive and collaborative manner (Burwell 2005). Gaunt (2017) highlighted continua of different dimensions that teachers and students within one-to-one instrumental teaching contexts can use to impact or shift their relationships through adjusting learning orientations, roles and ownerships and acknowledging interpersonal dynamics. Interconnections between these dimensions, such as fostering interpersonal and mutual communication, may give the student more ownership and engagement; this suggests that different teacher-student relationships and modes of pedagogy can be shifted, intertwined and transitioned between. However, educators may not always be aware of the nuanced approaches within each continuum, of which teaching relationship they are applying, or what roles they, and their students, are deploying (Creech and Gaunt 2012). Issues such as the influence of their former education, a lack of available pedagogical training (Haddon 2009) and cultural norms reinforcing teacher-student hierarchy could further mean that the notion of teaching roles and modes as transactional and fluid might not necessarily be known, accepted or encouraged.

Transition across Cultures: Teaching Adaptation of Chinese International Students Studying in the UK

Globalization of educational markets has enabled Chinese students' enthusiasm for studying abroad; they recognize the value of acquiring overseas qualifications for improving career prospects (Li 2022). The educational differences they experience potentially facilitate their sensitivity towards variances within student-teacher dynamics, influenced by disparate cultural and value systems. International students who have received music education in systems prioritizing Confucianism or collectivism, such as in China, are likely to be influenced by apprenticeship teaching approaches emphasizing examination results and passive learning attitudes (Zheng and Haddon 2023). Through reviewing research into music education in China, Zhang, Leung and Yang (2023) argue that China's school curriculum reformation in response to globalization and the advocacy for student-centred pedagogy does not specifically examine how China's own cultural and educational traditions influence this implementation. Haddon (2024) investigated the perspectives of Chinese returnees who completed student-centred instrumental pedagogical training in their UK MA programme and returned to teach in China; those teaching in international institutions in urban cities seemed to experience fewer difficulties in terms of implementing student-centred approaches than those working in other contexts. However, returnees involved in private instrumental teaching in top-tier cities still encountered pressures from the prevailing expectations concerning master-apprentice, competitive and exam-oriented teaching (Haddon 2024). This indicates that there may be varied awareness and acceptance of student-centred teaching modes in music education within China.

Among Chinese MA students studying in a UK Music Education programme, the ingrained hierarchical master-apprentice structure of their previous instrumental learning and teaching experiences highlights the Chinese teacher's role as provider of knowledge, disseminating and transmitting knowledge to their pupils (Liu 2022). Pedagogical challenges arise for Chinese student-teachers after commencing their UK music education course, where they are required to tailor teaching approaches to their instrumental pupils' interests and employ potentially unfamiliar teaching modes, such as mentor-friend and student-centred approaches (Zheng and Haddon 2023). The adaptive process, which encompasses academic and reflective awareness of teaching habits and possibilities, supports the potential for transition between the master-apprenticeship and mentoring relationship across cultures. In this chapter, we explore how these students perceive this transition in two dimensions: teaching awareness and communication in one-to-one teaching contexts.

Methodology

This chapter draws on the first author's PhD research exploring the pedagogical adaptations of Chinese students in the MA Music Education: Instrumental and Vocal Teaching at the University of York, UK. Residing within a social constructivism paradigm (Creswell and Poth 2018), a qualitative research methodology uncovered the participants' experiences and perceptions. The first author was a former student in the same MA programme, where they taught piano during their UK studies. They have continued their exploration of challenges in cultural and pedagogical adaptation within cross-cultural music education as a PhD candidate, also serving as a graduate teaching assistant in the MA programme. These different sub-identities can offer both insider and outsider perspectives through self-reflecting on the learning from the MA programme, the challenges faced both on the MA and afterwards when applying ideas from this to piano teaching in the one-to-one context in China and considering the programme from a different perspective as a member of the MA teaching team. Insights from these positions have been supported by considering how bias may be reduced in order to think dispassionately about the programme and learning (Dwyer and Buckle 2009).

Ethical approval was obtained from the University of York Arts and Humanities Ethics Committee, and thirteen semi-structured interviews were conducted by the first author with Chinese postgraduates who had completed approximately one term of their MA studies from September 2021 to December 2021. These interviews were conducted in Chinese Mandarin to ensure that participants could naturally and accurately express their ideas instead of being hesitant to provide answers due to using their second or additional language (Jiang 2018). Participants subsequently reviewed and approved their Chinese interview transcripts, and the researcher then translated the interview data into English. Prior to the thematic analysis, the translated transcripts were sent to each participant for further review to ensure the accuracy and integrity of the data.

Nine of the thirteen participants had been employed as one-to-one instrumental teachers in music training organizations in China, with four of them also working as group instrumental teachers in similar settings. Additionally, four participants had worked as online piano practice assistants, aiding beginner pupils in their technical development, while two participants had completed music internships in primary schools. At the onset of the second section of each interview, participants were asked to describe their previous instrumental teaching through an open-ended question: 'Could you please describe the instrumental lessons that you taught in China? (How did you teach when you were in China?)'. This was followed by another question aimed at eliciting specific information about their pre-masters teaching approaches: 'Were there any specific teaching approaches you used?' The data was analysed by following the thematic analysis steps outlined by Braun and Clarke (2006), with MAXQDA software employed for coding and thematizing. The findings illustrate the adaptive transitions concerning pedagogical differences between students' pre-MA habitual teaching approaches and those encountered within the MA teaching contexts and their perspectives of transition from an instructive, teacher-centred habit to a mentor-friend, student-centred mode.

Findings: Adaptive Perspectives from Instructing to Mentoring

Initial Awareness of the Use of Diversified Teaching Modes

The participants had developed varied teaching behaviours prior to commencing the MA programme. Some of them employed methods such as using stickers as rewards to enhance positive teacher-pupil relationships. They facilitated pupil practice by isolating sections and instructing repetition for technical development, sometimes in conjunction with reviewing pupils' practice videos for post-lesson guidance. Many participants indicated that their teaching approaches were predominantly influenced by replicating those of their former instrumental teachers in China; for example, counting or clapping beats alongside their pupils during lessons. Several participants adhered to a fixed teaching pattern involving task presentation, pupil playing and response and the teacher's demonstration, correction and feedback sequence in their instrumental lessons.

A consistent theme emerged across multiple interviews, where the utilization of demonstration or modelling to assist pupils in identifying and overcoming difficulties and mastering techniques was perceived as the 'main' and 'easiest' approach that they used most frequently. This preference stems from the belief that a teacher's proficiency in demonstration and the frequency of corrections during lessons signify a high level of professional competence and constitute effective teaching practices in the Chinese context. However, some participants felt worried and perceived a lack of diversity and creativity in this approach following exposure to reflective teaching during the MA course. One participant expressed a lack of confidence in this approach:

> In every first lesson with beginners, I would repeatedly teach the recognition of [the] keyboard and notes as well as the handshape in a standardized way because [this was] the initial step [in] my piano learning ... I'm worried about whether I could fully control the lesson as I did not have too much confidence about the copied teaching style. I would wonder if the instruction I gave was accurate and reasonable, if it was clearly expressed, and if the pupil really understood that.

Furthermore, a vocal teacher also admitted to a tendency to imitate their former teacher by mirroring their use of piano accompaniment without considering the pedagogical rationale behind such a choice:

> I was used to listening to accompaniment played by my vocal tutor during the lesson, so it was natural for me to play some chordal accompaniment for the pupil in my [MA] assessed lesson ... I did not think about the reason for using the piano accompaniment method before I studied the MA as I was imitating my former vocal lessons with my undergraduate tutors.

These perceptions suggest that despite variations in participants' teaching behaviours, many began by imitating and transferring teaching patterns and approaches from their former teachers. This aligns with the findings of Haddon (2009) regarding the replicative approaches of student-teachers. An instructing style that combines teacher demonstration with student imitation was perceived by these student-teachers as the primary method for instrumental technique development because of its potential representation of professional competence. Although some participants recognized that they were replicating teaching habits from their former teachers, they lacked confidence in their ability to ensure that their teaching was effective and understood by their pupils. This also indicates how prior educational experiences might serve as barriers, impeding student-teachers' awareness of varied teaching modes and their confidence to transition between them.

First Step to Transition: The Refinement of Questioning

In response to MA course content, the use of open-ended questions was perceived by several participants to be a practical teaching technique supporting transitioning from an instructional approach to a mentoring mode. One student-teacher remarked that the variety of questions delivered by MA teaching staff in instrumental lessons that they observed was an 'easy' initial way to adapt to a mentoring approach, useful when teaching students of varying proficiency levels. Consequently, this technique became a method that was 'most frequently used'. However, another participant felt that pupils who 'used to be led and taught in a way that every step has been told by the teacher' might be 'overwhelmed' if their teacher changed their approach from instructing to mentoring and started asking more questions. For these student-teachers, the primary challenge arising from the use of questioning resided in the difficulty of crafting open-ended questions and working with pupils who exhibited limited enthusiasm for discourse; a third participant felt that the effectiveness of employing questions to enhance interactive teaching relies on the active engagement and responses of pupils, as 'it can be time-consuming and useless if the pupils reported no ideas about the question asked'.

A related challenge pertains to potential disturbance of the teaching pace and lesson aims through questioning. One participant felt 'disrupted by pupils' hesitation and silent response, and felt [they] lost control of the lesson time and teaching pace'. Another participant considered that their instructional effectiveness would diminish if every teaching decision required student interrogation. They also suggested that pupils' parents might perceive extensive questioning redundant if too much time was devoted to questioning and reasoning: 'If the teaching purpose is to help the student to play well, then what is the point of wasting so much time asking questions?' These perceptions suggest that parents might prioritize direct and immediate learning and performing outcomes over developing learner metacognition and independence through questioning-based facilitation.

In addition to challenges related to their pupils' responsiveness and adaptability to questioning, student-teachers discussed strategies for managing potential disruptions caused by the use of questioning. One participant proposed allocating time for their pupils' answers by 'cutting down some teaching content', while another suggested simplifying questions, initially posing 'closed-ended questions with selective answers' before transitioning to open-ended inquiries.

Three participants expressed confidence in using questioning techniques, highlighting the importance of open-mindedness regarding their future post-MA use of this technique. However, one participant perceived that this enthusiasm needed to be balanced with an understanding of the learning expectations and purposes of students raised in the Chinese educational context. Nuances emerged as participants shared insights regarding attempts and refinements in implementing questioning as a teaching strategy. One participant recognized the importance of considering the quantity and quality of questions after engaging in course content on Socratic questioning, highlighting that they initially focused on 'increasing the number of questions' but 'after accessing the lecture … realized that the questions involved could be systematic and various': 'I could ask another question upon a question, such as, "why did I ask you this question?", "What is the purpose of asking this question?"' Another student-teacher observed that 'the quality of questions, the way of asking questions, the content of the questions, and how to make responses' to their pupils' answers needed to be taken into account. This echoes another participant who remarked on the importance of 'carefully' responding to pupils' questions and answers: 'If your pupil provides an answer that is completely different from what you expected, you need to explore why he or she had this answer, rather than ignoring it with panic and blindly moving on.'

Perspectives of Transitioning between Different Modes

Three participants reported a reflective and flexible approach when adapting to the pedagogical differences. Their reflective awareness led them to feel that the decision between employing teacher-directed or student-centred approaches in instrumental teaching is contextually driven; one participant felt that 'the teaching approaches suggested in the MA are appropriate for the Western or UK teaching context but are not appropriate for China's music education context'. Another participant considered combining the two teaching modes and employing them for different teaching purposes: 'I think it might be useful if a teacher could use student-centred approaches during the lesson and use master-apprentice guidance ... to help with their practice.' However, this seemed to be 'difficult' as 'the teacher needs to be very good at both teaching modes; otherwise, the pupil needs to understand the importance of both modes'. This participant also worried that their attention to the ideas and feelings of pupils may not necessarily have a relevant or positive response:

> Some very young children are not necessarily disciplined if you teach them in a friendly, student-centred manner ... many children in China need a strict, even somewhat impersonal teacher to regulate their lesson behaviour and practice at home. For example, if I ask my pupils whether they enjoyed the lesson or not, they are likely to respond, 'I would be really happy if I never had to learn piano again and never had to take piano lessons.'

This appears to contrast with research suggesting that qualities such as warmth and empathy are as important as musical abilities for those teaching beginners (Sloboda and Howe 1991). However, given that Chinese parents may make the decision for children to learn piano (Cui 2023), the pupils' motivation for learning piano may be externally driven, leading to potential resistance or lack of learner interest.

In addition, the choice between teacher-directed and student-centred modes appears to be specifically dependent on whether the teaching purpose drives towards rapid mastery or focuses on immediate outcomes and enjoyment, as one participant observed:

> If you [your pupils] would like to achieve a high professional level in a short period of time, you may just hold a few opportunities to be happy in the learning process; however, if you would like to enjoy the learning process, you may need to give up something related to immediate learning outcomes. Having said that, however, I always believe that a learning process [that] blended happiness and productiveness can exist as they are not mutually exclusive.

Another participant felt the teacher-directed and the student-centred modes 'were extremely different', such as the communication type characterized in each mode:

> A learner-centred mode suggests multi-directed and equal communication; however, a teacher-centred transmission suggests single-directed and top-down communication. So, I don't think my previous teaching habit is wrong, but I hope to find a balance between different pedagogies suggested by the MA and [those that have] developed in China ... I need to flexibly adjust, adapt and progress.

The perceptions from these three students indicate that their choice between the habitual teacher-directed and the implementation of a more student-centred mode was influenced by different contexts, their pupils, their teaching and learning purposes and their knowledge of both teaching modes. This reveals some of their considerations in developing understanding of negotiating between different pedagogies, emphasizing reflection, flexibility and adaptation.

Discussion and Implications

Participants navigated the adaptive process by reflecting on their pre-MA experiences, considering their experience of learning to use open-ended questions during their MA study, and the challenges of exploring mentoring approaches within their instrumental teaching. Initially seen as conflicting and distinct from their former educational experiences, the mentor-friend approaches appeared to complement the more instructive habitual approaches, even within just one term (three months) of experience of the MA course. Aligning with the continua summarized by Gaunt (2017), the intercultural and transitional perceptions of the Chinese student-teachers in this MA course revealed further nuances within the specific continuum of transitioning from teacher-directed instruction to student-centred mentoring: challenges in moving from dominating teacher instructions to questioning-led facilitation, and the concerns relating to immediate results, mastery and enjoyment-orientated teaching and learning. These align with Haddon's research (2019), indicating a transition from teacher-directed technical instruction to a more person and process-oriented and diverse pedagogical approach, exploring alternative perspectives in learning and teaching.

Using open-ended questions, assisted by reflection on their teaching, appears to support teachers moving between teacher-centred and student-centred approaches. The crafting of questions and their pupils' responses are challenges that potentially influence their transition process. Further combined with their lack of received student-centred approaches as instrumental learners pre-MA, as well as language barriers as they adapt and develop teaching strategies in their second language, English (see Chapter 9), their perceptions might reflect more difficulties and tensions, including parental expectations and concerns of professionalism. Despite the additional difficulties concerning cultural and linguistic differences, three students showed a flexible teaching mindset, indicating that the instructing and mentoring modes can be transitioned between, aligning with the idea that an individual's flexibility, openness and constant reflection are connected to their adaptability (Valmisa 2021).

The adoption of student-centred approaches by participants in this research shows potential for a collaborative learning process between teacher and student; both are learning from each other. This supports the idea that teachers should consider moving to models that promote students' independence, such as from an apprenticeship model to mentoring by decreasing teacher dominance (Burwell 2005). However, questioning techniques could be perceived as redundant by some Chinese parents and cause confusion because they tend to believe that teacher-centred and instructive approaches are beneficial to achieve immediate learning outcomes. Therefore, considering and understanding parental expectations would be useful for striking a balance during the teaching transition, particularly as notions of professionalism have implications for ongoing employment and for the potential reinforcement of teacher guidance by parents in at-home practice sessions.

Potentially, it could be argued that 'student-centred' may mean different things in different contexts and that the mentor-friend mode is more nuanced than merely utilizing questions. Educators could be encouraged to reflect on whether there are universal understandings of concepts, to consider how we have derived our understanding of concepts and approaches, what our expectations are in regard to using these within our teaching and to reflect on the resultant outcomes in our students. Therefore, it is possible that in the Chinese context, 'student-centred' could be regarded as pedagogical approaches that support the expectations for instructive approaches aiming for the rapid achievement of mastery, as opposed to a mentor-friend approach, which may foster a different orientation towards learning which could potentially be viewed as less constructive. As Ford (2020) observes, 'In addition to differences in reflective traditions and in students' understanding of how they should perform themselves to their teachers as international students in a new cultural context, a major problem with "what the student does" is that more often than not, it is dependent on a teacher defined outcome.' This has two relevancies for the present research: firstly, a double-layered presentation: that of the pupil and that of the teacher across cultures and contexts; secondly, the privileging of the educator's perspective over that of the learner. How might students understand the concept of 'student-centred' teaching, particularly in a context where competition remains endemic for learners (Guo and Cosaitis 2019)?

We could also reflect on – and discuss with those with whom we work – whether there are needs for specific approaches due to cultural expectations, in which case, would changing these be positive, and if so, in what ways might change be approached? The participants in this research saw development in their understanding of the value of a mentor-friend approach through using questioning, underpinned by their observation of instrumental lessons given by MA tutors and by their own reflection on teaching after just a few months of studying. However, this needs to be reconciled with concerns of professional competence, particularly relevant in competitive contexts in which a proliferation of teachers may lead to a saturated market with concerns for those who operate against the status quo. Nevertheless, building awareness and confidence in utilizing different teacher-student relationship modes could lead to the ability to draw on the most appropriate mode for the different situations of each learner as they progress, recognizing that movement along the master-apprentice and mentor-friend continuum is a flexible, responsive, versatile approach to instrumental teaching which can aid adaptation to different contexts and individuals and can facilitate development of both learner and teacher.

Conclusion

Chinese students taking part in the first author's research embarked on a journey of discovering and implementing student-centred teaching approaches during their UK MA study. Through exposure to a student-centred, mentoring approach advocated by the MA course, they came to perceive their habitual instructive teaching approaches as lacking diversity and creativity. Becoming aware of and negotiating barriers posed by their ingrained cultural and educational habits pre-MA, their main strategy was to improve communication with their pupils by asking more open-ended questions. This signifies their transition from instructing to mentoring approaches, although refining the questions asked and responding to pupils' perspectives posed further challenges linked to teaching in English as an additional language. Future research could delve deeper into the meaning of student-centred teaching as understood by those within different cultures, particularly as perceived by learners. It could also probe the effectiveness and implementation of student-centred pedagogies across cultures and specifically explore the impact of different mentor-friend approaches and their applicability across diverse cultural and educational contexts.

References

Braun, V., and V. Clark (2006), 'Using Thematic Analysis in Psychology', *Qualitative Research in Psychology*, 3 (2): 77–101.

Burwell, K. (2005), 'A Degree of Independence: Teachers' Approaches to Instrumental Tuition in a University College', *British Journal of Music Education*, 22 (3): 199–215.

Creech, A., and H. Gaunt (2012), 'The Changing Face of Individual Instrumental Tuition: Value, Purpose, and Potential', in G. E. McPherson and G. F. Welch (eds), *The Oxford Handbook of Music Education, Vol. 1*, 698–700, Oxford: Oxford University Press.

Creswell, J. W., and C. N. Poth (2018), *Qualitative Inquiry and Research Design: Choosing among Five Approaches*, 4th edn, London: Sage.

Cui, C. (2023), 'Measuring Parental Involvement as Parental Actions in Children's Private Music Lessons in China', *Frontiers in Psychology*, 13: 1061765.

Dwyer, S. C., and J. L. Buckle (2009), 'The Space Between: On Being an Insider-Outsider in Qualitative Research', *International Journal of Qualitative Methods*, 8 (1): 54–63.

Ford, B. (2020), 'Can Culturally Specific Perspectives to Teaching Western Classical Music Benefit International Students? A Call to Re-examine "What the Teacher Does"', *Frontiers in Education*, 5 https://www.frontiersin.org/journals/education/articles/10.3389/feduc.2020.00113/full.

Gaunt, H. (2017), 'Apprenticeship and Empowerment: The Role of One-to-One Lessons', in J. Rink, H. Gaunt and A. Williamon (eds), *Musicians in the Making: Pathways to Creative Performance*, 28–56, Oxford: Oxford University Press.

Guo, W., and L. J. Cosaitis (2019), 'A Cutting Edge Method in Chinese Piano Education: The Xindi Applied Piano Pedagogy', *Higher Education Studies*, 10 (1): 7–15.

Haddon, E. (2009), 'Instrumental and Vocal Teaching: How Do Music Students Learn to Teach?', *British Journal of Music Education*, 26 (1): 57–70.

Haddon, E. (2019), 'Perspectives of Chinese Students on Studying MA Music Programmes in a UK University', *ORFEU*, 4 (2): 30–58.

Haddon, E. (2024), 'Negotiating Pedagogical Cultures: Adaptive Challenges Facing Music Education Graduates on Their Return to China', in R. Prokop and R. Reitsamer (eds), *Higher Music Education and Employability in a Neoliberal World*, 159–72, London: Bloomsbury.

Jiang, M. (2018), 'Chinese Students' Adjustment to Studying in UK Higher Education: Academic Self-efficacy and Psychological Well-Being', PhD diss., University of York, UK.

Jorgensen, E. R. (2008), *The Art of Teaching Music*, Oxford: Oxford University Press.

Jørgensen, H. (2000), 'Student Learning in Higher Instrumental Education: Who Is Responsible?', *British Journal of Music Education*, 17 (1): 67–77.

Lehmann, A. C., J. A. Sloboda and R. H. Woody (2007), *Psychology for Musicians: Understanding and Acquiring the Skills*, Oxford: Oxford University Press.

Li, J. (2022), *Shaping Education Policy Discourse: Insights from Internationalization of Education Development in China*, New York: Springer.

Liu, X. (June 2022), 'Intercultural and Adaptive Pedagogical Developments of Chinese PG Students before, during and after Studying Music Education in the UK', conference paper presented at *China in the Social Sciences: Emerging Research from the North of England (ChiNESS)*, Sheffield, UK.

McWilliam, E. (2009), 'Teaching for Creativity: From Sage to Guide to Meddler', *Asia Pacific Journal of Education*, 29 (3): 281–93.

Qi, S. (2024), 'Analysis of the Effects of Cultural Differences on Teaching and Learning Styles and the Impact on Teaching and Learning in China', *International Journal of Education and Humanities*, 12 (2): 40–3.

Sloboda, J. A., and M. J. Howe (1991), 'Biographical Precursors of Musical Excellence: An Interview Study', *Psychology of Music*, 19 (1): 3–21.

Valmisa, M. (2021), *Adapting: A Chinese Philosophy of Action*, Oxford: Oxford University Press.

Yeh, C.-S. (2001), 'China', in D. J. Hargreaves and A. C. North (eds), *Musical Development and Learning: The International Perspective*, 27–39, London: Continuum.

Zhang, L.-X., B. Leung and Y. Yang (2023), 'From Theory to Practice: Student-Centred Pedagogical Implementation in Primary Music Demonstration Lessons in Guangdong, China', *International Journal of Music Education*, 41 (2): 271–87.

Zheng, X., and E. Haddon (2023), 'Pedagogical Transformation and Choice-Making: A Longitudinal Study of Chinese Pre-Service Guzheng Teachers in the UK', *Asia-Pacific Journal for Arts Education*, 22 (special issue): 1–33.

9

Understanding Subject-Specific Language Challenges for Music Learners with English as an Additional Language (EAL): What Are the Impacts and How Can Teachers Provide Support?

Hang Li and Xinpei Zheng

Introduction

Students who were 'exposed to a language at home that is known or believed to be other than English' and those who have English as an additional language are defined as EALs (Department for Education 2020: 4). This group comprises students from diverse cultural backgrounds and varied levels of English proficiency (Oxley and de Cat 2021). Recent years have witnessed a continuing increase of EALs in the UK: in the academic year 2023–4, EALs formed 20.8 per cent (1.7 million) of the total student headcount (8.5 million) across UK nurseries and schools (Department for Education 2024); in tertiary institutions, non-UK domiciled students formed 24 per cent (0.6 million, including full-time and part-time undergraduates and postgraduates) of the total student population (2.8 million) in 2021–2, of whom 22 per cent (0.1 million) were from China (HESA 2023). These students are referred to by different terms in literature: *English language learners* (ELLs) (Abril 2003; Eros and Eros 2019; Scherler 2006), *English learners* (ELs) (Eros 2015) or 'LEP' for those with *limited English proficiency* (Yudkin 1995). In this chapter, EAL is used to indicate this heterogeneous student group.

The growing culturally diverse study body necessitates providing accommodating teaching strategies and targeted support, which require teachers' awareness and understanding of students' specific concerns and needs (Scherler 2006). Drawing upon the findings from a case study on Chinese students in the MA Music Education: Instrumental and Vocal Teaching at the University of York, this chapter unveils these EALs' challenges with music specialist vocabulary and introduces targeted support provided by the course tutors, leading to implications for music teachers' practices in supporting EALs.

Literature Review

EALs' language concerns might lead to their reduced engagement and participation in music classrooms (Scherler 2006) and school music programmes (Elpus and Abril 2019). Although the demonstration of students' musical competence may not necessarily require English proficiency, EALs are 'frequently unable to discern the meaning behind much of the verbal discourse in the classroom and sometimes perform at a menial level or not at all' (Carlow 2006: 26). Abril (2003) asserts that an absence of teachers' supporting interventions may risk limiting EALs' learning opportunities; the situation is worsened particularly when the EAL has not yet attained English proficiency for student-teacher communication (Yudkin 1995). However, even with the best intentions to support their pupils, pre- and in-service music teachers face challenges due to the paucity of systematic guidance addressing working with EAL students (Durgunoğlu and Hughes 2010; Scherler 2006). These findings would also apply to tertiary music education.

To aid music teachers' effective supporting strategies, literature highlights the importance of understanding the stages of EALs' English language development. Drawing on the five-stage model developed by Krashen and Terrell (1998), scholars provide insights into the music teacher's practices (Bannerman 2023; Galván 2023). In EALs' three early stages – *Silent Period*, *Early Production* and *Speech Emergence* – of the five-stage model, a great deal of the teacher's intentional instructional support (e.g. visualization of instructions) is crucial for the EAL's comprehension and engagement (Galván 2023); the teacher's questions should be tailored congruently with the EAL's capacity to verbalize English at each stage (Bannerman 2023). For example, the teacher could ask questions that allow EALs to respond nonverbally in their *Silent Period*, while questions requiring a short-sentence answer are more appropriate for EALs in *Speech Emergence* (ibid.). Progressing to *Intermediate Fluency* and *Advanced Fluency*, EALs need the teacher's support and monitoring of their understanding of more nuanced content-specific English (Eros and Eros 2019). This concerns EALs' Basic Interpersonal Communication Skills (BICS) and Cognitive Academic Language Proficiency (CALP) (Cummins 1999): the development of CALP takes a longer time and more effort than BICS, thus EALs' fluency of BICS (i.e. informal spoken social language) does not indicate their equivalent proficiency in CALP (e.g. using music vocabulary). This warrants the teacher's caution concerning their content-specific instructions as EALs' demonstration of proficient BICS might cloud the teacher's awareness of their CALP gaps (Eros and Eros 2019). Bannerman (2023) elaborates on music teachers' instructional practices by referring to Gottlieb's (2016) categories of sensory, graphic, linguistic and interactive support, which echo the recommended strategies in previous studies (Abril 2003; Eros 2015).

The focus of much of the available literature centres around Hispanic students in US music classrooms, providing implications for English-speaking teachers working with EALs. The scholars mentioned above unanimously recommended teachers' conscious instructional modifications concerning their pace of speaking, verbal repetition and the use of multiple modalities. However, the aspect of musical terms warrants more context-specific consideration: some Italian terms are close to Spanish with similar pronunciation and spelling (e.g. *legato* and '*ligado*'), and some terms already exist in Spanish musical instructions (e.g. *sonata*), making them more easily understood by Hispanic EALs (Galván 2023); this might not apply to EALs from other regions, such as China.

Ward (2014) delineated three ways used to convey the understanding of Western musical terms in the Chinese-speaking context: transliteration, free translation and footnoted translation. Transliteration is generally used as 'transcription' of the sound of composers' names; free translation is usually used for musical genres and forms, and footnoted translation combines the sound of the original words with an aiding character or word for the meaning (see examples in Table 9.1). The translated terms are used in teachers' instructions to students, but the original forms of the terms are printed in students' workbooks and performance scores. Thus, extra verbal support is needed to enable students' comprehension of the techniques, interpretations and other necessary performance directions written on the score. Ward asserts that the distance between Chinese and Western musical terms places Chinese EALs 'at a

Table 9.1 Examples of Translation of Western Musical Terms in Chinese

Type of translation	Western musical terms	Translation in Chinese
Transliteration	Bach	巴赫 (bāhè)
Free translation	Sonata	奏鸣曲 (zòumíngqǔ)
Footnoted translation	Ballet	芭蕾舞 (bāléiwǔ)

Adapted from Ward (2014: 12–13).

distinct disadvantage' (2014: 11) in the global context where English is the lingua franca for communication.

At tertiary level, while research investigates EALs' broad language challenges and effective language support, little attention has been paid to music EALs. Kovačević (2019: 396) contends that the reason lies in 'the fact that art music is primarily observed in relation to the practical acts of musical performance, while the theoretical aspects of art music remained neglected and below-the-radar in terms of serious and detailed linguistic investigation and research'. Whichever pathway they study, music students will require this area of working professional knowledge (Kovačević 2018; Lesiak-Bielawska 2014; Marić 2022). For EALs who have previously engaged with the area of expertise in a language other than English, challenges are present and should be addressed.

At the Fryderyk Chopin University of Music in Poland, Lesiak-Bielawska (2014: 14) reported domestic students' (Polish EALs) pressing need for language support for musical terminology. Student questionnaire responses disclosed that this area of knowledge is 'what they needed most' in their degree study and was supported by the results of a subsequent competency test for students. Data collected from students and teachers informed the design of a corresponding English for Specific Purposes (ESP) programme, a field in which music has historically been neglected (Marić 2022) and 'has not managed to establish its place completely' (Kovačević 2019: 396). This links to the research gap regarding music EALs' subject-specific language challenges; the following study offers insights supporting a growing understanding of students' needs and relevant teaching approaches.

Context

The MA Music Education: Instrumental and Vocal Teaching at the University of York, UK, was established in the academic year 2015–16 by Dr Elizabeth Haddon. The course involves theoretical and practical modules exploring areas of music pedagogy. Students are required to carry out teaching practice throughout the course, and the practical modules require students to record a fifteen- to twenty-minute instrumental lesson with a pupil, submitting this and a reflective written lesson commentary as part of the summative assignments. Since its establishment, the course has seen a considerable increase in the number of enrolled EALs, most of whom are Chinese students. 'Talking about Music' (TAM) sessions were initiated by a lecturer who has considerable experience of working with Chinese students. These optional sessions support students' vocabulary of musical terms and pedagogical language skills and are delivered to students in groups of six to eight, led by a lecturer or graduate teaching assistant (GTA). Within the three one-hour sessions taking place across three consecutive weeks, students participate in discussion-based activities with the tutors facilitating the use of music subject-specific language.

Methodology

This study of TAM students and tutors constitutes a subunit of the first author's PhD research project – a case study on Chinese MA instrumental music education students, investigating the language challenges experienced by these students within their programme, the language support provided and perceptions of the value of this support. Ethical approval was obtained from the University of York Arts and Humanities Ethics Committee. The first author conducted non-participant observations in TAM groups in 2020–1 and 2021–2, recording the students' language concerns and tutors' corresponding approaches. The first author then interviewed the five observed TAM tutors (T1, T2, T3, T4 and T5) who also deliver MA session content and mark students' assignments. Interview questions explored tutors' perspectives on Chinese students' language challenges and staff practices in providing support. TAM students' perspectives were collected through a self-completed qualitative questionnaire, focusing on their perceptions of their language issues and their experience of TAM. Thirty-one Chinese students out of fifty-four TAM students responded to the questionnaire (S1, S2, S3 and so on). Data analysis was thematic, utilizing the processes of Braun and Clarke (2022). This chapter focuses on students' challenges with specialist music vocabulary and TAM tutors' supporting practices, which are also discussed in relation to the implications for instrumental teaching practices.

Findings

Students' Subject-Specific Language Challenges

Regarding their reasons for taking TAM and their expectations for the sessions, twenty-one respondents were motivated by learning musical terminology. One respondent specified their concerns with this area of knowledge in an EAL environment: 'I don't think I'm very familiar with the technical vocabulary of the English language' (S4); some respondents envisaged the benefits of knowing musical terms in English for their own instrumental teaching and music performance. Other motivations included the opportunity to communicate with classmates, the relevance of TAM to their course and improving their teaching skills in general. Answers to a question about any particularly challenging aspects of TAM disclosed some respondents' concerns with pronunciation: 'Many of the words are Italian pronunciation, so it is challenging for me to accurately say the words' (S3). S18 found it difficult to identify the equivalent terms between Chinese and English; S13 and S15 reported that the theoretical aspect (i.e. analysing the score) is 'difficult'.

In interviews, TAM tutors voiced their awareness of Chinese students' subject-specific language concerns. As T2 observed, musical terminology stood out as a primary issue that Chinese students struggled with in their assessed lessons. The example below could reflect some students' limited vocabulary of musical terms and resultant communication difficulties with their pupils:

> They (MA student) might say 'Can you tell me the strength of this phrase?', and I realized that they were trying to use the word 'dynamics', but they didn't have that word … I saw that particular word coming up, and the pupil looking confused and [the MA student] spending five minutes of a 20-minute lesson just trying to put across the question. (T1)

As T1 considered, limited knowledge of specialist vocabulary might have led to some students' avoidance of using musical terms in their lessons: 'I thought if only they knew what that word (the term *cantabile* on the score) meant, that could have been linked in (within the student's teaching).' Additionally, mispronunciation of musical terms stood out in some students' assessed lessons, which often led to the pupil's confusion. Within TAM, T5 recalled instances concerning dynamics: 'I was talking about dynamics, and students didn't respond about dynamics but something completely different. I don't know if that was me not explaining it, or the concept of dynamics wasn't quite understood.'

Interviewees considered that these challenges might be related to the instructions that students received in their home country, the pressure when students encounter terms in other languages in addition to English (e.g. Italian) and the nature of students' development of BICS and CALP: 'They have worked hard to develop their language skills in general speech, but musical vocabulary is a separate thing' (T1).

Observational data from the TAM sessions indicated students' challenges with specific terms. Issues with English vocabulary and musical terms were voiced by students within their pair or group class discussions, particularly in the first TAM sessions. In Group 1, a discussion group had been using the Chinese words 附点 (*dotted notes*) and 颤音 (*trill*) in their discussion, but they struggled to locate their equivalent words in English. A similar situation was observed in a discussion pair in Group 3 concerning 延长音 (*fermata*), 弱起 (*anacrusis*), 切分音 (*syncopation*) and the character of the tempo of the given piece (e.g. *andante*). Some students voiced conceptual issues concerning particular terms; for example, the difference between a notated *tie* and a *slur* and identifying the type of chords on a music score in their discussion in Chinese. Pronunciation issues were frequently observed with Italian terms such as *acciaccatura, fermata, arpeggio* and *diminuendo,* and some words serving particular musical meanings such as *triad* and *minor*. Furthermore, when searching for terms to answer tutors' questions, six students voiced their struggles with pronouncing the terms to their peers.

The Provision of Support

The tutors who designed TAM set the objectives as 'building up students' vocabulary of musical terms and specific praise and feedback to their pupils'. Accordingly, TAM is structured as three sessions: 'Describing What You Hear', 'Describing What You See' and 'Describing a Performance'. In each session, students work in pairs or small groups to discuss questions addressing aspects of music (e.g. rhythm) and pedagogy (e.g. giving specific praise to pupils), with a tutor's facilitation and the use of supporting documents 'Useful Musical Terminology' and 'Praise Phrases', created by the tutors. Key session questions are generated and based on selected pieces from ABRSM aural training in practice (Grades 6 to 8)[1] and a Grade 3 'merit' piano performance video from Trinity College London Examinations.[2] TAM students are encouraged to bring the pieces they are working on with their pupils to Session 2, as part 2 of the session. The progression of questions encourages students to practise the musical terms involved in the previous parts. This is exemplified in Table 9.2, which presents the key questions in 'Describing What You Hear'.

TAM tutors support students' development of subject-specific vocabulary, giving instructions and demonstration of term pronunciation, the provision of alternative word choices (e.g. *crushed note* for *acciaccatura*) and explanation of the distinction

Table 9.2 Key Questions in 'Describing What You Hear'

Part 1 audio material: Grade 8, Lyadov (piano)
• How would you describe the character, emotion, or mood of this piece? • Does this piece create a picture in your mind? • Could you suggest a title for this piece? (tutor asks follow-up questions and introduces relevant terms based on students' prior knowledge)
Part 2 audio material: Grade 7, Handel (piano)
• From listening to this piece, how would you describe the rhythm, tonality and harmony, texture, dynamics, tempo and pulse to a pupil? (tutor asks follow-up questions and encourages students to answer in more detail)
Part 3 audio material: Gershwin (voice)
• From listening to this piece, how would you describe the rhythm, tonality and harmony, texture, dynamics, tempo and pulse to a pupil? • How do the aspects you are describing affect the mood, character, emotion of the piece? • What Style or Period do you think this piece was written in? • What characteristics and musical features did you hear that informed this decision?

between UK and US musical terminology (e.g. *semiquaver* and *sixteenth note*). Terms were sometimes introduced by drawing connections to similar English words that students might be more familiar with, such as *moderato* and 'moderately'. Some tutors shared their tips for developing this area of knowledge: building up a 'bank' of terminology with the use of the pieces that they worked on with pupils (T2) and through materials such as 'Useful Musical Terminology' (T1, T4, T5). Additionally, tutors proactively elicited students' practice of the introduced terms through follow-up questions: 'What is the other word for *sixteenth notes*?', and 'What musical term can be used for "getting quieter in the last two bars"?' Tutors also played an important role in relating the terms to students' teaching, allowing space and time for students to practise using the terms in teaching scenarios and through reminders in tutors' summary sections before progressing to subsequent activities.

Tutors utilized multiple strategies to optimize their instructions and students' engagement. Linguistic modifications for instructions were used by all tutors. For example, T4 would consciously avoid verbiage in their questions; T5 would paraphrase some task questions before the session to make them easier for students to comprehend. Tutors' linguistic modifications in response to students' reactions to questions were also observed. For example, T1 provided example antonyms 'cheerful' and 'sad' when they sensed that students were confused by the question 'How would you describe the character of this piece?' Tutors often used gestures, movement and the piano in the classroom for students' visual and audio reference for conveying key terms or phrases. For example, T5 vocalized *crescendo* and *diminuendo* by singing with gradually changing volume alongside moving their hands further apart and closer together. Additionally, tutors made a conscious effort to encourage every student to talk. Some tutors varied the format of discussions within a session by shuffling pair group members or by alternating pair discussion and plenary discussion.

TAM Students' Reception of Support

Students were asked about their perspectives on the value of TAM and its relationship to their MA activities; related questions concerned their comments on the aspects of TAM and their tutors' delivery. Responses indicated appreciation of these programme-specific language support sessions, particularly in their development of specialist vocabulary in the EAL environment. Some respondents considered that TAM provided them with an additional opportunity to practise their English communicative skills, observing that this subject-specific context is more focused and practical for their degree than the pre-sessional language courses provided by the university. TAM also benefited respondents' other MA activities such as essay writing (S5, S9), instrument learning (S1) and their confidence in group discussions (S5, S18). Most respondents identified TAM as helpful for their teaching: 'In many ways it

(TAM) has helped me to communicate better with students in my instrumental music lessons. Also, in some of the lectures, the tutor mentioned specialist vocabulary that I could understand' (S4); 'I am able to teach students with relative proficiency in the language of the profession. In addition, I am more confident in explaining definitions and answering students' questions about music that I was previously unfamiliar with. It was really helpful!' (S5).

Tutors' delivery of TAM sessions received positive feedback, indicating approaches which respondents found useful and accommodating, such as the tutors' demonstrations of the pronunciation and use of musical terms (S4, S17, S20); additionally, the tutors' guidance allowed space for extra terms in addition to those within the session materials (S4). Moreover, further approaches were particularly welcomed by respondents: the use of visual support (S4, S20), the provision of opportunity for peer and tutor-student interactions (S5, S19, S24) and the sharing of experiences regarding the discussed topics from a subject specialist's perspective (S5). S11 noted enhanced confidence in speaking in the EAL environment through their tutor's encouraging approaches. For the further development of TAM, increasing the number of sessions, adding further variety of task materials and theoretical aspects were mentioned.

Discussion

These findings provide empirical information concerning Chinese MA students' subject-specific language challenges and the provision of target support from the host programme. The use of multiple methods allowed different perspectives to be obtained, providing specificity concerning music and EAL students. Although situated in a higher education context, the discussion of the findings provides implications for music teachers working with EALs across school and tertiary levels.

An individual's terminological competence refers to their proficiency with the subject terminology in receptive (e.g. listening to a subject lecture) and productive (e.g. generating a terminologically rich speech) activities (Botiraliyevna 2020; Lavrentieva et al. 2020), constituting 'the main part of professional competence' (Botiraliyevna 2020: 63). Findings showed that some Chinese students demonstrated the dissonance between their terminological competences in their first and an additional language; that is, through the frequently observed instances of students using correct terms in their discussion in Chinese, but struggles emerged when terminologically based answers were required in English. This resonates with Ward's (2014) concerns with the disadvantages stemming from the monolingual Chinese-based instructions for Chinese learners' engagement with Western musical terminology. Findings also suggested that there were music theory gaps for some students, which may hinder their course engagement. This concerns these students' music theoretical development before the MA. However, very little was found in available literature on the consideration of this aspect. Woodrow (2018) emphasized that a student's prior subject knowledge significantly influences the design and delivery of targeted language support. Therefore, teachers are recommended to be aware of EALs' previous musical trajectories that might differ from those of their counterparts and to navigate the issues related to students' language concerns. Such information could be obtained through teacher-EAL conversations. A collaborative dialogical journal between the teacher and EAL (Carlow 2006) could provide a low-stakes channel in this regard; additionally, it could be helpful for teachers to develop an information record of the EAL's linguistic and musical background – a template is given in Eros (2015: 423–4) – to aid their teaching practices.

Findings concerning the TAM tutors' approaches augment the necessity of subject specialists' involvement in supporting EALs' development of English for Specific Purposes (ESP). 'Subject knowledge undoubtedly enhances the teaching of ESP' (Woodrow 2018: 57), and subject specialists' involvement helps build EALs' stronger connection to their disciplines (Thorpe et al. 2017). Scholars have also addressed the importance of collaboration between music teachers and language specialists (Eros 2015; Scherler 2006). For example, music teachers could consult with English language teachers to develop language support strategies to accommodate students at Krashen and Terrell's (1998) five different phases of foreign language development – silent period, early production, speech emergence, intermediate fluency, and advanced fluency. Additionally, the TAM tutors' strategies reflected some essential components in line with relevant literature. First and foremost, empathy plays an important role in teaching and learning (Cooper 2011), which informs more effective strategies to support EALs (Zhang 2017). Tutors' empathy was demonstrated in their understanding of the studied EALs' language tensions and their facilitating practices. Within the sessions, tutors demonstrated the integration of instructional support strategies (Gottlieb 2016), linguistic support (e.g. using simpler words in questions), sensory support (e.g. using gestures and piano) and interactive support (e.g. shuffling pair members). Questionnaire responses indicated that these strategies were welcomed by the EALs, which lends support to the existing practices outlined in the literature review. Notably, the explicit teaching of subject-specific vocabulary benefits both English-only and EAL pupils (Oxley and de Cat 2021) in a mixed class: graphic and linguistic support can be used to develop school EALs' musical vocabulary, for example, through the student-teacher collaborative creation of a word bank or word wall in the classroom (Bannerman 2023). Teachers could also encourage and facilitate their development of personal learning dictionaries of subject-specific vocabulary (Harding 2007), in which EALs can include terminology-related information that is useful for them.

Conclusion

EALs' language barriers are a crucial aspect that warrants teachers' awareness and responding strategies. As revealed by the findings, the studied EAL students' challenges with music terminology suggest that this area requires targeted support, which contributes to their terminological competence within their HE programme. The importance of being capable and confident in using musical terms in teaching practices is indicated by tutor and student participants; the provision of targeted support was perceived by these EAL student-teachers as helpful. Moreover, this chapter offers implications for music teachers facing a linguistically and culturally diverse student body: the TAM tutors' strategies exemplified some recommended practices in related literature, with the studied EALs' feedback disclosing their reception of these support strategies. 'Music and the other arts are curricular areas where language need not stand as an obstacle to learning' (Abril 2003: 39), but this cannot be realized without the teacher's proactive supporting practices stemming from their awareness of EALs' language challenges. The research presented in this chapter depicted Chinese music EALs' subject-specific language challenges in order to raise educators' awareness and understanding and provides actionable insights into the teacher's practices aiming to ensure equitable learning opportunities for all students in the music classroom or studio setting, relevant to those working in instrumental pedagogy, and in higher music education across cultures and contexts.

Notes

1. Source: ABRSM, 'Aural Training in Practice: ABRSM Grades 6-8' (2012).
2. Source: https://www.youtube.com/watch?v=3o1Cve7nwWo.

References

Abril, C. (2003), 'No Hablo Ingles: Breaking the Language Barrier in Music Instruction', *Music Educators Journal*, 89 (5): 38–43.
Bannerman, J. (2023), 'Supporting English Learners in Music Classrooms', *Music Educators Journal*, 110 (1): 27–33.
Botiraliyevna, B. H. (2020), 'Formation of Terminological Competence in ESP Education', *JournalNX*, 6 (11): 63–8.
Braun, V., and V. Clarke (2022), *Thematic Analysis: A Practical Guide*, London: Sage.

Carlow, R. (2006), 'Building Confianza: Using Dialogue Journals with English-Language Learners in Urban Schools', in C. Frierson-Campbell (ed.), *Teaching Music in the Urban Classroom*, 25–34, Oxford: National Association for Music Education.

Cooper, B. (2011), *Empathy in Education: Engagement, Values and Achievement*, New York: Continuum.

Cummins, J. (1999), 'BICS and CALP: Clarifying the Distinction', *Institute of Education Science*. Available online: https://files.eric.ed.gov/fulltext/ED438551.pdf (accessed 23 June 2024).

Department for Education (2020), 'English Proficiency: Pupils with English as an Additional Language'. Available online: https://www.gov.uk/government/publications/english-proficiency-pupils-with-english-as-additional-language (accessed 23 June 2024).

Department for Education (2024), 'Schools, Pupils and Their Characteristics, Academic Year 2023/24'. Available online: https://explore-education-statistics.service.gov.uk/find-statistics/school-pupils-and-their-characteristics (accessed 23 June 2024).

Durgunoğlu, A. Y., and T. Hughes (2010), 'How Prepared Are the U.S. Preservice Teachers to Teach English Language Learners?', *International Journal of Teaching and Learning in Higher Education*, 22 (1): 32–41.

Elpus, K., and C. Abril (2019), 'Who Enrols in High School Music? A National Profile of U.S. Students, 2009–2013', *Journal of Research in Music Education*, 67 (3): 323–38.

Eros, J. (2015), 'Modifications of Music Curriculum and Assessment for English Language Learners', in C. Conway (ed.), *Musicianship-Focused Curriculum and Assessment*, 401–24, Chicago: GIA Publications.

Eros, J., and R. Eros (2019), 'English Language Learners', in C. Conway, K. Pellegrino, A. Stanley and C. West (eds), *The Oxford Handbook of Preservice Music Teacher Education in the United States*, 558–74, Oxford: Oxford University Press.

Galván, N. (2023), 'Enriching Spanish-Speaking English Learners' Experiences in the English Music Classroom', *Journal of General Music Education*, 37 (3), 1–9.

Gottlieb, M. (2016), *Assessing English Language Learners: Bridges to Educational Equity*, 2nd edn, Thousand Oaks, CA: Corwin.

Harding, K. (2007), *English for Specific Purposes*, Oxford: Oxford University Press.

HESA (2023), 'Higher Education Students Statistics: UK, 2021/22 – Where Students Come From and Go to Study'. Available online: https://www.hesa.ac.uk/news/19-01-2023/sb265-higher-education-student-statistics/location (accessed 23 June 2024).

Kovačević, D. (2018), 'Pedagogical Conceptualization of Content Knowledge in Teaching Art Music Related ESP', *Journal of Teaching English for Specific and Academic Purposes*, 6 (3): 333–9.

Kovačević, D. (2019), 'Design of an Art Music Related ESP Course Syllabus in the Contemporary Context', *Journal of Teaching English for Specific and Academic Purposes*, 7 (3): 395–404.

Krashen, S. D., and T. D. Terrell (1998), *The Natural Approach: Language Acquisition in the Classroom*, London: Prentice Hall.

Lavrentieva, O., V. Pererva, O. P. Krupskyi, I. Britchenko and S. Shabanov (2020), 'Issues of Shaping the Students' Professional and Terminological Competence in Science Area of Expertise in the Sustainable Development Era'. Available online: https://ssrn.com/abstract=4325144 (accessed 23 June 2024).

Lesiak-Bielawska, E. D. (2014), 'English for Instrumentalists: Designing and Evaluating an ESP Course', *English for Specific Purposes World*, 15 (43): 1–32.

Marić, S. J. (2022), 'Teaching English in Professional Music Education (EPME) in the Digital Era', *Методички видици (Methodical Perspectives)*, 13 (13): 141–61.

Oxley, E., and C. de Cat (2021), 'A Systematic Review of Language and Literacy Interventions in Children and Adolescents with English as an Additional Language (EAL)', *Language Learning Journal*, 49 (3): 265–87.

Scherler, K. (2006), 'Elementary Music Teachers Instructing Hispanic English Language Learners: Reflection on Practice', in M. E. Cavitt (ed.), *Texas Music Education Research 2006*, 28–45, Texas: Texas Music Educators Association.

Thorpe, A., M. Snell, S. Davey-Evans and R. Talman (2017), 'Improving the Academic Performance of Non-Native English-Speaking Students: The Contribution of Pre-Sessional English Language Programmes', *Higher Education Quarterly*, 71 (1): 5–32.

Ward, L.-J. (2014), 'An Approach to Chinese-English Bilingual Music Education', *Victorian Journal of Music Education*, 1: 11–16.

Woodrow, L. (2018), *Introducing Course Design in English for Specific Purposes*, New York: Routledge.

Yudkin, J. (1995), 'Language Barriers and Teaching Music', *Music Educators Journal*, 81 (6): 23–6.

Zhang, Y. (2017), 'Walking a Mile in Their Shoes: Developing Pre-service Music Teachers' Empathy for ELL Students', *International Journal of Music Education*, 35 (3): 425–34.

Part III

Skills-Building

10

Improvisation: Developing Skills and Confidence as Teachers and Learners

Alexis Cairns, Nina Kümin and Helen Madden

Introduction

Music improvisation involves creating new music spontaneously to generate novel musical ideas (Biasutti 2017). In music education, improvisation enables pupils to demonstrate their original musical ideas while concurrently fostering their general musicianship (Gruenhagen and Whitcomb 2014). Pupils who wish to pursue performance assessments including improvisation can work towards graded examinations offered by UK music examination boards that might include elements of improvisation: the Associated Board of the Royal Schools of Music and London College of Music Examinations offer jazz music grades, while Trinity College London offers jazz, rock and popular music grades; Rockschool offers grades for both classical and contemporary genres. Despite opportunities for instrumental music pupils to develop their skills, musical improvisation is not an activity that all teachers feel comfortable implementing in lessons (Whitcomb 2013); improvisation may be viewed as challenging to teach and less worthy than other musical skills (Stringham, Thornton and Shevock 2015). Other factors contributing to the challenges concerning improvisation in instrumental teaching include its infrequent inclusion in teachers' musical learning when they were pupils (Cossey 2024), the lessening of teachers' confidence in teaching improvisation due to more advanced improvisation criteria from the required curriculum for pupils in middle and high schools compared to elementary level (Ward-Steinman 2007) and teachers' lack of personal experience and familiarity with improvising (Koutsoupidou 2005).

In this chapter, a brief history of Western art music improvisation leads to descriptions of strategies that teachers can use to facilitate pupils to improvise in classical music, followed by contemporary genres of jazz, rock and pop improvisation methods. These strategies may not only enable pupils to improvise but could also aid in developing instrumental teachers' confidence in teaching a style of playing that they may be unfamiliar with. As a result, teachers might develop their skills in music improvisation along with their pupils.

Western Classical Improvisation

Scholars argue that the first musical utterances must have been improvised, and there are already references to improvisation in fourth-century church music (Alperson 1984). Later references, particularly throughout the sixteenth to nineteenth centuries, concern preluding, counterpoint, cadenzas, ornamentation, figured bass and longer pieces (Barton n.d.; Tinctoris [1477] 1961; Villavicencio 2008). Improvisation has fallen out of practice in current Western classical performance, however. Exceptionally, organists have continuously improvised in services, and historically informed performers have added improvised ornamentation (Moore 1992). Some keyboardists, including David Dolan, John Mortensen and Robert Levin, have taken this further, reviving larger-scale historical improvisation such as lengthy preludes, fugues and fantasias, but these are in the minority; very few classical musicians are taught to improvise whole pieces (Barton n.d.; Dolan 2024; Levin 2002; Mortensen 2020, 2024).

Scholarship is increasingly providing stylistic guidance for Baroque improvisatory practices. Yoo (2015) suggests exercises to teach Baroque improvisation in classrooms, but although designed for upper-elementary students, these could be prohibitively difficult for beginners unfamiliar with music theory. Callahan's reflections on teaching improvised Baroque counterpoint are limited to higher education keyboard students, requiring confident theoretical knowledge of harmony, voice leading and figured bass (Callahan 2012). The Scroll Ensemble provides practical videos on Baroque improvisation, some of which are adaptable for beginners (2020). In general, however, research is largely focused on advanced performers, usually keyboardists (Collins 2017; Dolan 2024; Gross 2013; Larson 1995; Mortensen 2024). Recent exceptions include advice on improvising a fantasia on the violin (Kümin 2023) and flute (Barbetti 2020), but these are still aimed at technically advanced players. There is, therefore, a gap concerning teaching historical improvisation to beginner and intermediate students in one-to-one lessons which this section seeks to begin to address through reflections on a small case study.

The general considerations and suggested games included in this chapter reflect the initial experiences of one of the authors (Nina Kümin – referred to as NK in the text) teaching Baroque improvisatory practices in peripatetic, individual, face-to-face violin lessons to students of ages eight to fifty, levels pre-ABRSM Grade 1 to post Grade 8, over a period of two months in the UK. These observations are not representative of larger trends, all levels or instruments; this is a huge topic requiring detailed analysis of student feedback and further empirical research beyond the scope of this introduction. Nevertheless, this section seeks to provide inspiration to support teaching Baroque improvisation to beginner and intermediate melody instrumentalists. While designed for Baroque improvisation, some of the suggested games could be easily adapted for other time periods and other instruments. These are by no means an exhaustive list but provide initial ideas for teachers to develop.

General Considerations

To avoid tasks seeming overwhelming, follow each individual's pace (Small 1979). From NK's experience, gradually lengthening improvisations builds explicit knowledge of stylistic considerations and tacit technical ability. Likewise, setting a timer to encourage longer improvisations can be a rewarding challenge. Sociologist Anna Bull (2019: 70) argued that classical musicians are constantly concerned with 'getting it right'; moving away from notated music can initially seem daunting, a response which NK encountered frequently. Considered language use is, therefore, imperative; phrases such as 'now see if you can' or 'what happens if' encourage students to take risks. NK's students were always enthused when particularly successful features were pointed out, such as using their full instrument range, varied phrase lengths or contrasting articulation. Some preferred to initially improvise with NK to feel less exposed. Honestly sharing NK's own experiences and celebrating the constant learning process of improvisation also reassured students. To build stylistic knowledge, creating *Style Scrapbooks* proved helpful: each student identified common features from pieces they were playing or knew of, categorizing these into rhythmic, melodic, structural and other features. Students and teachers can keep returning to and adding to these lists to build their stylistic confidence.

Games

Using games to aid learning has been promoted by many scholars (Broadhead and Burt 2012; Fleer 2011). Applying this to classical improvisation, NK has created the following games (listed from easiest to hardest), which proved accessible introductions to Baroque improvisation in her teaching:

1. *Give me an "A"!* – Students pick and play any note. Following this, ask for another and another. Then indicate to students to continue. Reassure students afterwards that they have already improvised successfully. This was often most successful when students were unaware that improvisation was the aim.
2. *Getting from A to B* – Students pick two notes and then find different ways to get between them: at first add rhythms and then other notes (scales, arpeggios or trills). Once confident, students can extend this to three or four notes, improvising a whole phrase.
3. *Doodling around* – Applying the skills learnt from game 2, experiment with adding notes or rhythms to a notated piece, ornamenting passages.
4. *Up the stairs, down the stairs* – Play a scale but alter the rhythm slightly. Then, add ornamentation as practised in games 2 and 3. Repeat, using an arpeggio. Finally, students can combine altered scales and arpeggios to create a Baroque-style prelude. Identify scales and arpeggios in pieces students are learning to show that these are the foundation.
5. *Get it wrong!* – Deliberately get things 'wrong' in a version of game 4 (such as playing a note not in the scale) and practise making it sound intentional by:
   a. Repeating, holding the note or adding rhythms
   b. Repeating and varying the last few notes
   c. Resolving up or down
6. *Trading phrases* – Create improvised dialogue. Each player improvises a few bars inspired by the previous contribution using skills from games 4 and 5.
7. *Medieval mayhem* – Create counterpoint by asking for short improvised phrases using the Dorian mode ending with a long note. During the long notes, the teacher then improvises a short phrase, building on the student's ideas, and again ending with a long note, allowing alternation between teacher and student.
8. *Finish the sentence* – Play the opening bars of a piece and then ask the student to continue, improvising their own ending. Students can also improvise theme and variation pieces by choosing a famous melody and seeing how many ways they can alter this (speed, major or minor tonality, ornamentation, etc.). Identify features that create different characters and add these to students' *Style Scrapbooks*.
9. *Dance the night away* – Use characteristic Baroque dance rhythms to create dance-style improvisations. Identify these from pieces that students know or suggest simple versions and add them to students' *Style Scrapbooks*.
10. *Loop the loop* – Improvise over a simple ground bass such as I-IV-V-I. Write out the notes in each chord. Invite students to choose one note from each chord, then to apply their skills from game 3 to find ways to get between each note and create a melody. Encourage students to focus on different features in different versions such as rhythm, pitch, character and ornamentation. Experiment with the effect of speed. It can be helpful here for teachers to play the bassline alongside the student's improvisation. Threading together different sections in different characters can create a longer piece.

In conclusion, these suggestions provide introductory approaches for beginner- and intermediate-level musicians to experience Baroque improvisatory practices. They encourage experimentation and creativity in opposition to a pedagogy of correction and provide an opportunity for teachers to learn alongside students. Students can learn much about style through these exercises and through creating their own *Style Scrapbooks*. For several pupils these exercises helped to reinvigorate enthusiasm for practice and playing. Students' instrumental technique and confidence also grew at a faster rate than in previous lessons. In order to enable more historical improvisation in performance, teachers need to reintroduce a pedagogy of classical improvisation into instrumental teaching. More research is needed to test these approaches in varied settings, but these games proved popular and successful within this small case study. Further research in this avenue would be beneficial for students and teachers, as well as eventually audiences through exploring responses to improvised classical concert material, building on the work of Dolan et al. (2013).

Jazz Improvisation

In contrast to the long history of Western classical improvisation, jazz improvisation emerged in the early twentieth century when US jazz musicians, specifically from New Orleans, predominantly learned jazz repertoire by memorizing melodies by ear, enabling their embellishment through strategies such as altering the phrasing or playing off-beat rhythms (Monson 2003). Instrumental music teachers can provide strategies to enable aspiring jazz pupils to improvise that are effective and encourage creativity; this can also support the development of instrumental technique (Henley 2024) and learner autonomy (Wright and Kanellopoulos 2010). Jazz improvisation can be a simple and enjoyable process for pupils and teachers alike, and teachers can nurture their pupils' learning by equipping themselves with exercises and activities that enable learners to have fun and feel a sense of achievement. The following section describes pedagogical strategies used by some instrumental jazz educators experienced in teaching beginner jazz improvisation pupils, collected through semi-structured interviews with twelve teachers as part of one of the authors' doctoral research studies (Cairns, forthcoming). The research participants detailed the activities listed:

Incremental Strategies

Incremental strategies refer to breaking down musical elements within jazz music and utilizing one component to help pupils start improvising. This simplifies the improvisation process as teachers can gradually add more elements as learners develop their improvisation skills. Examples of this strategy include the following:

  a. Focus on rhythm: pupils use one pitch to create rhythmic ideas. If pupils feel comfortable using one pitch, teachers could recommend adding a second pitch to continue developing their improvisation ideas, then a third, a fourth, until pupils eventually use every pitch of a scale or chord when improvising.
  b. Consider the harmony of a chord: for example, using pitches from the Dorian mode to improvise over a minor 7th chord (played by the teacher or a backing track) to understand the relationship between the notes and the harmony. This activity could benefit pupils who are confident using a small number of pitches and want to improvise using a whole scale.

Teachers might wish to ask pupils to assess their improvisations after they play. Inviting pupils to appraise their improvisations could facilitate them to consider what they played, to see if they can repeat it, plus reflect on how they could develop their improvised phrases to improve their improvisation skills.

Restrictive Options

Similar to incremental strategies, teachers could employ restrictive options for pupils to develop skills in jazz improvisation. Examples of this strategy are as follows:

  a. Give pupils a small number of pitches to improvise with. A reduced set of pitches may seem counterintuitive to encouraging pupils' creativity; however, this strategy can avoid learners feeling overwhelmed through reducing the number of aspects to think about. Teachers can reassure pupils that they do not have to use every note that they have learned, nor use the whole range of their instrument if they are not yet proficient. This strategy could also help learners structure their improvisations by focusing on two, three or four specific pitches.
  b. Gradually adding one pitch at a time could help pupils develop their skills as they focus on using a restricted number of notes. This exercise is similar to one of the incremental strategies mentioned above, as the given pitches relate to a specific scale or chord rather than a random selection of notes.
  c. Restrict the duration for improvising. Depending on pupils' level and confidence, they could improvise over a set number of bars or beats, such as four bars or four beats. Similar to using a small number of pitches, a restricted timeframe could facilitate pupils to think about how to fill a small space with their improvisation instead of feeling overwhelmed by thinking they have to improvise over many bars.

These restrictive options could enable pupils to consider how they might structure their improvisations by observing set limitations as they gradually become more used to improvising. Using limited rhythms, pitches or duration might reduce anxiety and support creative improvisation. These activities could also support pupils joining jazz ensembles; they might initially improvise over a short duration, then gradually improvise over larger passages as their confidence grows.

Modelling

Modelling, or demonstrating, could be a beneficial strategy when teaching jazz improvisation to pupils who are unsure how to begin improvising. Seeing and hearing a teacher model examples of jazz improvisation could encourage learners to have a go. Teachers' examples of how to employ modelling as a strategy were as follows:

a. Playing jazz improvisation does not have to be 'right'. The concept of playing something 'correct' or 'incorrect' can be diffused if teachers are willing to model jazz improvisation and embrace any supposed mistakes. Teachers may need a degree of confidence in themselves to model improvisation, plus demonstrate and convey what they perceive to be a 'mistake' as being of no concern. This approach might assure pupils there is no 'right' way to improvise, that improvisation is a natural aspect of being a musician, and there is no reason to fear it. It can also support the teachers' observations of pupils' understanding of jazz improvisation.

b. Demonstrating short examples of jazz improvisation could reassure pupils that they do not have to play unnecessarily long improvisations. Seeing their teacher provide examples of short improvisations, perhaps over two or four bars, could inspire learners to have a go because they might consider the short duration as more manageable compared to the potentially infinite space they initially may have thought they needed to fill.

c. Provide suitable modelling at an appropriate level. Some pupils might perceive a teacher's playing as too complex, which could put them off wanting to learn to improvise as they may hear what they perceive to be challenging jazz improvisations beyond their capabilities and consider that they will never reach the same standard. Gauging the level of the student and modelling at an appropriate level could prevent learners from being reluctant to improvise.

Teacher-Pupil Interaction

The teacher-pupil interaction strategy involves the teacher and the pupil playing together. Activities within this strategy are as follows:

a. A call-and-response exercise involves the teacher improvising a short phrase on their instrument ('call') and the pupil answering on theirs with their own improvisation ('response'). When the pupil is more confident, they could initiate the call, with the teacher playing the response. There is no limit to how long the call-and-response activity lasts, so the teacher may use it for a short time to help the pupil become more comfortable with improvisation or for as long as the pupil has fun with it.

b. Imitation involves the teacher improvising a short phrase followed by the pupil repeating what they heard, like an echo. Similar to the call-and-response activity, the pupil could also create short, improvised phrases for the teacher to copy.
c. The term 'trading fours' refers to musicians exchanging improvised phrases lasting for four bars (Sawyer 2008). This activity is similar to call-and-response, but here players improvise over a set number of bars (in this instance, four). Teachers could include this activity in lessons once they feel pupils can improvise for more bars. Teachers and pupils could start trading four bars, then eight, then twelve, then sixteen bars or more. Teachers and pupils could start playing two bars each to help bridge the gap between call-and-response and trading fours.

Jazz Overview

The strategies mentioned above that are drawn from the practice of experienced jazz educators are suggestions rather than mandatory for all pupils wishing to learn jazz improvisation. They require a student-centred teaching approach, as educators consider which might suit one pupil but not necessarily another. Some pupils may have a classical background where reading notation is typical practice; however, the above activities require no notation as they encourage pupils to trust their musical instincts and develop aural skills while learning jazz improvisation. As with classical improvisation, the notion of scaffolded constraints can support the engagement and confidence of the improviser: restricting choices and options yields creative freedom (Berkowitz 2010). These strategies might help instrumental tutors develop their skills in jazz improvisation if they have little to no experience in this, which could enrich their personal development.

Rock and Pop Adaptations

Techniques for improvising in a rock or pop style are very similar, borne from the blues and jazz tradition. Creating an additional section specifically dedicated to incorporating improvisation into a rock style might lead to unnecessary repetition of concepts. However, there are some additional aspects which may be more pertinent to a rock or pop situation but could also intersect with the jazz style. Improvisation, at the heart of its nature, is grasping a groove and matching that feel with a relevant *stylistic* note and rhythm set. When instructing a student in the fundamentals of improvisation, be it rock or jazz, the above processes would be at the heart of the sessions. However, the following additional points offer further approaches when focusing on rock and pop, from beginner to advanced level.

Tone and Confidence

Producing a rock solo might sometimes require a more confident and brighter tone compared to certain elements of jazz. Teachers could consider discussing with students the significance of first impressions, as the initial note of a solo can greatly impact the confidence of both the listener and performer. Therefore, emphasizing the practice of entry notes is essential for ensuring a strong beginning to a solo. Starting a solo effectively helps create a positive impression: the first note serves as the player's introduction – an opportunity to assert themselves with confidence. Hence, it is vital to practise the initial notes, paying attention to tone, volume and overall assurance. Musicians can reflect on whether the aim is for a powerful high note or a more gradual approach that better suits the style of the chosen piece and can consider how this first note (pitch) fits within the corresponding triad or if adding a chord extension could create a more intriguing opening. This inaugural note establishes the foundation for an outstanding, even exceptional, rock solo.

Solid Chord and Scale Knowledge

A deep comprehension of chord construction is essential for successfully navigating complex improvisation situations (Levine 1989). The same principle applies to scales. Starting with major and minor scales, along with their pentatonic variations, establishes a strong foundational scale vocabulary. Mastery of these scales is crucial for instant recall during performance, eliminating the need for conscious note calculation. Theory converted into practice (Alexander 1989) serves as an invaluable resource for exploring improvisation. While beginners may struggle with complex keys, emphasis on the importance of scale and key knowledge, aiming to master scales in all keys equally, is to be encouraged. Similarly, familiarity with triad and 7th chord constructions across keys establishes a solid foundation when improvising spontaneously. Having knowledge of primary and secondary chords in every key provides a framework and a sense of security, especially when dealing with unfamiliar chord progressions. Students can work through the circle of fifths gradually, incorporating key and chord theory into their lessons one step at a time; this framework is invaluable as it supports 'real life' understanding of chord progressions and modulations (Levine 1989: 18).

In jazz, techniques such as 'enclosures'[1] and playing around key tones are often encouraged to add ambiguity and embellishment. Expanding chords by incorporating or modifying 9ths, 11ths and 13ths is also recommended in jazz improvisation. In contrast, rock solos often lean towards a more straightforward and dynamic style, avoiding more intricate harmonic variations. However, relying solely on pentatonic or blues scales can lead to predictability. Students can explore ways to infuse interest into their improvised solos while maintaining the genre's stylistic authenticity.

Feel and Emotion

When guiding students towards developing their soloing skills, it can help to remind them that musical expression often stems from their emotions and intuition (Cochrane 2008). While understanding scales and chords is vital for a solid foundation, the essence of a remarkable solo lies in its depth, connection and delivery through melody and tone. Students can embrace the learning process and expand their musical horizons by listening to a diverse range of solos, not limited to their own instrument or genre. Studying and playing solos by other musicians can enhance improvisational abilities and broaden musical repertoire. This leads to the value of playing transcribed solos and learning to notate accurately.

Transcriptions: Transcribing or Playing from a Score

There is tremendous value in transcribing solos (in any genre). Though it may require time and dedication, transcribing offers an in-depth exploration of rhythmic delivery, scale and chord usage, melodic shaping and tonal expression, greatly enhancing aural skills (Gamso 2011). While this method may seem analytical and not entirely reflective of the rock style's spontaneity, it is a crucial tool for becoming a well-rounded and confident musician. Students can play from existing transcriptions to encounter different sounds and soloing approaches. This practice is particularly beneficial for finding entry points into solos by observing how favourite instrumentals commence – is it through a gradual build-up, a sudden eruption or a slide-up to the flat 7th of the blues scale? Playing transcriptions aids an expansion of harmonic and stylistic vocabulary, supporting musical growth and innovation, and can commence at entry level by the teacher playing a simple phrase for the student to notate, building eventually to transcribing more complex recorded solos. Students can also play along with the recorded soloists and try creating their own solos in response.

Conclusion

The games, approaches and strategies mentioned in this chapter could encourage instrumental teachers to attempt musical improvisation with their pupils. An initial exercise using one or two notes may give pupils a taste of what improvisation entails and show that it is, perhaps, not as scary as they thought, supporting confidence to try more complex processes. These activities enable anyone curious about improvisation to explore varied ways of playing music and support creativity. Additionally, demonstrating and collaborating with pupils through these approaches may help instrumental teachers grow confident in their own ability to improvise and to draw on diverse styles of music with their pupils.

Notes

1 In jazz improvisation, enclosures refer to a technique where the musician approaches a target note by playing surrounding notes above and below it. This adds colour, tension and interest to the improvisation by creating various melodic embellishments and resolving the target note. Enclosures are commonly used to create a smoother and more engaging musical line during improvisation.

References

Alexander, C. (1989), 'Instructing the Improviser', *Fontes Artis Musicae*, 36 (3): 220–3.

Alperson, P. (1984), 'On Musical Improvisation', *Journal of Aesthetics and Art Criticism*, 43 (1): 17–29.

Barbetti, M. (2020), 'Reviving the Ghost: A Method for Baroque Improvisation Modelled through Telemann's Twelve Fantasias for Flute without Bass (1727–1728)', MA diss., University of Western Australia.

Barton, B. (n.d.), 'Improvisation: Its Importance to the 21st Century Musician', *Academia EDU*. Available online: https://www.academia.edu/7370528/Improvisation_Its_Importance_to_the_20th_Century_Musician?email_work_card=title (accessed 31 July 2024).

Berkowitz, A. (2010), *The Improvising Mind: Cognition and Creativity in the Musical Moment*, Oxford: Oxford University Press.

Biasutti, M. (2017), 'Teaching Improvisation through Processes. Applications in Music Education and Implications for General Education', *Frontiers in Psychology*, 8 (911): 1–8.

Broadhead, P., and A. Burt (2012), *Understanding Young Children's Learning through Play: Building Playful Pedagogies*, Abingdon: Routledge.

Bull, A. (2019), *Class, Control, and Classical Music*, Oxford: Oxford University Press.

Cairns, A. (forthcoming), 'Jazz Improvisation Pedagogy for Beginner Jazz Improvisers in the UK One-to-One Lesson Setting', PhD diss., University of York.

Callahan, M. (2012), 'Teaching Baroque Counterpoint through Improvisation – An Introductory Curriculum in Stylistic Fluency', *Journal of Music Theory Pedagogy*, 26 (1): 61–100.

Cochrane, T. (2008), 'Expression and Extended Cognition', *Journal of Aesthetics and Art Criticism*, 66 (4): 329–40.

Collins, P. (2017), *The Stylus Phantasticus and Free Keyboard Music of the North German Baroque*, Aldershot: Ashgate.

Cossey, C. (2024), 'An Investigation into the Factors Influencing Teachers' Inclusion of Improvisation in Piano Lessons', *British Journal of Music Education*, 41(2): 157–67. doi:10.1017/S0265051723000396.

Dolan, D. (2024), 'Teaching Classical Improvisation', *David Dolan Piano Classical Improvisation*. Available online: http://www.david-dolan.com/teaching-classical-improvisation/ (accessed 31 July 2024).

Dolan, D., J. Sloboda, H. Jensen, B. Crüts and E. Feygelson (2013), 'The Improvisatory Approach to Classical Music Performance: An Empirical Investigation into Its Characteristics and Impact', *Music Performance Research*, 6: 1–38. Available online: https://david-dolan.com/wp-content/uploads/2021/09/mpr.pdf (accessed 31 July 2024).

Fleer, M. (2011), '"Conceptual Play": Foregrounding Imagination and Cognition during Concept Formation in Early Years Education', *Contemporary Issues in Early Childhood*, 12 (3): 224–40.

Gamso, N. M. (2011), 'An Aural Learning Project: Assimilating Jazz Education Methods for Traditional Applied Pedagogy', *Music Educators Journal*, 98 (2): 61–7.

Gross, A. (2013), 'The Improvisation of Figuration Preludes and the Enduring Value of Bach Family Pedagogy', *Journal of Music Theory Pedagogy*, 27: 19–45.

Gruenhagen, L. M., and R. Whitcomb (2014), 'Improvisational Practices in Elementary General Music Classrooms', *Journal of Research in Music Education*, 61 (4): 379–95.

Henley, J. (2024), 'Creativities in Instrumental Teaching and Learning: Unlocking Musical Imaginations', in N. Beach and G. Spruce (eds), *Instrumental Music Teaching: Perspectives and Challenges*, 115–29, London: Trinity College London Press.

Koutsoupidou, T. (2005), 'Improvisation in the English Primary Music Classroom: Teachers' Perceptions and Practices', *Music Education Research*, 7 (3): 363–81.

Kümin, N. (2023), 'Fantasising about the Past: A Baroque Violinist's Guide to Improvising Fantasias', PhD diss., University of York.

Larson, S. (1995), '"Integrated Music Learning" and Improvisation: Teaching Musicianship and Theory through "Menus, Maps, and Models"', *College Music Symposium*, 35: 76–90.

Levin, R. (2002), 'Improvising Mozart', *Bulletin of the American Academy of Arts and Sciences*, 55 (2): 87–90.

Levine, M. (1989), *The Jazz Piano Book*, Petaluma, CA: Sher Music.

Monson, I. (2003), 'Jazz Improvisation', in M. Cooke and D. Horn (eds), *The Cambridge Companion to Jazz*, 114–32, Cambridge: Cambridge University Press.

Moore, R. (1992), 'The Decline of Improvisation in Western Art Music: An Interpretation of Change', *International Review of the Aesthetics and Sociology of Music*, 23 (1): 61–84.

Mortensen, J. (2020), *The Pianist's Guide to Historic Improvisation*, Oxford: Oxford University Press.

Mortensen, J. (2024), 'cedarvillemusic', YouTube channel. Available online: https://www.youtube.com/channel/UCq0sDKI15IW8Fek6OqBhZ3w (accessed 31 July 2024).

Sawyer, R. K. (2008), 'Learning Music from Collaboration', *International Journal of Education Research*, 47: 50–9.

Small, A. R. (1979), 'Pace Yourself', *Music Educators Journal*, 65 (9): 30–3.

Stringham, D. A., L. C. Thornton and D. J. Shevock (2015), 'Composition and Improvisation in Instrumental Methods Courses: Instrumental Music Teacher Educators' Perspectives', *Bulletin of the Council for Research in Music Education*, 205: 7–25.

The Scroll Ensemble (2020), 'What Is Classical Music Improvisation Level 3 – Amateur Musician', YouTube video, posted by 'The Scroll Ensemble Classical Music Improvisation', 5 August. Available online: https://www.youtube.com/watch?v=oOa5ssiVmNg&list=PL8Zph-SkKedxl0CiTrRbGVFCaS-NR_JMV&index=4 (accessed 31 July 2024).

Tinctoris, J., and American Institute of Musicology ([1477] 1961), *Liber de Arte Contrapuncti*, trans. A. Seay, American Institute of Musicology.

Villavicencio, C. (2008), 'The Discourse of Free Improvisation: A Rhetorical Perspective on Free Improvised Music', PhD diss., University of East Anglia.

Ward-Steinman, P. M. (2007), 'Confidence in Teaching Improvisation According to the K-12 Achievement Standards: Surveys of Vocal Jazz Workshop Participants and Undergraduates', *Bulletin of the Council for Research in Music Education*, 127: 25–40.

Whitcomb, R. (2013), 'Teaching Improvisation in Elementary General Music: Facing Fears and Fostering Creativity', *National Association for Music Education*, 99 (3): 43–51.

Wright, R., and P. Kanellopoulos (2010), 'Informal Music Learning, Improvisation and Teacher Education', *British Journal of Music Education*, 27 (1): 71–87.

Yoo, H. (2015), 'Using Baroque Techniques to Teach Improvisation in Your Classroom', *Music Educators Journal*, 102 (1): 91–6.

11

Music Theory in the Instrumental Music Lesson: Built In or Bolted On?

Owen Burton and Anca Eskandar

Introduction

The current place of music theory within the larger context of music education seems uncertain. In recent years, questions have been asked on public platforms concerning its identity and relevance in the music industry,[1] and its deep connection to the music of the Western canon has also proved contentious (Attah et al. 2024). While music theory forms an essential part of a holistic approach to music learning, many students appear to approach it as a means of passing an exam rather than recognizing its deeper value (Rogers 2004). For the chapter authors, theory has formed a pivotal part of our musical lives as students and now teachers of music across varied educational contexts. We are conscious and appreciative of the resources to which we have had access (across various geographical locations) and the influential tuition we have received.

In this chapter, we consider the specific relationship between music theory and the instrumental lesson. Compartmentalization of theory and practice in instrumental teaching is often evident (Palmer 2014), with separate lessons, teachers and resources often provided for each. While effective, this can reduce engagement with theory within practical instrumental teaching contexts. This separation does not necessarily encourage dialogue around and practical recreation of theory-grounded concepts (such as scales, rhythm and articulation), which can build a deeper understanding of musical styles. We reflect upon this shared concern – which resonates with our own teaching practices – in the light of literature. While much scholarship addresses approaches to music theory pedagogy within the music theory classroom, we are concerned with a grey area, one which has received less explicit emphasis – the integration of theory alongside, or even *within*, the one-to-one instrumental lesson and the impact on holistic learning. Despite acknowledging the variety of experiences – in the learning context and each individual learner – there is potential for creative and rewarding teaching, with opportunities for pupils to attain and apply knowledge as part of their wider musicianship.

This chapter begins with a broader view on approaches to music theory pedagogy, identifying some issues of consistency and variable senses of curriculum, before briefly analysing the relationship between music theory and practice from the perspective of UK-based graded examination boards. It concludes with a real-life practical example from a one-to-one beginner piano lesson, bringing these broader considerations into a more focused context. Our reflective approach draws attention to perspectives which could support and empower teachers. Naturally, we end with more possibilities than certainties, which is something we celebrate and hope could inspire other colleagues.

Consistency in Incorporating Theory: The Curriculum for Music and the Cultural Supremacy of the Western Classical Tradition

As current literature indicates, music theory is taught in various ways within settings including state and private schools, specialist music schools, after-school programmes and private tuition. The diverse approaches to teaching music theory include the complete separation of theory and practice, various degrees of inclusion and its enmeshment within the instrumental lesson.

Since the introduction of the National Curriculum for Music in 1992, various aspects of music theory alongside composing, performing, listening and appraising music have been a part of the curriculum for primary and secondary school children in England (Mills 1994). A series of inspections made by Mills (1994) in several schools in England revealed issues including very low expectations from pupils, lessons taught by non-specialist music teachers in primary settings and a diminished sense of knowledge progression and applicability from primary to secondary level. Similar issues are still being raised in more recent reports holding the UK government responsible for the reduced statutory curriculum time for music at Key Stages 1–3 as well as diminished 'opportunities for children to pursue music to GCSE and A Level'

(All-Party Parliamentary Group for Music Education and Incorporated Society of Musicians and University of Sussex 2019: 3). The same report states that this has taken effect owing to policy changes and the introduction of the English Baccalaureate (EBacc) which drove the teaching and learning attention towards core subjects (English, maths and the sciences). Moreover, the idea of delivering a comprehensive and balanced curriculum in all state-funded UK schools has been greatly depleted due to the '"academisation" of many schools, together with the establishment of Free Schools' (Savage and Barnard 2019: 9) where following the National Curriculum for Music is no longer a requirement.

Theory also finds itself part of a larger context of addressing narratives of cultural supremacy in music, which adds to the complexity and issues of consistency in its application to educational settings. Although adhering to the idea that reading staff notation is generally considered valuable for musicians performing various styles and genres, by associating staff notation mostly with the Western classical tradition, Bate (2020) considers it to be a less inclusive aspect of music education that should be preceded and supported by aural training and practical skill development (beneficial at all levels but especially in the early stages). Enforcing musical literacy in the National Curriculum for Music could suggest the idea of cultural supremacy of the Western classical tradition and ignorance towards other musical ideologies. In contrast, a complete abandonment of – or limited attention to – Western art music and its replacement by more modern and popular styles of music would mean disregarding the very foundation that supports music theory as a discipline and might only convey false ideas of 'politically-motivated associations with capital-rich elitism' (Whittaker 2020: 26). What Whittaker (2020) suggests here is that while aspects of Western classical music theory continue to bring an added value to music education, the understandable concerns around a problematic 'elite' could be avoided through a creative and inclusive approach to the delivery of theoretical knowledge. In this way, deploying a more complex teaching process could avoid a decline in the development of the educational system.

While supporting the commendable efforts that have been and continue to be made in conservatoires and university music departments across the globe towards diversifying the instrumental and vocal repertoire, Palfy and Gilson (2018) suggest that music undergraduates continue to be interested in studying prominent figures of the Western classical tradition as they consider this to be 'the integral, defining genre for music theory as a field' (2018: 1), while Snodgrass (2020) advocates that grasping written music notation enables students to freely converse about music. In a study conducted at the University of Sheffield, UK, regarding students' sociocultural and learning experience, Dibben (2006) reveals that nine students out of forty-one online survey respondents and ten interview participants were concerned with the level of harmony being taught in their undergraduate studies, with a comment from a respondent saying that 'more lessons in music theory in 1st yr for anyone who's behind' (2006: 105) would be beneficial. The views of undergraduate music students towards music theory relate closely to the way the subject is taught and the course tutor's attitude and enthusiasm while delivering the course (Kang 2006). A more recent study involving 290 undergraduate students showed that 'undergraduate music theory has been a largely positive experience for students, who overall view the subject of music theory as highly beneficial, useful, and as providing a competitive edge for a musical career' (Gutierrez 2018: 16). The study also reveals that if the theory class is designed to encourage creativity and to be easily adaptable to students' personal goals, it is more likely to be viewed as a valuable addition to the overall curriculum.

Where do ABRSM[2] and other boards' graded music examinations in the UK stand in this discourse of whether there remains a place for music theory and literacy in the music education of future generations? In a UK context in which instrumental teaching is not regulated by a governing authority (Barton 2019; Boyle 2021; Stakelum 2024), selecting which aspects of music theory and in what format to deliver them remains each teacher's decision after having considered a wide range of factors. These could include student's level, goals (of taking or not taking performance and theory graded examinations), length of lessons, parental priorities, financial accessibility to longer or additional lessons to cover theory, understanding of the importance of theory, the teacher's willingness and preparedness to teach it and whether or not theory is included in the student's school music experience.

At a swift glance, the ABRSM syllabus for music theory (and that of other graded music board examinations) has very similar requirements to the UK National Curriculum for Music (Department for Education 2021), GCSE music (Department for Education 2015a) and A-Level music (Department for Education 2015b) and could be seen as a supplementary source of access to music education in times where provision in schools is seeing a considerable decline (Savage and Barnard 2019). However, there are concerns about potentially lowered standards in the ABRSM music theory grades 1–5 syllabus resulting from the ABRSM's online format and content in response to the Covid-19 pandemic in 2020. Barriers towards accessibility were also identified for students who may not have an internet connection or a quiet room in their home where they can sit the exam without interruption (Barton n.d.). Furthermore, the transition from ABRSM's digitized Grade 5 music theory examination to a fully paper-based examination at Grade 6 raises consequential difficulties for students who may have paid less attention to their music notation writing skills. In this sense, returning to the assertion that music literacy has an inferior significance in the early stages of music education compared to aural training and practical skill development (Bate 2020), how might some of these practical or aural emphases be reconciled with more traditional theoretical and notational principles? Abrahams (2015: 97) considers music literacy as being an 'ability not only to decode notation but also to make sophisticated decisions about what to listen to and how to categorize those choices'; this holds vital importance for instrumentalists and underscores the concept of whole musician or musicianship underpinned by music theory.

Theory, Practice and Examinations

A balance between rigour and openness to the benefits of adaptive strategies for practical integration of music theory appears important within instrumental lessons in the UK. Graded theory examinations offer clear and structured provision; this separation of theory and practice within the assessment process for instrumental learning can be beneficial insofar as it might allow focused engagement with concepts, which can then be transferred to performance. ABRSM seems to be aware, though, that theory might not be met with intrinsic interest, a perception also highlighted by Björk, Granfors and Ruthmann (2023). In a short introductory video called 'What's the point of music theory?', ABRSM observes that it might be thought of as a 'dry, irrelevant, complicated thing to learn; something that feels more like maths than music, something to get through' (ABRSM 2023a). The video goes on to express that understanding theoretical ideas leads to increased musicality, opening 'more possibilities' in the performance. To achieve this ambition, exam boards have become receptive to the possibility that having more options in the exam format can support overall musical development. In general, there is consistency across UK exam boards in articulating the value of theory and its integration, but variation in the amount of flexibility afforded to the learner in doing this. For example, to progress to ABRSM practical Grades 6 and above, candidates must pass Grade 5 in one of the following: Music Theory, the Practical Musicianship exam, or a Jazz Practical grade to ensure 'all-round musical knowledge' (ABRSM 2023b). This formalized milestone is not required by other examination boards such as Trinity College London, but Trinity emphasizes that 'theoretical musical knowledge works to enhance and support practical studies' (Trinity College London 2024).

Actively integrating theory alongside the physical domain of the musical instrument can help navigate concepts. This is true for singers too, as they might connect concepts to the piano or guitar – the instruments most likely to accompany them. In its practical performance exams, Trinity offers various supporting tests, including 'Musical Knowledge' (from Initial to Grade 5), involving targeted questions relating directly to pieces being performed, building in a bite-size theoretical dimension as part of a broader, practical musical experience in the performance exam. Examples of such questions at Grade 1 level include: 'What is the value of this note?' and 'What does this symbol mean?' ABRSM also offers a series of graded Practical Musicianship exams, while MTB (Music Teachers' Board) has 'interactive' music theory tests, where students answer questions within an online learning environment. Both of these ABRSM and MTB syllabi provide alternative formats to written exam papers. In the MTB tests, students can listen to music and use a virtual piano keyboard within the interface, as well as place notes on a stave, much like a composer or arranger would when using notation software (Music Teachers' Board 2024). Conversely, it is interesting to note the requirement in ABRSM and Trinity's online theory exams that candidates should not have sight of a keyboard or piano as a visual aid (ABRSM 2023c; Trinity College London 2023), presumably to replicate the exam conditions of the paper-based version. However, a question emerges about the extent to which the piano enjoys primacy as the instrument associated with music theory and whether pianists have an advantage when it comes to linking theory with their playing. The visual immediacy of the keyboard is apparent for grasping pitch-based concepts, and it is perhaps for this reason that MTB begin their Grade 1 Music Theory syllabus with a segment called 'The Piano Keyboard' (Music Teachers' Board 2024). While there are benefits to visual, notation-based understandings, making the most of how theory can be applied, practically realized and used will be explored further in the next section.

Questioning Techniques, Informality and a Practical Example

Informal approaches to integrating and raising awareness of music theory can take place during the instrumental lesson. We understand the one-to-one lesson to have 'formal' characteristics if, for example, it follows a recognized syllabus and acts on predetermined learning goals. Indeed, music examinations can be regarded as a kind of formal learning (Green 2002), which has since evolved in non-classical genres through practical grades for pop or rock performance by Rockschool and Trinity College London (Boyle 2021). For Folkestad (2006: 143), informal learning 'is not sequenced beforehand; the activity steers the way of working/playing/composing, and the process proceeds by the interaction of the participants in the activity.' Informality, in our view, emerges from a lack of enforced consistency or standardized curriculum design in using certain theory-targeted strategies within the instrumental music lesson.

One way in which informality might surface in the one-to-one practical lesson is through theory-related discussion using questions. Questions can help learners achieve deeper understanding, becoming more actively involved and self-reflective in their learning (Dirkse 2014). Research on effective questioning in the music theory classroom provides useful context for considering how theory-targeted questions might be handled in the practical lesson. For Dirkse (2014), effective questions are not vague and students know what is expected of them. This essential idea – of making theory-based questions targeted where there are a limited number of correct answers – has clear applicability to the teacher who wishes to incorporate theory into the wider learning goals. It also challenges the pupil to consider a theoretical aspect that is immediately relevant to the larger practical task at hand and has value in addressing musical issues that can sometimes deviate from the immediate task of learning to play a piece and realizing a score. Ideally, such questions would invite the pupil to respond with freedom and share their thought process, as reflected in a study by Burt and Duker (2022), which introduced a 'Question Formulation Technique' designed to guide learners towards being able to formulate their own questions, increasing further their creative engagement (2022: 1–2). For example, if a teacher wants a pupil to understand musical keys, a simple question would be: 'What key is this piece in?', though even better might be the variants 'How do we find out what key this piece is in?' or 'How many sharps or flats are there in the key signature?', thus guiding the student through dialogic conversation. The same tactic could apply to the task of identifying and recalling intervals. Hearing the characteristic sound of particular intervals might help pupils understand their function in a deeper, musical sense. Because of this, it seems vital to actively encourage the linking of aural, spatial and visual understanding by playing these on an instrument or singing them aloud. Labelling different musical intervals – easily a dry task when removed from musical application – becomes more significant when understanding that they do much to construct the sound character of a piece of music.

Such cross-connections can increase the ability to recognize other musical techniques in wider repertoire and create more ownership and agency for the pupil. The question, though, is how much emphasis is to be placed on these discussions in a practical lesson. Ward's (2007) belief in attaining 'musical understanding' in instrumental lessons supports consideration of this point. For Ward, musical analysis and performance teaching have shared goals, including musical understanding, communication and problem-solving. Ward also observes negative perceptions among performance teachers, especially concerning accessibility to analytical concepts and terminology (2007). In light of these ideas, we consider a real-life example, a teaching scenario of a piano lesson with a child learner working on a piece composed for the Trinity College London Grade 2 exam syllabus (*Fun Fair Blues* by Naomi Yandell), shown in Figure 11.1. As the title suggests, the style is 'Blues' and as such the left-hand chords are mainly structured around the root notes F, B-flat and C, frequently outlining the common 'Bluesy' interval of a minor seventh. Unremarkable though this might seem, such chords help build a defining expressive feature of this genre. While the overall key might be referred to as 'F', the boundaries of this key are quite unfixed, as it frequently introduces extra chromatic – or 'blue' – notes not found in F major. Given the prevalence of such features in much popular music,

Fun Fair Blues

Naomi Yandell
(b. 1961)

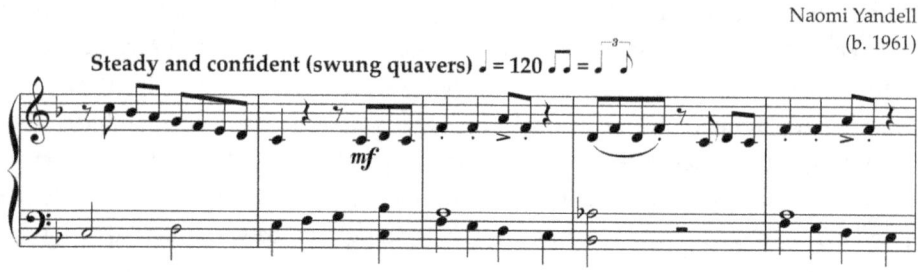

Figure 11.1 *Fun Fair Blues* by Naomi Yandell. Copyright © 2020 Trinity College London Press Ltd. From 'Trinity College London Piano Exam Pieces Plus Exercises From 2021 Grade 2'. All rights reserved. Reproduced by permission.

and the capacity for re-creation (possibly through improvisation), addressing them as part of a holistic understanding enables theory to deepen the understanding of musical practice.

Clearly, the pupil does not need to consider these issues in great depth. The point is that this notated piece introduces a left-hand chord shape that is common in Blues piano music. The pupil's hand becomes more familiar with how this minor seventh *feels*, the sound it produces, and the fact that it can be moved around in a looping fashion. As well as isolating instances of this chord type and practising moving along the chord progression, the possibility emerges that the name of this interval can be linked with a broader musical and theoretical context. This might require using the question 'How do we work out what interval that is?' and a discussion around its larger identity and character.

This example helps in considering the individual strengths of the practical (learning the piece) and the theoretical and whether their combination can produce more than the sum of their parts. This calls for a balance between formal and informal approaches to teaching and learning. In a formal music theory context, identification of intervals can be pedagogically valid and efficient, affording task focus and providing space for connecting visual recognition from notation. But without the built-in practical element, it can potentially lack context. Informality, then, is a means to a more holistic understanding, bringing theory into close proximity with awareness of playing style, performance practice and genre. It also provides another dimension to understanding, as well as targeting overall musicianship. But with informality comes risk. In the scenario above, introducing theory questions could take the lesson temporarily away from the more immediate 'focus' of learning the piece – if the lesson is conceptualized in this way. It might therefore risk an inefficient transference of theory knowledge as there might be less space to ensure understanding, less guarantee that it will be returned to in a structured manner, and a teacher might not focus on all relevant aspects of harmony. The theoretical learning might also require adaptability to compensate for the pupil's response, which impacts lesson planning.

Not all aspects of music theory appear equal when it comes to informality in the one-to-one lesson. Considering rhythm, for example, *Fun Fair Blues* uses a common device of notating 'straight' quavers, with the instruction that these equate to groups of triplets. But the essential meaning is that quavers should be 'swung'. This concept is easier to relay through demonstration than the above task of recreating intervals. The pupil can 'feel' the idiomatic rhythm – with its long-short alterations – but the 'theory' in this case also seems more immediately connected to a practical aim of the lesson, in recreating the music accurately. Perhaps the same can be said for realizing the rhythmic accents in bars 9–10.

Another challenge might be getting pupils to engage actively with musical form (or how a piece of music is shaped and put together), which might take place across various levels of detail. In discussing musical form in popular music, Middleton (1990) identifies repetition as the smallest form of difference. This way of thinking about how music is shaped – as an organization of varying degrees of what sounds the same, similar or different – could be applied to a piece such as this. Similarly, Ward's (2007) 'toolkit' includes a strategy targeted at rhythm and structure, including tasks such as asking the pupil to identify the number of times a rhythm occurs. Building on this principle, using questions such as 'can you find any other places where that figure occurs?' and asking the pupil to mark this in some way, relates directly to the practical goal of realizing these musical units in performance but also works to build a larger picture of the overall shape of the piece.

These factors echo the question of what a sufficient way of handling theory within the practical lesson is. Returning to Folkestad (2006), the need to be open-minded and accepting of the informal – that formal-informal exists on a spectrum, both present to varying degrees and working in dialectic fashion – would apply to one-to-one instrumental teaching situations. To enjoy the benefit, though, teachers would also need to accept less control and predictable outcomes.

Conclusion

We have drawn attention to an intriguing lack of consistency across the UK sector in how music theory might relate to the instrumental lesson. While this has been a point of shared concern, we also feel that some of the most interesting directions are not necessarily the most obvious within widely disseminated curricula or syllabi, which understandably place a certain emphasis on handling theory and practice separately. With this inconsistency comes a range of options, demonstrating that no one way fits all in terms of teaching and learning. In reflecting on some of the uses of theory in wider educational settings and the more focused one-to-one instrumental lesson, we recognize an open avenue for teachers to decide which practice (or combination of practices) is best suited for their individual pupils. With informality comes a greater potential for inequality of opportunity among students; however, contributing to an ongoing discussion is an important step towards continued inclusivity of theory within practical learning. We return, therefore, to the issue of holistic learning and being receptive to the bridging of experiences. In this spirit, we close with a quotation from Abrahams (2015), whose broader view of music education resonates strongly with our own perspectives, which, in turn, have led to the points raised about instrumental contexts considered here. The value of Abrahams's reflection comes from recognizing that instrumental teaching can be just as meaningful as music education in schools, given its potential for tailored, informal focus for individual learners across different knowledge areas:

Music education is a discipline that should empower musicianship and in the process transform both the students and their teacher. It is a field of study to enrich and change the knowledge, understanding, and perceptions that students and teachers have as individuals and as members of society. Music education in school provides a crosswalk to connect formal music learning inside school with informal music learning outside school. It provides a window into the cultural history of the past, records the cultural history of the present, and sets the foundation for a cultural history of the future. (Abrahams 2015: 98)

Notes

1 For an example of a public-facing contribution to this discussion, see The Crow Hill Company, 'Music Theory, Do We Need it?', YouTube video, 11:13, posted by "The Crow Hill Company", 25 January 2018, https://www.youtube.com/watch?v=aGJnNvw6SOA&t=246s, accessed 29 July 2024.
2 Associated Board of the Royal Schools of Music (ABRSM), a UK examination board offering music performance and theory exams.

References

Abrahams, F. (2015), 'Another Perspective: Teaching Music to Millennial Students', *Music Educators Journal*, 102 (1): 97–100.
ABRSM (2023a), 'About Music Theory Exams', *ABRSM*. Available online: https://www.abrsm.org/en-gb/music-theory/about-music-theory (accessed 29 July 2024).
ABRSM (2023b), 'Practical Grades', *ABRSM*. Available online: https://www.abrsm.org/en-gb/practical-grades/about-practical-grades (accessed 29 July 2024).
ABRSM (2023c), 'Music Theory Guidance', *ABRSM*. Available online: https://www.abrsm.org/en-gb/music-theory/guidance (accessed 29 July 2024).
All-Party Parliamentary Group for Music Education and Incorporated Society of Musicians and University of Sussex (2019), 'Music Education: State of the Nation', *ISM*. Available online: https://www.ism.org/images/images/State-of-the-Nation-Music-Education-WEB.pdf (accessed 29 July 2024).
Attah, T., E. Cavett, B. Dueck, S. Miller and L. Redhead (2024), 'Teaching Music Theory in UK Higher Education Today: Contexts and Commentaries', *Music Education Research*, 26 (1): 71–81.
Barton, D. (2019), 'The Autonomy of Private Instrumental Teachers: Its Effect on Valid Knowledge Construction, Curriculum Design, and Quality of Teaching and Learning', PhD diss., Royal College of Music, London.

Barton, D. (n.d.), 'ABRSM Theory Exams: The End of an Era?', *David Barton Music*. Available online: https://www.davidbartonmusic.co.uk/abrsm-theory-exams-the-end-of-an-era/ (accessed 29 July 2024).

Bate, E. (2020), 'Justifying Music in the National Curriculum: The Habit Concept and the Question of Social Justice and Academic Rigour', *British Journal of Music Education*, 37 (1): 3–15.

Björk, C., M. Granfors and A. Ruthmann (2023), 'Learning Music Theorising through Inspiration and Curiosity. Insights from Emergent Lesson Design in an Upper Secondary School in Finland', *British Journal of Music Education*, 41 (1): 3–19.

Boyle, K. (2021), *The Instrumental Music Teacher: Autonomy, Identity and the Portfolio Career in Music*, Abingdon: Routledge.

Burt, P., and P. Duker (2022), 'Student-Driven Music Theory: How the Question Formulation Technique Can Promote Agency, Engagement, and Curiosity', *Journal of Music Theory Pedagogy*, 36 (1): article 2.

Department for Education (2015a), 'Music GCSE Subject Content', *GOV.UK*. Available online: https://assets.publishing.service.gov.uk/government/uploads/system/uploads/attachment_data/file/397559/GCSE_subject_content_for_music.pdf (accessed 29 July 2024).

Department for Education (2015b), 'GCE AS and A Level Music', *GOV.UK*. Available online: https://www.gov.uk/government/publications/gce-as-and-a-level-music (accessed 29 July 2024).

Department for Education (2021), 'National Curriculum in England: Music Programmes of Study', *GOV.UK*. Available online: https://www.gov.uk/government/publications/national-curriculum-in-england-music-programmes-of-study/national-curriculum-in-england-music-programmes-of-study (accessed 29 July 2024).

Dibben, N. (2006), 'The Socio-Cultural and Learning Experiences of Music Students in a British University', *British Journal of Music Education*, 23 (1): 91–116.

Dirkse, S. (2014), 'Effective Questioning Strategies for the Music Theory Classroom', *Journal of Music Theory Pedagogy*, 28 (4): 69–84.

Folkestad, G. (2006), 'Formal and Informal Learning Situations or Practices vs Formal and Informal Ways of Learning', *British Journal of Music Education*, 23 (2): 135–45.

Green, L. (2002), *How Popular Musicians Learn: A Way Ahead for Music Education*, Aldershot: Ashgate.

Gutierrez, J. A. W. (2018), 'Students Evaluate Music Theory Courses: A Reddit Community Survey', *College Music Symposium*, 58 (2): 1–27.

Kang, Y. Y. (2006), 'Defending Music Theory in a Multicultural Curriculum', *College Music Symposium*, 46: 45–63.

Middleton, R. (1990), *Studying Popular Music*, Milton Keynes: Open University Press.

Mills, J. (1994), 'Music in the National Curriculum: The First Year', *British Journal of Music Education*, 11 (3): 191–6.

Music Teachers' Board (2024), 'Interactive Music Theory', *Music Teachers' Board*. Available online: https://www.mtbexams.com/music-theory/ (accessed 16 July 2024).

Palfy, C. S., and E. Gilson (2018), 'The Hidden Curriculum in the Music Theory Classroom', *Journal of Music Theory Pedagogy*, 32 (1): article 5.

Palmer, M. (2014), 'Learning Basic Music Theory through Improvisation', *College Music Symposium*, 54: 1–10.

Rogers, M. R. (1984, rev. 2004), *Teaching Approaches in Music Theory: An Overview of Pedagogical Philosophies*, Carbondale: SIU Press.

Savage, J., and D. Barnard (2019), 'The State of Play: A Review of Music Education in England 2019', *Musicians' Union*. Available online: https://musiciansunion.org.uk/MusiciansUnion/media/resource/Guides%20and%20reports/Education/MU_The-State-of-Play_WEB.pdf?ext=.pdf (accessed 29 July 2024).

Snodgrass, J. (2020), *Teaching Music Theory: New Voices and Approaches*, New York: Oxford University Press.

Stakelum, M. (2024), 'Music Literacy and the Instrumental Teacher', *Music Education Research*, 26 (1): 47–57.

The Crow Hill Company (2018), 'Music Theory, Do We Need It?', *YouTube* [Video]. Available online: https://www.youtube.com/watch?v=aGJnNvw6SOA&t=43s (accessed 29 July 2024).

Trinity College London (2023), 'Digital Music Theory: A Candidate's Guide', *Trinity College London*. Available online: https://www.trinitycollege.com/resource/?id=10168 (accessed 29 July 2024).

Trinity College London (2024), 'Theory of Music', *Trinity College London*. Available online: https://www.trinitycollege.com/qualifications/music/grade-exams/theory (accessed 29 July 2024).

Ward, V. (2007), 'Teaching Musical Awareness: The Development and Application of a "Toolkit" of Strategies for Instrumental Teachers', *British Journal of Music Education*, 24 (1): 21–36.

Whittaker, A. (2020), 'Investigating the Canon in A-Level Music: Musical Prescription in A-level Music Syllabuses', *British Journal of Music Education*, 37 (1): 17–27.

12

Embodiment in Music Learning and Teaching

Jennifer Cohen, Caroline Owen, Edwina Smith, Xin Liu and Rosemary Lynch

Introduction

Musicking (Small 1999) is an embodied experience. Whether engaging as a listener or performer, we are active participants in shaping and interpreting sound combinations to create a meaningful musical experience. As an instrumentalist or vocalist we manipulate our instrument or voice to this end; as a performer we choreograph phrases and structures to communicate musical messages – as true for a parent singing to an infant (Doja 2014) as for a professional musician on stage. It is not, however, just the making and manipulating of sound that happens within our bodies: music may induce an array of bodily responses from foot tapping to dancing to intense emotional reactions (Brower 2000). Even imagining music can induce vivid bodily experiences. The huge variety of music-evoked responses, from imagined narrative (Margulis et al. 2022; McAuley et al. 2021), visual imagery, colours or textures (Curwen 2018) to visceral and emotional feelings, highlights the embodied foundations of our musical experiences (Aksnes 2001).

Embodied experience permeates our musical language. We speak of tension and release; a warm tone; a rough or smooth texture. We might feel a musical pulse; a sense of excitement or calm; a mood or an emotion. Music 'moves' us: conceptual metaphors relating to bodily movement are ubiquitous in the language of music (Eitan and Timmers 2010; Zbikowski 2009). In the Western world, we describe pitch spatially or in terms of its height; phrases in terms of their direction or speed. A musical style might be bouncy, dance-like or relaxing. We talk of a musical work evolving, taking the performer or the listener on a journey. Malloch and Trevarthen (2018: 1) describe music as 'the sounds of human bodies and minds moving in creative, story-making ways'. Conceptual metaphors are thought to derive from our need to explain new experiences in terms of familiar ones and are often based on bodily movement or interaction with the environment (Lakoff and Johnson 1980). At the most fundamental level, learning depends on relating new information to a previously lived experience.

Our embodied 'communicative musicality' (Trevarthen 2002: 22) begins before we are born: infants respond to voices and music *in utero* and recognize them after birth (Hepper 1991). Adults sing to, and rock infants to engage or calm them, and use a specially musical form of prosody with exaggerated contours and rhythms in infant-directed speech (Papoušek 1994). Infants engage in dialogic communication with their caregivers using 'wordless structured gestural narratives' (Malloch and Trevarthen 2018: 4). As infants develop control over 'their music-like utterances' (Schiavio et al. 2017: 1), they begin to use their bodily actions within their environment as a form of expression beyond communicating with their caregivers, learning to create and manipulate sound autonomously. Schiavio and colleagues refer to these early sonic explorations as 'teleomusical acts' (2017: 1).

Music-making is learned through the body and developed by *doing*. Experimentation, repetition and practice allow us to develop fluency and ultimately to craft music in meaningful ways. It might seem intuitive that the body is the medium through which we create, manipulate and make sense of sound; it is also the site that hosts all our musical experiences: the rise and fall of melody, the tension and release of harmony or the musical pulse. Beyond this, embodiment may be understood as a process that is fundamental in all mental life (e.g. Fuchs 2017; Gallagher 2015). For classically trained musicians, however, it has been suggested that emphasis on theory-based learning (such as reading printed notation) may focus attention away from the lived experience of musicking and from the physical movements and creativity needed to make it meaningful (Hess 2018; Smith 2020). Dalcroze (1865–1950) considered that contemporary teaching methods focused too narrowly on intellectual skills and did not afford students the physical *experience* essential for developing musical understanding (Anderson 2012). To help them develop aural awareness, Dalcroze devised games and exercises based on spontaneous gestures his students made as they sang or listened to music. His approach, 'eurhythmics' (from the Greek roots '*eu*' and '*rythmos*' meaning 'good flow') is now appreciated worldwide. Dalcroze had recognized the vital role of embodiment in understanding: literally, sense-making via the senses.

In music, as in other creative arts, we often speak of 'embodiment' in terms of the process through which we communicate expression, allowing listeners and other musicians to make sense of our musical messages, just as our expressive gestures enhance our verbal communication in non-musical contexts. However, it is important to distinguish between 'embodying' a musical style or character in this sense and the theory of embodied cognition, which holds that we make sense of the world around us through our dynamic brain-body system. This chapter considers the relevance of embodiment in musical learning and teaching from three perspectives: sense-making, expression and communication. Connecting these to learning, performing and teaching, the authors – instrumental teachers, professional performers and researchers – draw on scholarship and professional reflections.

Embodiment as Sense-Making

Lying in opposition to Cartesian dualism, which considers the body and mind as separate entities, theories of embodied cognition (Gallagher 2015; Merleau-Ponty [1945] 2010) highlight the vital role of the body in shaping our experiences and understanding. The body is the site of 'sense-making' (Silverman 2020). It is the vehicle through which we 'sense' (as in 'feel') both physically and intuitively, as well as 'make sense' of phenomena (in other words, create meaning and understanding). Theories of embodied cognition hold that meaning is generated through our physical and mental lived experiences, emphasizing the significance of action in sense-making (Herbert and Pollatos 2012; Schiavio and van der Schyff 2018). In this view, physical experiences in the world are fundamental in allowing us to conceptualize new ideas in terms of familiar ones, usually 'our most immediate bodily experience' (Adlington 2003: 302). This has important implications for learning, not just in terms of developing physical skills but also in generating image schemata – our mental imagery or conceptualization of physical movements and processes, such as playing a musical instrument.

Developing instrumental and vocal techniques exemplifies embodied learning. Posture, breath control, producing and manipulating sound and crafting a musical experience all involve bodily movement and understanding. Our embodied experience of music might include physically 'sensing' (i.e. 'feeling') the movement of our fingers or breath, or viscerally sensing the rise and fall of a musical melody, the direction or motion of a phrase, the tension and release of harmony or a particular emotion, for example.

Developing instrument-specific technique, such as drawing a bow across a string to produce a sustained tone, implies that these movements become intuitive: embodied knowledge about how to manipulate our instrument or voice to produce an intended sound that may result in a mental image or *schema* of aspects of technique, such as fingering, bowing or breath control. We also develop understanding of the expressive implications of these instrument-specific movements, which may also generate mental imagery – conceptualizations of musical elements such as phrase contours, harmonic structure or rhythmic shapes. In musical performance, we use this embodied knowledge as an expressive means to convey musical ideas, shapes, direction, character or feeling.

Embodied Expression as a Communicative Tool

Just as physical gestures are integral to social communication, musicians' expressive movements may offer visual representation of their musical interpretation (Cohen 2018). Our expressive movements can work in collaboration with other musicians too, allowing us to coordinate structural elements such as beginning and ending together or speed changes, as well as interpretative aspects. As these expressive movements communicate our musical intentions, they are decoded by listeners or fellow musicians via their own embodied understanding through a process of *simulation*.

Embodied Simulation

Following the discovery of mirror neurons (Di Pellegrino et al. 1992; Kohler et al. 2002), which activate when an action is observed or heard, as well as performed, Gallese's theory of embodied simulation (2005) proposed that inferring other people's mental states and emotions involves *simulating* these via our own cognitive system. As such, we may develop an intuitive understanding of the actions and sounds produced by others through unconscious imitation or embodied simulation of those actions and sounds with which we are familiar (Corness 2008; Gallagher 2015; Gallese and Sinigaglia 2011). Following this premise, Overy and Molnar-Szakacs (2009) explain how the mirror neuron system allows listeners to understand musicians' expressive intentions through their bodily movements. Importantly, embodied simulation is dependent on our motor skills: we simulate goal-directed movements that we have the capacity to execute ourselves (Overy and Molnar-Szakacs 2009). For all listeners, these could constitute the gestures and bodily movements that enhance our everyday communication. For expert musicians, such goal-directed movements may include some that are instrument-specific. A growing body of research shows mirror-like neural activity in the brain of skilled performers as they listen to music, corroborating the embodied simulation theory. Expert musicians can thus be seen to 'simulate' actions relevant to *producing* the music as they listen (see Schiavio, Menin and Matyja 2014). The significance of embodiment in all aspects of musicking has important implications for teaching and learning, and we explore these in the next section.

Embodiment in Learning and Teaching

Drawing on the writings of Delalande (see Delalande and Cornara 2010) and Piaget (1972), Schiavio et al. (2017) describe how infants and young children learn through exploration, expression and organization: first discovering the sonic possibilities of the voice or musical instruments, then learning to manipulate these in order to produce meaningful sound and ultimately being able to use this skill for more sophisticated musical creativity. This process is not unique to young children but is relevant in all aspects of human learning. Delalande proposes teachers can guide learners by *mirroring* the spontaneous sounds learners discover during exploration; *modelling* the means to produce intended sounds; and *scaffolding* these to further develop musical exploration (Delalande and Cornara 2010; Schiavio et al. 2017).

For musical learners, it is therefore important to develop an awareness of the body and its central role in sound production and manipulation, as learning takes place by *doing*. For teachers, this means facilitating processes of embodiment by incorporating strategies that use the body (e.g. activities that allow information to be felt physically, such as walking to a pulse, clapping a rhythm or using body percussion) and encouraging practice strategies that build on these. For learners, many scholars have underscored the importance of developing and embedding skills so that they become automatic or intuitive (Çorlu et al. 2015; Hadjimichael, Ribeiro and Tsoukas 2024; Myers 2002). Myers (2002) highlights the importance of attention within this process of developing intuition or *tacit* knowledge.

Embodiment as Tacit Knowledge

Broadly speaking, the literature divides knowledge into two main categories: explicit knowledge, describing information that can be easily articulated and shared, such as objective facts, and tacit knowledge (see Hadjimichael, Ribeiro and Tsoukas 2024), which is experiential, cannot be captured adequately in words and only exists within the individual.

Explicit knowledge is frequently exploited in order to initiate the learning of a skill, such as playing an instrument or understanding complex rhythms. As we begin to acquire such abilities in practice, there is a simultaneous obtaining of much deeper, tacit understanding. The essence of sense-making – the process by which explicit musical knowledge gains a tacit dimension – is embodiment (Cohen 2018). An example might be someone who can 'feel' or 'sense' a pulse or clap a rhythm without being able to explain it theoretically. This individual has *tacit* knowledge but has not yet codified their experiences explicitly. Conversely, the rhythm can be explained theoretically, for example, in terms of its mathematical foundations, generating *explicit* knowledge: an objective 'fact' that can be articulated and shared. Explicit knowledge alone is not sufficient for being able to play rhythmically: a student might understand the mathematical principles of rhythm without necessarily being able to apply them. To 'make sense' of rhythm, their explicit 'knowledge that' (a semiquaver or sixteenth note equals one quarter of a crotchet or quarter note, for example) must be developed into a more experiential tacit 'knowledge how' to feel the subdivisions in relation to the pulse. Learning requires a meaningful marriage of the explicit and the tacit.

Cohen (2018) explains that as knowledge becomes deeply ingrained in an individual through practice and repetition, it becomes intuitive, or accessible without conscious thought, leaving attention to be directed elsewhere. Embodiment, incorporating the body (experiential knowledge by doing) and the mind (engraining explicit knowledge into our subconscious or subattention so that it becomes intuitive) is the process by which explicit knowledge develops a tacit dimension.

Implications for Learning and Teaching

The more expert the musician, the more tacit knowledge they have intuitive access to, as Myers (2002: 56) explains: 'Experts' knowledge is more organized than novices', in ways that enable them to access it efficiently. Novices see information in isolated pieces; experts see large meaningful patterns.' Such patterns, or image schemata, allow musicians to relate physical movements to sonic outcomes. Learners achieve this as they 'repeatedly practise an activity, using materials and tools, under the guidance of more experienced others' (Hadjimichael, Ribeiro and Tsoukas 2024: 546).

Beginner musicians, then, need to be able to focus their attention on the basic processes required to produce and manipulate sound using their instrument or voice in order for these processes to become intuitive and automatic. Furthermore, as Çorlu et al. (2015: 497) note, automating technique through practice alleviates some of the cognitive load involved in performance, leaving more cognitive resources for expressive playing 'rather than sound-producing gestures'.

Developing Embodied Awareness

In the following section, we explore some of the ways in which teachers might help learners to develop awareness, not only of their bodily movements and how these influence their musical production and expression but also of how their musicking is represented cognitively and psychologically: how their physical movements and musical intentions manifest themselves conceptually in their mind's eye. We share some examples from our own teaching and learning experiences that have led us to reflect on the embodied nature of musicking. The quotes we share emerged through individual reflections and group discussions.

Embodied Cognition

In modern Western society where much school-based learning is focused on the written word, learners might expect to approach music in a similarly academic way. With the convenience and ubiquity of printed notation in Western educational settings, it can be tempting for teachers to introduce notation and reading at an early stage of the learning process. Furthermore, the appeal of producing evidence of musical 'achievement', such as passing a graded examination (also see Chapter 16), might understandably lead keen students to prioritize 'mastering' repertoire of a particular level of difficulty over developing mindfulness of the process of musicking itself. However, some educators, including Kodály and Dalcroze, have strongly advocated developing holistic musical understanding through singing, listening and movement as foundational to instrumental learning. Several of the scholars discussed earlier in this chapter at the very least endorse the teaching of technique to connect mind and body from the early stages. Approaches for understanding effective body use include Dalcroze's *Eurhythmics* (Anderson 2012), the Alexander Technique (Kleinman and Buckoke 2013) and body mapping (Buchanan and Hays 2014), among others, while the work of Kodály, Orff and Suzuki continues to offer inspiration and guidance in holistic musical learning and teaching. Pedagogical approaches such as Kindermusik and the Suzuki[1] school encourage very young children and their families to explore their natural musicality through movement, dance and song and to develop concepts of musical pitch and rhythm through movement and gesture.

Schiavio and Nijs (2022: 2) emphasize the importance of creativity, interaction and bodily movement in developing 'meaningful relationships with the instrument' as well as with the music itself. In instrumental and vocal lessons, we might encourage beginners to develop a visual image of aspects of technique, guiding them to connect the sound they produce with the fingering, embouchure, breath control, bowing or posture required to produce it. Learners with any degree of experience may already be aware of image schemata and able to describe mental conceptions of technical and musical processes, whereas others may benefit from being encouraged to explore how they conceptualize movements and sounds. Guiding our students to reflect on how they successfully manipulate their technique to achieve a particular sonic outcome can also help them develop independence and agency in their practice, empowering them to find their own way to achieve a desired musical outcome rather than relying on a teacher to tell them if their sound or technique is 'correct'.

Conceptualizing embodiment may be instrument-specific: for example, vocalists and wind players might intuitively develop a deep connection between their body and instrument through breathing, compared with keyboard players. Conversely, as pianists engage with the keyboard and pedals, their arm weight, touch sensitivity, hand, arm and foot coordination and wrist use for phrasing and agility might engender a different sort of conceptual connection to the music from that experienced by wind or string players.

Embodying Musical Expression

Embodiment might also result in expressive movement in response to a musical idea or character. Although some students might need encouragement to develop the freedom to move expressively, less self-conscious learners may instinctively embody music with glorious abandon, as one author shared: 'Several of my very young students demonstrate their embodied awareness of musical styles without any prompting and regularly dance the style of their piece before playing it. When I ask them how the music makes them feel, it seems to come naturally to them to dance their answer.' This beautifully illustrates Delalande's *explorative* and *expressive* conducts (see Delalande and Cornara 2010) and might inspire a lesson based on experimenting with how to translate these dance movements into expressive playing or a discussion about what qualities within the music inspired those particular movements.

Guiding students to think about what they want to communicate through playing or singing, perhaps through imagery or storytelling, may help them develop deeper connections to the music by creating their own interpretation and also strengthen their sense of autonomy and conviction. Asking 'If this music were a person, what would they be like?' might inspire conversations about how the character moves, what they are doing, even how they are dressed and what age they are, or be extended to a 'cast' of musical characters, encouraging students to immerse themselves in contrasting personae at different points in a piece of music.

This approach may lead to greater confidence in performance and even relieve performance anxiety. For example, one author found that encouraging a student to embody a 'concerto performer' led to a more extrovert and communicative performance, while suggesting they embody a conductor resulted in the student taking greater responsibility for their own rhythmic pulse and directing an accompanist with greater clarity. Assuming a different persona also led to an unexpected discovery for one (female) author when performing in male costume: 'Once dressed as a man I found myself embodying a more male character, standing differently and playing in a more extrovert way, allowing myself to be free of the idea that "girls don't show off" – an idea that I didn't even know was in my head until the male costume and assumed persona freed me of it.'

Creating a 'safe' space in lessons for students to explore expressive movement can help them develop their own creative ideas and aid their understanding of how body movements influence their musical performance in practical as well as expressive terms. Sometimes, teachers may need to guide students to explore their movements consciously, for example, if expressive movement disrupts airflow, disturbs finger patterns or creates additional tension. Careful, empathic teaching may help them reassess embodied habits to improve playing fluency or even mitigate against injury. Van der Schyff (2015: 11) advocates encouraging learners to 'attend to the moment' to enhance their kinesthetic awareness; we can also help learners better understand the physical aspects of technique by encouraging practice in front of a mirror or through modelling within our own playing.

Although bodily movement may enhance the expression we create through sound, it cannot replace it. Awareness of this may be especially important if teaching through demonstration. One of us reflects on working with 'advanced students who sincerely thought they were observing dynamic changes when they were merely crouching down or raising their eyebrows for *piano*, and standing up tall or frowning for *forte*, having copied these gestures from other performers in the past', while a colleague from China notes: 'Some students and teachers may focus on the goal of students being able to perfectly mimic the teacher's body motions, but they often fail to holistically explain the connection between our minds, bodies or those specific movements that need to be imitated, and dynamic expression.' Examples like these highlight the significance of embodied learning for musicians and the importance for teachers to empower learners to develop their own embodied understanding.

Conclusion

We have seen how musicians' attention may be focused in different ways at different stages of learning, whether directed towards the physical skill required to produce a particular sonic outcome or towards the musical expression they wish to communicate. Embodied learning is the process by which explicit knowledge develops a tacit dimension – through which we develop an intuitive feel for our instrument or voice. Embodied understanding of how to use our instrument or voice to shape sound into music and music into performance enables us to communicate our musical intentions to others for their own embodied experience.

Embodied cognition emphasizes the importance of active participation in learning. As infants, we learn how to manipulate and shape sounds by exploring, experimenting and creating; however, in Western 'classical' musical education we may be tempted to ignore these vital early stages by the allure of producing a measurable musical 'result'. As learners, teachers, listeners and musickers in any capacity, it is worth keeping in mind the exploratory nature of our early musical experiences and allowing our students and ourselves to indulge in 'such embodied exploration through sound making, improvisation, … and by maintaining the deep connection between music, dance, song, and storytelling' (van der Schyff 2015: 7).

Notes

1 See https://www.kindermusik.com/ and https://www.suzukischool.com/.

References

Adlington, R. (2003), 'Moving beyond Motion: Metaphors for Changing Sound', *Journal of the Royal Musical Association*, 128 (2): 297–318.

Aksnes, H. (2001), 'Music and Its Resonating Body', *Danish Yearbook of Musicology*, 29. Available online: https://www.dym.dk/dym_pdf_files/volume_29/volume_29_081_101.pdf (accessed 5 August 2024).

Anderson, W. T. (2012), 'The Dalcroze Approach to Music Education: Theory and Applications', *General Music Today*, 26 (1): 27–33.

Brower, C. (2000), 'A Cognitive Theory of Musical Meaning', *Journal of Music Theory*, 44 (2): 323–79.

Buchanan, H. J., and T. Hays (2014), 'The Influence of Body Mapping on Student Musicians' Performance Experiences', *International Journal of Education & the Arts*, 15 (7): 1–28.

Cohen, J. (2018), 'Playing with Time: The Creative Embodiment of Knowledge in the Performance of Baroque Flute Music', PhD diss., University of York.

Çorlu, M., C. Muller, F. Desmet and M. Leman (2015), 'The Consequences of Additional Cognitive Load on Performing Musicians', *Psychology of Music*, 43 (4): 495–510.

Corness, G. (2008), 'The Musical Experience through the Lens of Embodiment', *Leonardo Music Journal*, 18: 21–4.

Curwen, C. (2018), 'Music-Colour Synaesthesia: Concept, Context and Qualia', *Consciousness and Cognition*, 61: 94–106.

Delalande, F., and S. Cornara (2010), 'Sound Explorations from the Ages of 10 to 37 Months: The Ontogenesis of Musical Conducts', *Music Education Research*, 12 (3): 257–68.

Di Pellegrino, G., L. Fadiga, L. Fogassi, V. Gallese and G. Rizzolatti (1992), 'Understanding Motor Events: A Neurophysiological Study', *Experimental Brain Research*, 91: 176–80.

Doja, A. (2014), 'Socializing Enchantment: A Socio-Anthropological Approach to Infant-Directed Singing, Music Education and Cultural Socialization', *International Review of the Aesthetics and Sociology of Music*, 45 (1): 115–47.

Eitan, Z., and R. Timmers (2010), 'Beethoven's Last Piano Sonata and Those Who Follow Crocodiles: Cross-Domain Mappings of Auditory Pitch in a Musical Context', *Cognition*, 114 (3): 405–22.

Fuchs, T. (2017), *Ecology of the Brain: The Phenomenology and Biology of the Embodied Mind*, Oxford: Oxford University Press.

Gallagher, S. (2015), 'Reuse and Body-Formatted Representations in Simulation Theory', *Cognitive Systems Research*, 34: 35–43.

Gallese, V. (2005), 'Embodied Simulation: From Neurons to Phenomenal Experience', *Phenomenology and the Cognitive Sciences*, 4: 23–48.

Gallese, V., and C. Sinigaglia (2011), 'What Is So Special about Embodied Simulation?', *Trends in Cognitive Sciences*, 15 (11): 512–19.

Hadjimichael, D., R. Ribeiro and H. Tsoukas (2024), 'How Does Embodiment Enable the Acquisition of Tacit Knowledge in Organizations? From Polanyi to Merleau-Ponty', *Organization Studies*, 45 (4): 545–70.

Hepper, P. G. (1991), 'An Examination of Fetal Learning Before and After Birth', *Irish Journal of Psychology*, 12 (2): 95–107.

Herbert, B. M., and O. Pollatos (2012), 'The Body in the Mind: On the Relationship between Interoception and Embodiment', *Topics in Cognitive Science*, 4 (4): 692–704.

Hess, J. (2018), 'Musicking Marginalization: Periphractic Practices in Music Education', in A. M. Kraehe, R. Gaztambide-Fernández and B. S. Carpenter II (eds), *The Palgrave Handbook of Race and the Arts in Education*, 325–46, Cham: Palgrave Macmillan.

Kleinman, J., and P. Buckoke (2013), *The Alexander Technique for Musicians*, London: Bloomsbury.

Kohler, E., C. Keysers, M. A. Umiltà, L. Fogassi, V. Gallese and G. Rizzolatti (2002), 'Hearing Sounds, Understanding Actions: Action Representation in Mirror Neurons', *Science*, 297 (5582): 846–8.

Lakoff, G., and M. Johnson (1980), 'The Metaphorical Structure of the Human Conceptual System', *Cognitive Science*, 4 (2): 195–208.

Malloch, S., and C. Trevarthen (2018), 'The Human Nature of Music', *Frontiers in Psychology*, 9: 1–21. Available online: http://dx.doi.org/10.3389/fpsyg.2018.01680 (accessed 5 August 2024).

Margulis, E. H., P. C. Wong, C. Turnbull, B. M. Kubit and J. D. McAuley (2022), 'Narratives Imagined in Response to Instrumental Music Reveal Culture-Bounded Intersubjectivity', *Proceedings of the National Academy of Sciences*, 119 (4). Available online: https://www.pnas.org/doi/full/10.1073/pnas.2110406119 (accessed 5 August 2024).

McAuley, J. D., P. C. Wong, L. Bellaiche and E. H. Margulis (2021), 'What Drives Narrative Engagement with Music?', *Music Perception: An Interdisciplinary Journal*, 38 (5): 509–21.

Merleau-Ponty, M. (1945/2010), *Phenomenology of Perception*, trans. D. Landes, Abingdon: Routledge.

Myers, D. (2002), *Intuition: Its Powers and Perils*, New Haven: Yale University Press.

Overy, K., and I. Molnar-Szakacs (2009), 'Being Together in Time: Musical Experience and the Mirror Neuron System', *Music Perception: An Interdisciplinary Journal*, 26: 489–504.

Papoušek, M. (1994), 'Melodies in Caregivers' Speech: A Species-Specific Guidance towards Language', *Early Development and Parenting*, 3 (1): 5–17.

Piaget, J. (1972), 'Development and Learning', in C. S. Lavatelli and F. Stendler (eds), *Readings in Child Behavior and Development*, 3rd edn, 38–46, New York: Harcourt Brace Jovanovich.

Schiavio, A., and L. Nijs (2022), 'Implementation of a Remote Instrumental Music Course Focused on Creativity, Interaction, and Bodily Movement. Preliminary Insights and Thematic Analysis', *Frontiers in Psychology*, 13: 899381. Available online: https://www.frontiersin.org/journals/psychology/articles/10.3389/fpsyg.2022.899381/full (accessed 5 August 2024).

Schiavio, A., and D. van der Schyff (2018), '4E Music Pedagogy and the Principles of Self-Organization', *Behavioral Sciences*, 8 (8): 72. Available online: https://www.mdpi.com/2076-328X/8/8/72 (accessed 5 August 2024).

Schiavio, A., D. Menin and J. Matyja (2014), 'Music in the Flesh: Embodied Simulation in Musical Understanding', *Psychomusicology: Music, Mind, and Brain*, 24 (4): 340–3.

Schiavio, A., D. van der Schyff, S. Kruse-Weber and R. Timmers (2017), 'When the Sound becomes the Goal. 4E Cognition and Teleomusicality in Early Infancy', *Frontiers in Psychology*, 8: 1585. Available online: https://doi.org/10.3389/fpsyg.2017.01585 (accessed 5 August 2024).

Silverman, M. (2020), 'Sense-Making, Meaningfulness, and Instrumental Music Education', *Frontiers in Psychology*, 11: 837. Available online: https://doi.org/10.3389/fpsyg.2020.00837 (accessed 5 August 2024).

Small, C. (1999), 'Musicking – the Meanings of Performing and Listening. A Lecture', *Music Education Research*, 1 (1): 9–22.

Smith, G. D. (2020), 'Embodied Experience of Rock Drumming', *Visions of Research in Music Education*, 35 (1): 12.

Trevarthen, C. (2002), 'Origins of Musical Identity: Evidence from Infancy for Musical Social Awareness', in R. A. R. MacDonald, D. J. Hargreaves and D. Miell (eds), *Musical Identities*, 21–38, Oxford: Oxford University Press.

van der Schyff, D. (2015), 'Music as a Manifestation of Life: Exploring Enactivism and the "Eastern Perspective" for Music Education', *Frontiers in Psychology*, 6: 129898. Available online: https://doi.org/10.3389/fpsyg.2015.00345 (accessed 5 August 2024).

Zbikowski, L. M. (2009), 'Music, Language, and Multimodal Metaphor', in C. J. Forceville and E. Urios-Aparisi (eds), *Multimodal Metaphor*, 359–81, Berlin: Mouton de Gruyter.

13

Hurdles Not Brick Walls: Supporting Students to Overcome Physical and Mental Barriers to Instrumental Practice

Rosemary Lynch, Marianna Cortesi, Jennifer Cohen and Sara Norouzi Iranzad

Introduction

Regular practice is crucial to learning and improving performance on a musical instrument (Araújo 2016), and having an adequate environment in which students can practise regularly is essential to achieve this (Creech 2010). The authors of this chapter are instrumental teachers as well as academics and performers, from diverse international backgrounds, who teach young learners through to octogenarians. Through varied instrumental teaching experience gained in various international settings, they all see the encouragement of self-regulatory behaviours as their overriding objective in enabling learners of any age to practise effectively and efficiently. In doing so, the learner takes ownership of their own goal setting, and by equating practice with improvement, the cognitive connection between these can be nurtured from the start of a learner's instrumental journey. An abundance of literature on this topic exists, including Bartolome (2009), McPherson, Miksza and Evans (2017), McPherson and Zimmerman (2002) and Pike (2017), building on Dewey's (1859–1952) pursuit of the importance of a collaborative process in the learning environment. The teacher is not authoritarian therefore, acting rather as a vehicle through which their expertise can guide and promote self-reflection and self-regulation within the learner.

The following sections set out some of the environmental and cognitive barriers to practice experienced by our students and consider where (and how) these intersect. We then discuss some of our strategies, which are both reactive to a situation (as knowledge of individual students' needs emerge and evolve over time) and proactive: as our experience as teachers grows, so too does our toolkit to address obstacles and encourage effective practice. It is also pertinent to note that many of our strategies combine the mind (cognitive) and the body (doing and embodied), particularly as the field of embodied cognition[1] is growing and treatment of the body and mind as separate entities is diminishing (Saad and de Medeiros 2017). To address cognitive barriers to practice, the authors share some of their 'doing' strategies alongside (meta)cognitive strategies to encourage self-regulation in the practice environment.

Environmental Barriers

The Cambridge Dictionary (2024) defines practise as 'to do or play something regularly or repeatedly in order to become skilled at it'. As many students have busy weekly schedules, often including sports clubs and family commitments, we consider time constraints to be a major environmental factor for learners. Playing an instrument necessitates frequent practice, which can cause friction between the amount of time a student may have to dedicate to their musical pursuits and the time they ideally need. Thus, cognitive engagement with practice can be hampered. Students who do not have enough time to practise often deal with this deficit by running through their pieces aimlessly, with no clear purpose (Hallam 1997). This becomes their standard practice strategy and, therefore, a barrier to effective practice.

Ideally, learners would have an allocated space in their house where they can practise regularly without external distractions (such as parents, siblings or even electronic devices causing interruptions). Not all learners, however, have access to a dedicated home music room, or they may have to share that space with siblings who also need it, impacting the available practice time, particularly for those playing large instruments such as the piano, which are often situated in a communal room in the family home. Learners of these instruments may be unable to practise in alternative locations; therefore, a sense of unease or tension could be connected to their perception of practice. However, even those learning more portable instruments (such as flute or violin) could experience environmental barriers including the inconvenience or added time required to assemble the instrument, a music stand and their music books; these can manifest as cognitive barriers. This is particularly apparent among younger students or those with additional needs, who may need assistance to prepare their equipment (and clean their instrument before or after practice, particularly relevant for woodwinds). These examples show that a less-than-ideal physical space in which to practise can set up a detrimental cognitive connection to the idea of practice.

StGeorge's (2006) study into the correlation between practice and continuation rates for instrumental learning describes two participants' very different home practice environments. One can seek advice from his father, an experienced musician; for another, practice was completely self-motivated: 'No-one in my family really plays, and so I thought if I do more practice, I might be good at the flute' (2006: 6). In our experience, this is a common issue for our students: an environment where others play and music is heard can encourage practice. If no one else plays, however, or where there is a perception that no one can help, then practice can become an isolating and unenjoyable chore where, again, environmental and cognitive barriers converge. It is equally important to recognize that when parents are performers or music teachers themselves, they can become over-involved and too critical, creating another barrier for the student.

This extends to a consideration of EDI (Equality, Diversity and Inclusion) barriers. Independent practice at home may not be equally feasible for all students: as teachers, it is important to acknowledge that for some learners, particularly those who have difficult socio-economic and emotionally challenging home environments, it can be impossible for them to practise at home. It is imperative to note here that as instrumental teachers, we are not trained healthcare professionals, or privy to sensitive information that may explain some barriers that the learner cannot articulate verbally. While how they play and perform in any given lesson may provide cues, listening empathetically is not just about using our ears or 'listening' in the traditional sense but involves observing explicit and implicit cues from our students, absorbing and interpreting information rather than taking it at face value. While we cannot empathize in the sense of occupying a learner's particular environment and sharing a learner's unique 'lived experience', we can be present in an empathetic way, empowering us to collaborate effectively with the student to maximize other ways for them to practise.

Another EDI point is to consider the effects of geopolitical climates, which negatively impact some learners. While only Afghanistan's regime has completely banned music (Sameyee 2023), in other countries such as Iran, governmental controls and international sanctions limit access to useful resources and practice apps, potentially impacting a learner's range of choices for their practice schedule. Economic difficulties concerning cheap currency and no international banking access make purchasing music or apps online very difficult; the prohibitively high cost of instruments and externally sourced musical equipment such as metronomes exacerbate the challenges related to learning and practising. In addition, curfews make it more difficult for young learners in particular to schedule instrumental lessons after school or maintain regular practice sessions, and their interest in practising may therefore diminish.

Cognitive Barriers

Perhaps one of the most common barriers to practice is students' limited knowledge of *how* to practise effectively. The large body of literature demonstrates that effective practice is deliberate, goal-oriented and task-specific (Bartolome 2009; Hallam 2001; McPherson and Zimmerman 2002; Oare 2012; Pike 2017; Sloboda et al. 1996). However, these characteristics are often not reflective of the practice of our students whose complaints around practice include the solitary nature of practice, self-reported low attention span, which is often connected to practice feeling like a chore, as well as perfectionist tendencies which induce fear or paralysis around attempting a task. The authors recognize the issues around practising discussed in the writing of Oare (2012), Bartolome (2009), Pitts, McPherson and Davidson (2000) and Pike (2017) through both their teaching and their personal experiences of practice. For example, many of our students (particularly young beginners) appear to prefer to run through multiple pieces without error detection, without persistence and with a tendency to return to easier passages or move onto something else when things become difficult. Lacking 'a specific idea of what aspects of the music needed work' and 'unable to express' their learning goals (Oare 2012: 65), there is fundamentally 'no clear idea of why and how they should be learning' (Pitts, McPherson and Davidson 2000: 54).[2]

As Zimmerman (1986) notes, self-regulation occurs when students are 'active participants in their own learning process' (1986: 308). This is the start of them beginning to address the cognitive barrier: a lack of understanding of how to practise effectively. As instrumental teachers, how can we facilitate an understanding of deliberate, goal-oriented, task-specific practice for different students? We consider this a key discussion to have with every student at the outset of their instrumental learning journey and to review this during lessons, developing strategies and understanding as learners progress and as their circumstances change. As Ericsson, Krampe and Tesch-Romer's (1993) research demonstrates, expertise grows as practice accumulates over time. As teachers, we also need to be aware of the expectations of learners (McPherson 2000) which can come from perceptions of immediate reward, or perfectionist tendencies which could result in distress or underachievement throughout their life (Arbinaga 2023).

Strategies

The authors of this chapter consider discussing effective strategies with their students to be of paramount importance. Furthermore, being reflective in our own teaching and learning practice enhances our ability to engage empathetically with students' individual practice needs and goals. In the following sections, we discuss strategies which have materialized from the intersection between students' environmental and cognitive barriers to practice. We hope these will be of use to readers who may wish to incorporate or expand on some of these ideas in their teaching, acknowledging that as these often organically emerge in real world situations, they are somewhat imperfect and are merely offered as ideas to fuel the reader's own strategic handling of their students' practice barriers. Our suggestions are not intended as universally applicable: some may work for some students and not for others. One example of this is the use of technology in practice apps which can be beneficial to some learners (who might struggle with structuring their practice independently) whereas others find it another distraction or barrier to effective practice. Again, it is crucial for the teacher to tailor strategies to the individual circumstances of each student through empathetic listening and then collaborating on feasible goal-setting and relevant processes with the student.

Listening and Modelling

As music practitioners, it is prudent to have conversations with our students about what their expectations and motivations are around learning their instrument. Every student has a different home environment and ideas about what learning an instrument entails. From the outset, teachers can discuss and explore 'effective practice' with their students as part of the lesson. It is then possible to discuss and plan a realistic (and focused) practice schedule around the student's motivations and goals, rather than our pre-existing ideas. Checking in regularly to ascertain whether and how their motivation changes as they progress can then empower both teacher and learner to alter practice expectations as necessary, rather than adopting a 'top-down', blanket approach. For younger and teenage learners, we strongly advise also communicating with parents or carers so that if there is a disconnect between the student's motivation and the parents' or carers' expectations, these can be incorporated into the discussion around enabling practice and long-term goals. We stress the importance of communication extending beyond the duration of the lesson, building up relationships and awareness of practice (and equipment) needs for each student, thus ensuring a holistic approach. For example, environmental strategies can include chatting about and offering advice for the layout of a practice room, or the possibility of leaving instruments assembled and visible at home, so that less assembly preparation is required. Also, we advocate discussing the physicality of playing an instrument; modelling good posture and technique can reduce the likelihood of practice becoming physically uncomfortable and something to avoid. This also encourages longevity in learning, as it builds good practice from the start, so that physical discomfort is prevented further down the line.[3]

In our instrumental teaching, much strategizing involves the reiteration of quality practice, rather than quantity, and we advocate for honesty about our own experiences with managing our practice in our everyday lives where time and focus can be short. Sloboda et al.'s remarks on 'formal effortful practice' being 'a principal determinant of musical achievement' (1996: 287), and Pitts, McPherson and Davidson's assertion that 'Practice which is satisfying and enjoyable will in itself be a source of motivation' (2000: 54) have been impactful in how we have pragmatically developed strategies to foster self-motivation across these two components. At first glance, the 'formal' of Sloboda et al. (1996) may appear at odds with the enjoyment emphasized by Pitts, McPherson and Davidson (2000). Our strategies, however, mainly aim to improve self-regulatory behaviours by encompassing consistent commitment with a sense of fun and achievement, fostering an improved relationship with effective practice for our students. In so doing, they often take the form of games, 'chunking', acronyms for focus and recall and self-ownership by the learner recording their practice in a practice diary. Many learners are so used to online apps for schoolwork and social interactions that they will readily use online music apps in preparation for exams, such as aural trainer apps.[4] There are many practice diary apps which can help learners organize their practice effectively in a fun and engaging way. In our experience, however, while these apps can be a supportive tool in developing self-ownership in practice schedules, they can also become an added distraction or prohibitively expensive, thus another barrier to effective practice. This point again highlights the importance of conversations with our students, listening and responding strategically and sensitively to their individual practice needs and situations.

Gamifying Practice

All of the authors use 'Game-based learning' (Margoudi, de Oliveira and Waddell 2016: 426) to model fun ways to practise effectively at home. These games have emerged and evolved over time and are flexible so that individual learners can bring their own ideas to them too, enabling self-regulation and task ownership during their home practice sessions. The examples below are a snapshot of many variations in gamifying that the authors frequently use. One author uses dice as a means of goal-setting for sight-reading: each roll of the dice determines the number of short pieces a student should sight-read. A different approach consists of rolling the dice, then the student repeats a section of a piece they are finding difficult as many times as the number they rolled on the dice: each iteration is aimed at achieving a specific goal rather than mindless repetition. This game adds fun and purpose to a repetitive task. Another goal-setting challenge uses a sticker target game where five stickers are placed on a score that the learner is studying. Each sticker represents a different musical aspect that requires practice (e.g. dynamics or articulation). As their skill level grows, they colour the stickers in until all five are done; when it is deemed by both teacher and student to be a 'five-star piece', it is performance-ready.

One author uses the idea of a 'Concentration Hat', which a student can mime putting on when they recognize that they need to pay closer attention to a certain section of a piece. Others draw a hat above a specific score passage as a way to remember to focus on developing specific aspects of their playing. This is no different in principle from how musicians habitually annotate their scores, so this forms a good habit-forming strategy, particularly for taking ownership in responding to instructions from the conductor in ensemble settings.

For other technical challenges such as learning arpeggios, one author has found that younger students love making up silly associations with the note names that vary (sometimes wildly) from the common ways of remembering these. For example, instead of just learning C, E, G, as 'Cows Eat Grass' for C Major, students experiment with making up their own, such as 'Caterpillars Easily Glow' or in the case of A minor, one student suggested 'Astronauts Climb Everest'. The resulting comedic imagery in their imaginations means that 'boring' arpeggios become a source of fun, efficiently and effectively memorized.

Older learners are no less susceptible to the benefits of gamifying practice regimes, and games can be deployed and modified to suit older age ranges. Sometimes this can be as simple as varying rhythms during scales practice, challenging themselves to memorize a section or reward-based goal setting. For example, practising a technical exercise and rewarding themselves with playing a much-loved and much-played piece.

'Chunking'

All of the authors use chunking strategies as an essential practice tool to model for their students; recent research into its efficacy among beginners (Dueck 2023) builds on much diverse literature on the topic (Greher and Ruthmann 2012; Iott 2021). This term refers to sectioning off parts of a piece and practising them in more manageable chunks and is particularly useful for achieving effective practice in a short time period. It is a time-efficient exercise to model in a lesson and apply to individual practice: it demonstrates progress and can also reduce the tension or perfectionist anxiety that might build up in the learner's attitude towards the whole piece (and even the instrument) as a result of a challenging section. 'Chunking' can be as little as a part of a phrase or a greater chunk of a sizeable piece. Fun and effective ways to deviate from repeatedly playing the same section include using different rhythms, experimenting with articulation and 'gluing' chunks together. This promotes understanding of building a piece and can lead to further experimentation and conversation during lessons, which may explore specific musical features in different musical eras, a certain composer's style, articulation decisions, composing a short melody in the same style and so forth.

'Freestyle Playing'

Encouraging students to experiment and to play freely without notation can promote a relationship with their instrument that makes them want to practise. Many beginner learners, for example, enjoy making up tunes and often want to show their teacher what they have created during their home practice. Encouraging older or more advanced students to set aside practice time to express themselves freely with their instrument, with no audience, no judgement, just 'playing for playing's sake' can foster a flowing enjoyment and connection to their instrument. This can be particularly useful if they have been focused on exam or audition preparation.

De-Isolation Strategies

As mentioned in the environmental barriers section, a lack of self-motivation can manifest from feelings of isolation with the often solitary experience of practising, adding to the perception of practice being a chore. Therefore, one strategy is encouraging students to access ensemble playing as well as instrumental lessons, even if it is just practising at home with a sibling, a friend or a parent. We know from our own experiences and research such as McPherson (2000) and StGeorge (2006) that beginners of any age are likely to continue learning for longer if there is companionship in the learning environment. Even higher-level learners who are encouraged to play in ensembles alongside instrumental lessons tend to experience a better relationship with practice (Nielsen et al. 2018).

Through one author's experiences of reducing isolation for her students during Covid-19, a communal practice strategy has persisted in her music school. The idea was instigated by a student wanting to take ownership of their practice during this challenging time. Organizing online practice through a WhatsApp group, the author's piano students (and their parents) agreed to meet via Zoom at a designated time every evening. In the first session of the week, the students would each introduce the piece that they were going to practise, then mute their microphones and practise. The visual stimulus of others practising simultaneously made it a communal activity. During the week, they would also send video performances of their prepared pieces to the group, encouraging and being encouraged by each other with emojis and voice messages. These online appointments were very effective especially for students who struggled with self-regulation and helped them get into the habit of practising and, post-pandemic, preparing for concerts. At the suggestion of the teacher, it was decided that anyone who was experiencing difficulties with a piece should consult their classmates: sometimes a student who already knew a piece would play for them or would offer suggestions to solve their friend's challenges. This strategy can be called upon whenever any political turmoil in her country adversely affects regular access to face-to-face instrumental tuition.

Acronyms

Recent research into the efficacy of acronyms suggests that they can be useful in helping the brain focus on completing tasks, even after interruptions (Radović and Manzey 2019). This is useful to consider in the many varied intersections of the cognitive and environmental barriers to practice that students encounter, where frequent interruptions may be the norm. These may include stoppages for family commitments, space and attitudes towards practice at home, and self-created interruptions through social media engagement during practice. Townsend (2012) uses the acronym PRACTICE (Practice of Relevant Activities Causes Technical Improvement, and, Correct Execution). The authors of this chapter welcome this contribution to seeking to define the term 'practice' in a personalized, targeted way. However, unlike the acronym LEST (Listen Empathetically, Strategize Together), which emerged 'reactively' (and organically) from our many reflective experiential discussions, we found PRACTICE to be imposed on the word 'practice' making it challenging to remember its components and potentially weakening its intended goal of assisting teachers and students in instigating practice techniques. Acronyms may not be perfect or universally helpful; rather they give an indication of how often we find ourselves tailoring practice regimes in collaboration with our students and their particular learning goals. For example, one author mentioned how their acronym 'MITs' evolved: one particular learner needed a way of recalling and guiding the main areas for practice that had arisen from their lessons and so MITs (Most Important Things) was born. The learner has one Macro MIT, which is their main practice goal, and then Mini MITs within that overarching practice framework. Another author uses a similar idea, but not acronymized, in their 'theme for this week' which informs the practice content dependent on recurrent emergent aspects from the lesson such as 'dynamics!', or 'shape the musical story!' The author found that this works well for secondary school age and older learners, as well as those practising for a performance or an exam.

Conclusion

It is clear from the discussion above that the overarching barriers to practice are cognitive and environmental, and these factors interrelate. With adverse environmental practice conditions and without resources and knowledge of how to practise effectively, students can feel isolated, anxious, bored or 'triggered' by the expectations implied by the word 'practice', potentially leading to fear and avoidance behaviours.

We did not set out to add another acronym to the plethora of acronyms in our world today. However, during the many reflective conversations that the authors continue to have regarding practice barriers for their students, it became apparent that we all centre our efforts around listening in an empathetic way and then collaborating with students, parents and academic settings (when appropriate) to find strategies that support the individual student to manage and maintain effective and enjoyable practice. We offer the acronym LEST as a tool which instrumental teachers may find useful when considering their students' practice needs. As mentioned previously, we recognize that acronyms may not be universally beneficial and offer this only as a suggestion, particularly for early career practitioners. We see LEST as a word acting as a quick mental reminder to ourselves as teachers to engage with the changing landscape of our students' busy lives and practice needs, particularly at times when we may have concerns about our students' practice levels versus their expectations of success. We acknowledge that while we cannot put ourselves in our students' shoes in a sociocultural and economic context, for example, we can empathize as performers and lifelong learners ourselves, needing to manage the fluctuating demands in our own practice environment.

This chapter has provided experience-led information, assisted by drawing on a rich research portfolio in this area, and we hope that our strategies may forge ideas for early career practitioners to facilitate self-regulation behaviours in learners from the start of their instrumental tuition. With teachers who listen empathetically to implicit and explicit cues and collaboratively strategize, learners can access a positive feedback loop which encourages effective and enjoyable practice, bringing lifelong benefits. We look forward to continuing research in this area promoting understanding around the cognitive and environmental barriers to practice, particularly in a variety of international settings, so that practice is communally addressed as an enjoyable challenge rather than an additional chore in an environmentally and cognitively hostile space.

Notes

1. For a broader discussion of embodied cognition, see Chapter 12.
2. Other cognitive barriers to acknowledge are specific disabilities and learning needs, which can also be environmentally challenging; these are discussed in Chapter 14.
3. Rosset i Llobet and Odam's *The Musician's Body* (2007) is a useful tool for teachers, learners of all ages and parents for understanding the physical demands of many different instruments.

4   Such as ABRSM Aural Trainer (2024); see also Bishop (2023) for examples of other practice apps.

References

Araújo, M. V. (2016), 'Measuring Self-Regulated Practice Behaviours in Highly Skilled Musicians', *Psychology of Music*, 44 (2): 278–92.

Arbinaga, F. (2023), 'Resilient Behaviors in Music Students: Relationship with Perfectionism and Self-Efficacy', *PubMed, National Library of Medicine*, 13 (9): 722.

'Aural Trainer' (2024), ABRSM. Available online: https://www.abrsm.org/en-gb/for-learners/apps-and-practice-tools/aural-trainer (accessed 2 July 2024).

Bartolome, S. J. (2009). 'Naturally Emerging Self-regulated Practice Behavior among Highly Successful Beginner Recorder Students', *Research Studies in Music Education*, 31 (1): 37–51.

Bishop, E. (2023), 'Staying On-Task: Practice Apps', *Music Teacher Magazine*, 1 September. Available online: https://www.musicteachermagazine.co.uk/features/article/staying-on-task-practice-apps (accessed 2 July 2024).

Creech, A. (2010), 'Learning a Musical Instrument: The Case for Parental Support', *Music Education Research*, 12 (1): 13–32.

Dueck, R. W. (2023), 'Developing a Progressive Chunking Technique in Musical Literacy: An Analysis of the Method Books and Sight-Reading Materials for Beginner Piano Students', MA diss., University of Ottawa, Canada. https://ruor.uottawa.ca/server/api/core/bitstreams/485d049a-7a08-45fd-9d48-cadcd384ddc5/content.

Ericsson, K. A., R. T. Krampe and C. Tesch-Romer (1993), 'The Role of Deliberate Practice in the Acquisition of Expert Performance', *Psychological Review*, 100 (3): 363–403.

Greher, G. R., and S. A. Ruthmann (2012), 'On Chunking, Simples, and Paradoxes: Why Jeanne Bamberger's Research Matters', *Visions of Research in Music Education*, 20 (3): 1–11.

Hallam, S. (1997), 'The Development of Memorisation Strategies in Musicians: Implications for Education', *British Journal of Music Education*, 14 (1): 87–97.

Hallam, S. (2001), 'The Development of Metacognition in Musicians: Implications for Education', *British Journal of Music Education*, 18 (1): 27–39.

Iott, S. (2021), *Thinking and Playing Music: Intentional Strategies for Optimal Practice and Performance*, London: Roman and Littlefield.

Margoudi, M., M. de Oliveira and G. Waddell (2016), 'Games-Based Learning of Musical Instruments: A Review and Recommendations', Available online: https://www.researchgate.net/publication/310149327_Game-Based_Learning_of_Musical_Instruments_A_Review_and_Recommendations (accessed 2 July 2024).

McPherson, G. E. (2000), 'Commitment and Practice: Key Ingredients for Achievement during the Early Stages of Learning a Musical Instrument', *Bulletin of the Council for Research in Music Education*, 147: 122–7. http://www.jstor.org/stable/40319399.

McPherson, G., and B. J. Zimmerman (2002), 'Self-Regulation of Musical Learning: A Social Cognitive Perspective', in R. Colwell and C. Richardson (eds), *The New Handbook of Research on Music Teaching and Learning*, 327–47, Oxford: Oxford University Press.

McPherson, G., P. Miksza and P. Evans (2017), 'Self-Regulated Learning in Music Performance', in D. H. Schunk and J. A. Greene (eds), *Handbook of Self-Regulation of Learning and Performance*, 2nd edn, 181–93, New York: Routledge.

Nielsen, C., R. K. Struder, H. Hildebrandt, U. M. Nater, P. Wild, B. Danuser and P. Gomez (2018), 'The Relationship between Music Performance Anxiety, Subjective Performance Quality and Post Event-Rumination among Music Students', *Psychology of Music*, 1 (46): 136–52.

Oare, S. (2012), 'Decisions Made in the Classroom: A Qualitative Study of Middle School Students' Thought Processes while Practicing', *Application of Research in Music Education*, 30 (2): 63–70.

Pike, P. (2017), 'Self-Regulation of Teenage Pianists during At-Home Practice', *Psychology of Music*, 45 (5): 739–51.

Pitts, S., G. McPherson and J. Davidson (2000), 'Developing Effective Practise Strategies: Case Studies of Three Young Instrumentalists', *Music Education Research*, 2 (1): 45–56.

'Practise' (2024), *Cambridge Dictionary Online*. Available online: https://dictionary.cambridge.org/dictionary/english/practise (accessed 2 July 2024).

Radović, T., and D. Manzey (2019), 'The Impact of a Mnemonic Acronym on Learning and Performing a Procedural Task and Its Resilience toward Interruptions', *Frontiers in Psychology*, 10: 1–17.

Rosset i Llobet, J., and G. Odam (2007), *The Musician's Body*, Aldershot: Ashgate.

Saad, M., and R. de Medeiros (2017), 'The Continuum of Mind-Body Interplay – From Placebo Effect to Unexplained Cures', *Medical Science & Healthcare Practice*, 1 (1): 1–9.

Sameyee, K. (2023), 'Musicians in Afghanistan Live in Fear and Despair amid the Taliban Ban on Music', *Globalvoices*, 22 August. Available online: https://globalvoices.org/2023/08/22/musicians-in-afghanistan-live-in-fear-and-despair-amid-the-taliban-ban-on-music/ (accessed 2 July 2024).

Sloboda, J. A., J. W. Davidson, M. J. A. Howe and D. G. Moore (1996), 'The Role of Practice in the Development of Performing Musicians', *British Journal of Psychology*, 87 (2): 287–309.

StGeorge, J. (2006), 'The Relationship of Practice to Continued Participation in Musical Instrument Learning', Conference: *XXVVIIIth Australian Association for Research in Music Education*, January. Available online: https://www.researchgate.net/publication/258217591_The_relationship_of_practice_to_continued_participation_in_musical_instrument_learning (accessed 2 July 2024).

Townsend, B. (2012), 'Understanding PRACTICE: An Acronym for the Holistic Approach to Practice', *International Journal of Music Education*, 30 (4): 397–408.

Zimmerman, B. J. (1986), 'Becoming a Self-Regulated Learner: Which Are the Key Subprocesses?', *Contemporary Educational Psychology*, 11: 307–11.

Part IV

Inclusivity, Support and Resources

14

Specific Learning Needs: An Exploration of Inclusive and Accessible Approaches

Kristl Kirk, Bella Powell, Rosemary Lynch, Jennifer Cohen and Pete Dale

Introduction

Despite increased discussion of inclusive and accessible music teaching in recent years, barriers to learning or making music may still exist for a variety of students (Fautley and Whittaker 2018; Henley and Barton 2022). These barriers may manifest as physical, social and pedagogical issues, which may impact students' participation in musical activities. According to Sieber (2008: 53), 'Social attitudes and institutions determine, far greater than biological fact, the representation of the body's reality.' While our society often operates within the medical model of disability, viewing it as 'something that must be repaired or is a problem to solve' (Dobbs 2017: 52), there have been some recent exciting examples in the media of how disability does not need to prove a barrier to learning or performing music. Lucy, a blind teenager who won Channel 4's 'The Piano' competition in 2023, was supported by the Amber Trust, a charity focused on music opportunities for visually impaired students (Hall 2024). At the 2023 Proms, Felix Klieser, who was born without arms, impressed audiences at the Royal Albert Hall by playing the French horn with his toes (Jonze 2023). While these are inspiring examples, limitations may be imposed on students with disabilities, often due to societal attitudes and their educational experiences rather than by the disability itself (Spruce 2024). Oliver's (2013) social model of disability, which identifies barriers and the societal changes necessary to move towards equality for disabled individuals, underpins the practice of the authors in this chapter.

The Importance of Context

All disabilities and learning needs are different, and each individual's experience of a disability or learning need will be unique to them. Therefore, while it is not possible to discuss all aspects of accessibility within the scope of this chapter, the authors discuss some of the disabilities and specific educational needs they have encountered in instrumental teaching contexts. These settings range from one-to-one to group lessons, in primary through tertiary education within both the state and private sector, including music hubs and private practice. Although based in the UK, the authors' intention is that many of the issues and strategies discussed will be relevant to a wide range of students, including principles and approaches appropriate for international contexts. Our aim is to signpost good-practice strategies for *all* students, which may in turn benefit those students with disabilities or learning needs.

A Shared Process of Reflexivity as a Means of Deepening Understanding

'Reflection has a role in learning and informing action' and is useful for 'the building of theory to guide practice or action', particularly in complex situations (Moon 1999: 52). Through a shared reflective process, the authors recognize assumptions and beliefs needing to be challenged but also discover aspects of empathy, compassion and encouragement. By drawing and reflecting on specific examples from our practice, the authors seek to explore these experiences with an understanding of how they relate to core ideas in the existing research literature and pedagogy. The discussion of inclusive practices will be framed through Finkelstein, Sharma and Furlonger's (2019: 748) domains of 'collaboration and teamwork, instructional support, organisational support, social/emotional/behavioural support and determining progress'. The final section of this chapter signposts the reader to resources which are relevant to specific needs. Our hope is that this chapter will offer other music teachers personal and professional support in the area of inclusive teaching.

Identifying Barriers

Practical barriers for both instrumental teachers and their students may exist around the communication and exchange of information concerning pupils' specific learning needs. Challenges identified by the authors include communicating with schools and parents, interpreting students' behaviour and obtaining accurate knowledge about special educational needs or disabilities. Some conditions are immediately apparent, but others fall into the category of 'non-visible disabilities' and may not be readily observable by the teacher.

Author C related how neither school nor parents volunteered information and wondered whether their position as a music tutor caused them to be 'seen as an outsider from the school perspective' with disclosure about specific students 'deemed unnecessary by the school'. Other potential reasons for a lack of disclosure might include the procedures adhered to by schools in connection to data protection and safeguarding. Alternatively, in the case of a parent or guardian, a reluctance to share information might stem from a fear that the child will be labelled or stigmatized. Despite a positive perspective of this as an opportunity to build 'connection without preconceptions' and to develop a sense of trust and understanding with individual students, one teacher noted that a lack of knowledge about students' needs caused them to feel 'a sense of worry' with resulting implications for their teaching in the form of 'misconceptions and strategic planning issues'. They felt this prevented them from delivering the 'best possible tailored teaching for students'.

Other barriers related more specifically to teachers having accurate knowledge about specific issues and relevant effective strategies, as Author A, a piano teacher, noted in teaching a student with dyspraxia[1]:

> The first barrier was my own lack of knowledge about dyspraxia itself, which meant that I used the same teaching strategies I had always used with all students except I found they were not working with this student. The second barrier was a lack of knowledge about effective learning environments, materials, strategies and approaches for this specific student.

Presumptions about students' physical limitations when learning an instrument in addition to a lack of training led Author B to describe how they adopted a 'trial and error approach in conjunction with students to establish what worked best for them'. This raises the question of which type and amount of information should be shared with the instrumental music teacher for them to be able to provide relevant support to the student. It also raises the important point of considering how disclosure might be shared in a way that minimizes stigma for the student. The authors recognize that a lack of information from schools or parents might stem from an oversight or may be driven by fears of stigma or safeguarding breaches.[2] However, without sufficient information being communicated to the music teacher, teachers have found it challenging to provide individually tailored lessons for the specific student (Lindner and Schwab 2020).

In the following narrative, Author C described how a lack of communication affected their understanding of student and parental expectations for lessons:

> As the school organized the lessons, I had no direct contact with the parents. My misconceptions were that the parents and school expected me to deliver lessons in a way that got this child playing this instrument and reading music because that was my understanding of my primary role as a tutor. The school and parents' misconceptions were that I would understand the complexities of the child's special needs on first meeting and respond appropriately without specialist training.

This suggests that teachers need to be made aware not only of the disability but should also be entitled to have access to information regarding the student's usual ways of working in the classroom and specific areas of sensitivity and needs. Although not all general classroom information will overlap with music lesson contexts, it may prove to be a guide or even a starting point for the music teacher in their understanding of the student and the choices they make about repertoire and curricula, thus enabling a more individualized approach. Through discussions around a lack of training in relation to this within our own practice, however, the authors highlight a need for more systematic training.

Misconceptions

Misconceptions in the area of disability relate to both teachers' perceptions of students' capabilities and the strategies that might be applied in given situations. Author D described how this impacts both student and teacher:

> Misconceptions about disabilities (for example, deafness) are often very reductionist views rather than understanding the spectra and individual nature of disabilities ... The more these misconceptions persist, the more they become solidified as seeming 'truths' (for example, many D/deaf[3] people 'think' they can't do music) making it harder to make changes to presumptions and creating a negative feedback loop. Education is key for challenging presumptions and making this change.

This links to the need for greater awareness of accessible learning environments, materials and strategies and, most importantly, what works well from the student's perspective. This also highlights the complexity of co-occurring conditions and the spectrum nature of disability with implications and challenges for music teachers as a result. As an example, there is a high co-occurrence of attention, coordination and other sensory processing difficulties with dyslexia, which may have a bearing on the student's ability to concentrate and sustain motivation (Brimo et al. 2021). The spectrum across which many disabilities occur means that teachers must be careful to avoid not only preconceived ideas about the disability but also preconceived ideas about what the student is hearing, seeing or experiencing when learning music.

The misapplication of strategies may have potential consequences for students. For example, misconceptions surrounding visual stress in dyslexia are widespread. However, offering coloured overlays as a blanket solution may mask other serious visual issues which can only be diagnosed by specialists (Gilchrist, Holden and Warren 2018). Author C acknowledged a mixture of emotions when they observed two students' reactions to misapplied strategies:

> I soon realized that it was much more complicated for both students as their specific learning needs were so entwined with their teenage angst and their education in general. They were so aware of it as a difference that made them stand out in a way they didn't want to. I felt sad and under-informed that I had possibly contributed to their self-doubt by using over-simplistic methods in a space that should have felt separate from their general education (and labelled) environment.

Student responses to teaching can be complex, and it may be challenging to interpret them accurately and to identify the root causes or underlying needs.

Inclusive and Accessible Approaches

The previous sections provide evidence of a need for high-quality and inclusive pedagogical training for music teachers, which accurately informs teachers about disabilities, how students' music learning may be affected and effective strategies. The following sections discuss a number of inclusive and accessible approaches across the domains of inclusive teaching practice (Finkelstein, Sharma and Furlonger 2019: 748) as well as the potential development of the role of music hubs in offering continuing professional development (CPD) to inform and educate instrumental music teachers with up-to-date, relevant information.

Collaboration and Teamwork

The authors recognize that a number of factors may be outside of teacher control, including disclosure and the institutional learning environment; however, they agree that there is a need for greater openness in communication between the instrumental music teacher, parents and schools. The first domain of inclusive practice is 'collaboration and teamwork' (Finkelstein, Sharma and Furlonger 2019), and this refers to how teachers engage with other stakeholders in the educational process. This engagement and communication may provide reassurance to parents as well as confirm that their experiences are valuable and insightful for the teacher. As suggested earlier, instrumental music teachers may learn from other teachers in the school setting about how to support a student, but they may also offer insights of value to their non-music teacher colleagues by adopting a more collaborative and synergistic approach.

An example of this may be highlighting to the school leadership team and community the benefits to students from having a more unified approach in which the music teacher is also seen as a member of the team. We suggest that for all students (regardless of disclosed disabilities or learning needs), it can be useful for teachers to establish dialogue with schools and parents at the commencement of instrumental lessons; for example, asking if there is anything the instrumental teacher should be aware of (whether formally diagnosed or not) and then having ongoing conversations to ensure communication of the student's progress, needs and any changes within relevant aspects, such as institutional support.

Determining Progress

Planning lessons and assessing progress for a diverse range of students may be challenging for teachers; however, the use of a framework may assist teachers with this process and could also enable the development of a flexible student profile. The Sounds of Intent framework (Welch et al. 2009) consists of incremental measures of music development and is particularly suited to teaching students who have profound and multiple learning difficulties (PMLD). From a broader perspective, the Universal Design for Learning framework (CAST 2018) encourages teachers to consider:

1. 'How learners will engage with the lesson',
2. 'How the information is presented to learners',
3. 'How learners are expected to act strategically and express themselves.'

The principles of UDL are designed to encourage student goal-setting and self-reflection in the learning process. In addition, this may be useful for a teacher as a means to support the development of students' metacognitive skills and the importance of delivering feedback to students in a timely and sensitive manner. This framework also encourages the teacher to think and act as a reflective practitioner in order to identify positive areas of teaching as well as areas for change in a reflective cycle of ongoing development (Gibbs 1988).

Instructional Support

The second domain of inclusive practice refers to 'instructional support'. Existing pedagogy on general instrumental learning highlights the benefits of a student-centred approach in building student engagement and autonomy (Hallam, Cross and Thaut 2009; McPherson, Davidson and Faulkner 2012). The use of a student-centred approach also has implications when teaching students with additional learning needs or disabilities and can involve collaborating with students to develop techniques and strategies which work for them. As Author A reported:

> For me, personalized teaching begins by observing and working with the student to find their own ways of learning. Following on from this, I try to observe the dyslexic student's responsiveness to strategies, identify the barriers that interfere with their learning and encourage their learning potential when those barriers are removed, drawing on principles from Universal Design for Learning. (CAST 2018)

Author C described how 'developing personalized strategies' helped them 'to learn and reflect on what my role as a tutor is and can be', suggesting that this enabled them to feel empowered to collaborate with and advocate for the student. Specific strategies were reported by Author B involving collaboration with deaf or physically disabled students to remove learning barriers:

> [I began by] working with students to develop techniques and strategies which work for them (for example, using physical markers for tuning, when the pupil was struggling to hear differences between pitches). Similarly, for students with physical disabilities, working alongside them, using questioning and exploration of alternative techniques to find setups which work well from both physical comfort and technical perspectives.

Adaptations to instruction may include the time given to complete tasks, difficulty and participation level, expectations in terms of student outcomes, instruments and the teaching environment, according to Darrow and Adamek (2018). Adaptations to music notation or concepts could be considered, as well as differentiated formats for practice guidance and reminders. As some examples, practice reminders for dyslexic students might be best presented in ways that avoid lengthy text, such as audio-recorded notes or brief notes on a shared WhatsApp chat with the student's parents. For a blind student, the optimal presentation of music may be aurally or through the use of a braille score. While instruments may be adapted for physically disabled students, the authors recognize the tensions which might arise from desiring access for all students versus the ableist organology of most musical instruments, which may contribute to a sense of alienation or 'otherness' for disabled students.

The importance of using multisensory instructional strategies is also highlighted by the authors: music is a multimodal activity, and we learn aurally, visually, kinesthetically and socially. Strategies (e.g. embodied strategies and visual strategies) can be used in enhancing music education (for all learners). Embodied movements, such as those advocated by the Dalcroze approach, may help students to internalize aspects of the music and to connect themselves to the music in a holistic way through movement (Sutela, Juntunen and Ojala 2016). Teachers might address issues of cognitive load[4] by connecting smaller concepts to a wider framework and then breaking them down into smaller chunks to help students learn them. By providing students with scaffolded support, the teacher may be able to provide guidance and reassurance until the student is able to learn independently.

Organizational Support

Forms of organizational support which promote inclusive teaching include an awareness of appropriate and accessible learning environments. This includes considering how the student responds to transitions between activities and how lesson routines are established. As Author D related:

> With Deaf learners, specifically, it is important to be Deaf aware and consider communication issues including communicating clearly, setting the room up effectively, ensuring the listening conditions are optimal; but these things are good practice anyway.

Organizational support in the form of technology may include recording lessons, listening to recordings of music and making short recordings for the student to consult during the week. Other applications used by the authors of this chapter include those which develop specific skills such as rhythm and note-reading, aural training, music theory and composing software. This appeals to students who are motivated by games and technology, as well as encouraging autonomous decision-making in their learning.

Social, Emotional and Behavioural Learning Support

The following narrative describes the importance of accurate information to support Author C's ability to recognize the underlying nature or causes of behavioural issues in students:

> Another example is that of students who have not had a Statement of Special Educational Needs,[5] or are in the process of obtaining one. The misconceptions from the school are that they are 'naughty' or 'difficult' children and that their difficulties are primarily social because of their overt behavioural problems … so I began under the impression that [the pupil's] learning issues were summed up as behavioural. Through lessons, it soon became apparent that there could be special educational needs which were being masked by the difficult social behaviour.

If the student feels that information related to their identity is shameful or needs to be kept hidden, it may impact their identity and self-concept, affecting their willingness to be open with the teacher. The result may be a lack of motivation due to what Maier and Seligman (2016) refer to as 'learned helplessness', or passive reactions to repeated failure. Students who feel that a poor outcome is inevitable may disrupt the learning environment from sheer frustration at their challenges or embarrassment from a perception of not being able to keep pace with peers (Raufelder and Kulakow 2022).

Research has identified the risk of 'internalizing' and 'externalizing' behaviours in dyslexic children when they are faced with negative educational environments, suggesting that they may experience anxiety and feelings of aggression (Wilmot et al. 2023: 2). Similarly, challenges arising in connection with language and communication may correlate to behavioural and attention problems in deaf children, although these issues are by no means exclusive to deaf children (Barker et al. 2009). In a study of autistic children and adolescents, 'social camouflaging' behaviours were identified, including hiding signs of autism and attempting to fit in with others despite this being uncomfortable and exhausting for the autistic individual; the sense of needing to hide their authentic 'self' in the educational environment may lead to poor mental health outcomes for these students as a consequence (Ross, Grove and McAloon 2023). This further highlights the need for greater knowledge about specific disabilities to avoid misconceptions in teacher perceptions, which may contribute to negative spirals in learning.

Promoting students' positive behaviour begins with identifying and reminding students of their strengths, praising effort in the process of learning and reinforcing their belief in what they are capable of achieving (Patston and Waters 2015). Some students are not accustomed to hearing praise in learning environments, as Author A noted:

> Following praise for sight-reading efforts and progress in coordination skills, I noticed that the student downplayed what they had achieved. This signified to me how deeply-rooted their lack of confidence was and I felt sad that they did not recognize the importance of their strengths.

Drawing on Fredrickson's (2001) broaden-and-build theory of positive emotions, a shift from a deficit-focused to a strengths-focused approach has the potential to facilitate students' resilience despite their challenges and may give students an openness to new ideas and a greater sense of agency in the learning process. This may also contribute to the development of greater empathy and awareness on the teacher's part, as they recognize implications for students' motivation and self-belief; this, in turn, may play a part in putting the student on the pathway to a more positive learning journey.

Conclusion

Although the UK's National Plan for Music Education (Department for Education 2022) has established a commitment to inclusive education, the authors of this chapter recognize the need for more systematic training for music teachers in this area. Music hubs (regional structures in England for supporting the aims of the National Plan for Music Education), along with other specialist organizations such as those listed below, may play an important role in providing continuing professional development to better equip teachers to teach students with disabilities. Research indicates that by providing training opportunities in the area of special needs, teachers may have a greater sense of confidence in their ability to create adaptations for a wider range of students with additional needs (VanWheelden and Whipple 2005). By recognizing that all students can engage with music, inclusive teaching practices offer the student the 'chance to experience the joys of the subject and to progress in their learning of it' (Department for Education 2022: 42).

Notes

1. Also referred to as developmental coordination disorder, dyspraxia may affect coordination, balance and motor control.
2. See also Chapters 5 and 6 for further considerations of safeguarding.
3. The National Deaf Children's Society describes the use of 'Deaf' as referring to someone who sees themselves as part of the deaf community and who is likely to use sign language, while 'deaf' refers to the experience of hearing loss. https://www.ndcs.org.uk/information-and-support/glossary/glossary-d/.
4. Cognitive load is the amount of information a student may be able to process before they become overloaded.
5. A document stating the student's special educational needs, the support that should be provided and the type of 'educational setting they should attend' (EA Special Educational Needs 2024).

Further Resources and Information

Dyslexic Students:

British Dyslexia Association (2020), 'Music and Dyslexia'. Available online: https://cdn.bdadyslexia.org.uk/uploads/documents/000-BOOKLET-Dyslexia-music.pdf?v=1614338349 (accessed 23 August 2024).

D/deaf Students:

Holmes, J. A. (2017), 'Expert Listening beyond the Limits of Hearing: Music and Deafness', *Journal of the American Musicological Society*, 70 (1): 171–220.

Mason, K., T. Pozzo and P. Osborne (2018), 'Sounding Out: A Toolkit for Music Practitioners Working with Deaf Students', *Creative Futures*. Available online: https://www.creativefuturesuk.com/sounding-out-toolkit (accessed 23 August 2024).

National Centre for Early Music, 'I Can Download & Play'. Available online: https://ncem.co.uk/icanplay/ (accessed 23 August 2024).

National Deaf Children's Society (2024), 'Deaf-Friendly Music Teaching'. Available online: https://www.ndcs.org.uk/information-and-support/professionals/activities/music/ (accessed 23 August 2024).

SoundLINCS (2018), 'Good Vibrations Toolkit: Inclusive Approaches for Making Music with Deaf and Hearing Impaired Children and Young People'. Available online: https://www.soundlincs.org/_files/ugd/7e97c8_fcd16c9862fc4dd195b3a128597c91f5.pdf (accessed 23 August 2024).

Blind or Visually-Impaired Students:

The Amber Trust (2024), 'Amber Sound Touch: The Amber Trust's Online Resource for Teaching Music to Blind Children'. Available online: https://soundtouch.ambertrust.org/ (accessed 23 August 2024).

Autism Spectrum Students:

Hammel, A. M., and R. M. Hourigan (2020), *Teaching Music to Students with Autism*, New York: Oxford University Press.

Hourigan, R., and A. Hourigan (2009), 'Teaching Music to Children with Autism: Understandings and Perspectives', *Music Educators Journal*, 96 (1): 40–5.

Shaughnessy, C. (2022), 'Tuning In: Autism', Available online: https://www.tuninginautism.com/ (accessed 23 August 2024).

Neurodivergent Students:

Musicians' Union (2023), 'Neuro-Inclusive Music Teaching: How to Teach Music to Neurodivergent Students'. Available online: https://musiciansunion.org.uk/working-performing/education-and-teaching/career-development-as-a-teacher-en/neuro-inclusive-music-teaching (accessed 23 August 2024).

Disabled and Additional Support Needs:

Drake Music Scotland (2024), 'The Difference We Make'. Available online: https://drakemusicscotland.org/ (accessed 23 August 2024).

Complex Needs:

Sounds of Intent (2024), 'Sounds of Intent: An Inclusive Framework of Musical Engagement'. Available online: https://soundsofintent.org/en/home/index (accessed 23 August 2024).

References

Barker, D. H., A. L. Quittner, N. E. Fink, L. S. Eisenberg, E. A. Tobey and J. K. Niparko (2009), 'Predicting Behavior Problems in Deaf and Hearing Children: The Influences of Language, Attention, and Parent-Child Communication', *Development and Psychopathology*, 21 (2): 373–92.

Brimo, K., L. Dinkler, C. Gillberg, P. Lichtenstein, S. Lundström and J. Åsberg Johnels (2021), 'The Co-Occurrence of Neurodevelopmental Problems in Dyslexia', *Dyslexia: An International Journal of Research and Practice*, 27 (3): 277–93.

CAST (Center for Applied Special Technology) (2018), 'Universal Design for Learning Guidelines version 2.2' [Graphic Organizer]. Available online: https://udlguidelines.cast.org/static/udlg_graphicorganizer_v2-2_numbers-no.pdf (accessed 23 August 2024).

Darrow, A.-A., and M. Adamek (2018), 'Instructional Strategies for the Inclusive Music Classroom', *General Music Today*, 31 (3): 61–5.

Department for Education (2022), 'The Power of Music to Change Lives: A National Plan for Music Education'. Available online: https://assets.publishing.service.gov.uk/government/uploads/system/uploads/attachment_data/file/1086619/The_Power_of_Music_to_Change_Lives.pdf (accessed 13 August 2024).

Dobbs, T. (2017), 'Equity in Music Education: Being Schooled on Disability', *Music Educators Journal*, 104 (2): 51–3.

EA Special Educational Needs (2024), 'Statement of Special Educational Needs'. Available online: https://send.eani.org.uk/statutory-assessment/statement-sen (accessed 27 August 2024).

Fautley, M., and A. Whittaker (2018), 'Key Data on Music Education Hubs 2018'. Available online: https://www.artscouncil.org.uk/sites/default/files/download-file/Music%20Education%20Hubs%2C%20Key%20Data%20-%202018.pdf (accessed 13 August 2024).

Finkelstein, S., U. Sharma and B. Furlonger (2019), 'The Inclusive Practices of Classroom Teachers: A Scoping Review and Thematic Analysis', *International Journal of Inclusive Education*, 25 (6): 735–62.

Fredrickson, B. L. (2001), 'The Role of Positive Emotions in Positive Psychology: The Broaden-and-Build Theory of Positive Emotions', *American Psychologist*, 56 (3): 218–26.

Gibbs, G. (1988), *Learning by Doing: A Guide to Teaching and Learning Methods*, Oxford: Oxford Polytechnic.

Gilchrist, J., C. Holden and J. Warren (2018), 'Specific Learning Difficulties (SpLDs) and Visual Difficulties: A Guide for Assessors and SpLD Practitioners'. Available online: https://sasc.org.uk/media/fmpassi3/splds-and-visual-difficulties guidance-for-spld-practitioners-june-2018.pdf (Accessed 13 August 2024).

Hall, S. A. (2024), Who Is Lucy from The Piano? Blind and Neurodivergent Young Pianist Has a New Documentary', *ClassicFM*. Available online: https://www.

classicfm.com/discover-music/lucy-illingworth-blind-neurodivergent-the-piano/ (accessed 13 August 2024).

Hallam, S., I. Cross and M. Thaut, eds (2009), *The Oxford Handbook of Music Psychology*, Oxford: Oxford University Press.

Henley, J., and D. Barton (2022), 'Time for Change? Recurrent Barriers to Music Education', *British Journal of Music Education*, 39 (2): 203–17. doi:10.1017/S026505172200016X.

Jonze, T. (2023), '"My Life Is Beautiful": Felix Klieser, Who Plays the Horn with His Toes, on Making His Proms Debut', *The Guardian*. Available online: https://www.theguardian.com/music/2023/jul/25/my-life-is-beautiful-felix-klieser-who-plays-the-horn-with-his-toes-on-making-his-proms-debut (accessed 13 August 2024).

Lindner, K. T., and S. Schwab (2020), 'Differentiation and Individualisation in Inclusive Education: A Systematic Review and Narrative Synthesis', *International Journal of Inclusive Education*, 1–21, https://doi.org/10.1080/13603116.2020.1813450 (accessed 14 May 2025).

Maier, S. F., and M. E. P. Seligman (2016), 'Learned Helplessness at Fifty: Insights from Neuroscience', *Psychological Review*, 123 (4): 349–67.

McPherson, G. E., J. W. Davidson and R. Faulkner (2012), *Music in Our Lives: Rethinking Musical Ability, Development and Identity*, New York: Oxford University Press.

Moon, J. A. (1999), *Reflection in Learning and Professional Development: Theory and Practice*, London: Kogan Page.

Oliver, M. (2013), 'The Social Model of Disability: Thirty Years On', *Disability & Society*, 28 (7): 1024–6.

Patston, T., and L. Waters (2015), 'Positive Instruction in Music Studios: Introducing a New Model for Teaching Studio Music in Schools Based Upon Positive Psychology', *Psychology of Well-Being*, 5 (1): 10.

Raufelder, D., and S. Kulakow (2022), 'The Role of Social Belonging and Exclusion at School and the Teacher–Student Relationship for the Development of Learned Helplessness in Adolescents', *British Journal of Educational Psychology*, 92: 59–81.

Ross, A., R. Grove and J. McAloon (2023), 'The Relationship between Camouflaging and Mental Health in Autistic Children and Adolescents', *Autism Research*, 16 (1): 190–9.

Sieber, T. (2008), *Disability Theory*, Michigan: University of Michigan Press.

Spruce, G. (2024), 'Inclusive Approaches to Instrumental Teaching and Learning: A Social Justice Perspective', in N. Beach and G. Spruce (eds), *Instrumental Music Teaching: Perspectives and Challenges*, 141–9, London: Trinity College London Press.

Sutela, K., M.-L. Juntunen and J. Ojala (2016), 'Inclusive Music Education: The Potential of the Dalcroze Approach for Students with Special Educational Needs', *Approaches: An Interdisciplinary Journal of Music Therapy*, 8 (2): 179–88.

Van Weelden, K., and J. Whipple (2005), 'The Effects of Field Experience on Music Education Majors' Perceptions of Music Instruction for Secondary Students with Special Needs', *Journal of Music Teacher Education*, 14 (2): 62–70.

Welch, G., A. Ockelford, F.-C. Carter, S.-A. Zimmerman and E. Himonides (2009), '"Sounds of Intent": Mapping Musical Behaviour and Development in Children and Young People with Complex Needs', *Psychology of Music*, 37 (3): 348–70.

Wilmot, A., P. Hasking, S. Leitão, E. Hill and M. Boyes (2023), 'Understanding Mental Health in Developmental Dyslexia: A Scoping Review', *International Journal of Environmental Research and Public Health*, 20 (2): 1653.

15

Working with Transfer Students: Teachers' Experiences of 'Bridging the Gap'

*Edwina Smith, Polly Sharpe,
Elizabeth Haddon and Eleni Perisynaki*

Introduction

Instrumental students transfer between teachers for many reasons. The original teacher may stop teaching or become unavailable, or the student might change their place of education; the student may require a teacher who can take them to a more advanced level or teach a different musical style; or the transfer may be based on personal preference, parental decisions or financial considerations.

The authors of this chapter have worked with numerous students making this transition. We have all developed strategies to support a positive transfer and continue to explore new approaches through discussion with colleagues, consulting pedagogical material by other experienced teachers (e.g. Boyle and Widdison 2021; Denenburg 2018; Harris 2008, 2014; Watkins and Scott 2012) and visiting online blogs and teaching forums, where this is clearly a topic of interest. However, apart from work by Mio (2018, 2019), there is little academic research on this subject, described by Mio and Brenner (2023: 74) as an 'underdeveloped area of musical enquiry'.

With this in mind we devised a survey to ask other instrumental teachers about their experiences of working with transfer students in a one-to-one setting.

Following ethical approval from the University of York, information (including a link to the survey and details concerning data storage, anonymity and informed consent) was emailed to potential respondents and forwarded by them to other teachers, utilizing a snowballing method (Williamon et al. 2021). Thirty-two teachers replied, with experience ranging from under five years to over fifty years, covering vocal teaching and all the main Western instrumental categories except brass. Their students ranged from children under five years to adults and included beginners to professional musicians. All respondents taught in a variety of settings and formats, including privately, in schools, for music hubs, universities and conservatoires. Many taught both face to face and online in the UK and elsewhere. Twenty-one respondents (65.6 per cent) had received formal training in instrumental teaching, but only four reported that this included content specifically related to teaching transfer students.

Areas covered by the survey included reasons for students transferring to or away from the respondent; potential positive and negative effects on students' learning experience; benefits and challenges for teachers; and strategies for approaching the first lesson or for 'bridging the gap' between current capabilities and what the teacher considered necessary to enable the student to progress. We also asked how teachers felt about students transferring away from them and (if they knew in advance) how they prepared the student for this. A final section explored respondents' personal experiences of transferring between teachers as a learner and whether these had influenced their own teaching practice. We are indebted to the respondents for their generosity in giving considerable time and thought to the survey. Their responses, analysed thematically, have created a rich resource of experience and advice, which we share and discuss in this chapter.

Benefits of Transfer

A New Perspective

Survey responses indicated that a range of benefits might result from transferring to a new teacher. Frequently mentioned was the opportunity for experiencing a new perspective and different approach, which could 'stimulate a student's motivation and enthusiasm for learning as they experience something new and exciting' (T1)[1] and might lead them to be 'revitalised, challenged in a motivating way' (T2). A new teacher might have different priorities, encouraging the student to focus on alternative or previously neglected aspects of their playing; they might be more specialized, teach at a higher standard or simply 'unlock understanding' (T9) by 'saying similar things but in a different way' (T11).

Personal Development

Some respondents suggested that changing teacher might have a positive effect on the student's personal development and 'bring out different aspects of the student's personality' (T6), especially if their previous student-teacher relationship had 'become too comfortable', leading to a lack of progress (T17). It could also be an opportunity for 'personal growth and independence as students learn to navigate changes and adjust to new teaching dynamics' (T1). In addition, exposure to different teaching styles might encourage independent learning by 'enrich[ing] students' self-awareness in relation to what works well for them' (T5).

In some cases, a teacher with a wider range of experience might be more realistic than a previous teacher about the student's current standard and abilities. This could initially be uncomfortable for the student but, if handled with positivity and empathy, be beneficial for them in the longer term. Some students may also appreciate a new teacher who has 'no preconceived ideas' of them (T31), especially if their previous teacher had taught them since childhood. However, as one respondent observed, 'sometimes a new teacher is just a better fit for the student' (T26).

Several teachers remembered positive and beneficial transfers as students themselves: some moved from a good relationship only because the new teacher could take them to a more advanced level; others were happy to leave behind negative experiences with their previous teacher and start afresh, one even stating that a new teacher 'completely saved me ... her impact on me made me the musician and teacher I am today' (T32).

Benefits for Teachers

Many respondents noted reciprocal benefits, in particular the opportunity for their own personal and professional growth. Teachers commented on enjoying the challenge of developing new strategies to suit the transfer student, learning to adapt and be open-minded about different approaches and cultures and expanding their problem-solving skills. Teacher 2, welcoming this opportunity for continuing professional development, remarked that it encouraged them 'to refer to books [and] educational resources and therefore gain extra knowledge along the way' or to 'think "outside the box" and be extra vigilant, thinking of new ideas'. Others discovered new repertoire, teaching material or effective approaches via a student transferring to them, whether from notes in practice books or music or through discussion; as Teacher 19 commented, 'Sometimes, a student can explain an issue and technical solution in a way that I find really helpful ... The new teacher doesn't need to be threatened by the previous one – hopefully we are all building towards the same aim – the student doing better.' In a profession where isolation can be a challenge (Burwell, Carey and Bennett 2019), another teacher mentioned the 'insight into what my colleagues in the teaching profession are doing' as a particular benefit (T4).

Positive Relationships

Some teachers valued the chance 'to start a musical journey mid-way through' (T29), finding it 'exciting to plan the path ahead with a new student' (T23). Inevitably, some students transfer from a less-than-happy relationship with their previous teacher: one respondent mentioned the professional satisfaction of 'feeling like I'm making a really positive impact on a student who has been poorly taught or who has had a poor relationship with their previous teacher' (T26). Several wrote about the joy of seeing a student regain enthusiasm and motivation, one commenting that 'I have taken on so many students that have been on the brink of quitting and totally revitalized them, that I think it has become my speciality' (T32).

Challenges and Strategies

Disruption to Progress

Survey respondents frequently mentioned the challenge for students of disruption to progress during the period in which they became familiar with a change of approach or expectation after transfer. It was suggested that this might be accompanied by frustration or confusion, and perhaps a loss of confidence or motivation, as 'some students feel they have done something wrong because to them they feel as though they are "re-learning" how to play their instrument' (T7). As Teacher 10 reflected, 'If you're not careful, it can be deflating for the student if you don't handle that situation delicately and continue to praise what they're doing well' to avoid feelings of inadequacy and frustration, particularly if a previous teacher had given the student 'a false sense of achievement or allowed them to avoid scales and the "boring" elements of instrumental study' (T10).

Specific challenges could arise if a student moved from a non-specialist to a specialist on their instrument when basic techniques might have to be completely revised. Teacher 11 found it particularly helpful that their music hub had 'a resource bank of tips for non-specialist teachers' and that they could ask for advice and observe lessons to minimize the need for re-learning when a student transferred to a specialist.

The Need for Time and Empathy

Many respondents stressed the importance of patience, specific praise and encouragement; of giving transfer students time to understand and adjust; and of building trust through open dialogue, 'creating a discussion rather than a lecture'

(T20) and thus encouraging independent learning and exploration rather than demanding change without explanation. It was observed that even previously well-taught students might need time to adjust to a new teaching style, or to different standards and expectations, and that for some students, just changing to a teacher of a different gender might be initially unsettling. Conversely, a student might be initially positive about transferring but have unrealistic expectations of how quickly or easily they would make progress with the new teacher and then feel disillusioned if a magical 'quick-fix' did not transpire (T17). As Teacher 29 concluded:

> It's a very vulnerable and delicate time for a student – learning to trust someone new, feeling comfortable to make mistakes and being reciprocal to constructive criticism. It has to be handled with great care … and it is the teacher's responsibility to nurture and encourage during this time so that a student feels safe to explore their musical self and creativity.

Reflecting on challenges experienced when transferring as a student themselves, many respondents empathized with their own new students and adjusted their approach accordingly, although several now saw their earlier difficulties in perspective, recognizing that the initial challenges led to longer-term benefits. One remembered how, after a transfer, they had initially 'cried every lesson through frustration, hard work and desire to be better' (T32), while another described the move to a pre-conservatoire teacher as 'the hardest, most meaningful, and impactful learning experience of my entire life' (T5).

Emotional Attachment

Many teachers stressed the importance of recognizing possible emotional attachment issues and showing respect for the student's previous experiences. Children, in particular, might miss the 'familiarity and comfort of their previous teacher-student relationship' (T1), and the new teacher might feel challenged to 'live up to a previous much-loved teacher' (T18). Any student who had developed a positive rapport with a teacher might find it 'difficult to accept that this can happen again' (T8) or 'have to learn to negotiate a new and potentially different "unspoken contract" between teacher and student' (T3).

It was also suggested that some students might experience anxiety 'in case there is animosity between old and new teacher' (T5) or perhaps feel a sense of disloyalty if they had personally chosen to make the transfer or if they questioned what they had previously been taught. Above all, it was repeatedly stressed that the new teacher should never criticize previous teachers, 'both for the credibility of the [teaching profession] and for students' learning, to avoid confusion' (T5). However, it was observed that this could be particularly difficult if students still had occasional lessons with a previous teacher: one respondent stated that they were careful to check that students 'have extricated themselves from the previous commitment before they sign up for lessons with me' (T17).

Early Lesson Strategies

Most teachers felt that in early lessons after the transfer, it was necessary to identify areas for improvement, and possibly gaps in knowledge and technique, through discussion. Several recommended forward planning, in consultation with the student (and parents if applicable), to establish achievable goals that could help maintain motivation, although it was stressed by Teacher 23 that 'the explanation and the plan [need] to make the student feel valued and assured so that they can take a risk and change something, or step out of their comfort zone in order to develop'. Opinion was divided, however, on the value of making areas for improvement clear to the student immediately, some teachers preferring to be initially less direct and to work more subtly to address these. In either case, though, adaptability and understanding of the individual student's needs were recognized as vital; as Teacher 9 observed, deciding on the appropriate approach 'is a judgement call. Not challenging [a] student enough is [as] much a problem as challenging them too much.'

In the first lesson, most teachers encouraged new students to feel comfortable by asking them to play a piece they particularly enjoyed. In addition, one teacher suggested they 'might gently stretch [the student] with scales and arpeggios of increasing difficulty to find where their ceiling is' (T4); another commented that 'for musicianship skills I like to play pulse, rhythm, and scales games which show their current level of understanding (not to criticize but to find out where to build from)' (T6); a third said they 'positively explain what is working well and how I feel I can help' (T32). In later lessons, some teachers suggested moving sideways to different material of a similar, or perhaps easier, standard, or to 'work on missing skills via games and discovery' (T2), in order to pre-empt feelings of frustration or demotivation caused by struggling with new concepts in the context of previously learned, possibly over-demanding, material. Several teachers also assessed their new students' abilities by giving them repertoire to learn independently, which sometimes prompted discussion encouraging students to identify for themselves particular areas for improvement.

It was, however, considered important to be honest: one vocal teacher felt that when major changes were necessary, it was 'normally best to be very clear about this, after trust is established' rather than the student trying to 'apply new teaching to poor singing' (T9). Another respondent suggested that occasionally 'a new teacher might have to offer some home truths that perhaps that pupil is not quite the right standard for a specific grade yet' (T32), while a third stressed that sometimes a direct conversation was necessary to emphasize the importance of changing technique immediately to avoid developing major physical problems (T10).

Although several respondents had experienced a complete 'back-to-basics' approach when students themselves, some teachers felt this might be psychologically damaging, and only one (vocal) teacher recommended it in order to 'rebuild the voice from the ground up', adding that this would be accompanied by frequent reference to challenges the student had identified, and how working together on particular strategies could help resolve these (T20).

All challenges for both teacher and student were magnified if combined with exam pressure, especially when, as described by Teacher 24, the student had 'already been entered for an exam that I wouldn't have entered them for. I responded by having an open and honest discussion about expectations, time constraints, and lesson content before and after the exam.'

Initial Confusion or Resistance to Change

Several teachers suggested that initial confusion could arise from something as simple as 'using different language to explain technique' (T17) or when 'apparently contradictory information or ideas are confronted' (T9). Even if ultimately beneficial, careful handling of the immediate situation might be necessary to avoid conflict. It was observed that initial challenges could be mutual if a student resisted change, especially if they had not independently chosen to transfer. Strategies suggested by one teacher in this situation included reassurance about the value of work done with previous teachers combined with adaptation of their methods and resources 'whilst continuing to build on this with new, creative ideas' (T24). Another valued this approach as a way for students to 'experience a sense of "continuum"', based on their personal experience of transferring to a teacher who 'further enriched my background with her insights and never tried to undermine the work I did with my old teacher but tried to build on that' (T5).

Resistance to change might also come from students and parents if moving 'from a teacher who is extremely exam focused … without a holistic approach' (T26) to one who takes a longer-term view of development, a situation requiring the new teacher to have 'flexibility, adaptability, and commitment to fostering regular and open communication with students and parents' (T1). However, it was acknowledged by many respondents that in every transfer situation adaptability has to come from both sides. Even if convinced of the effectiveness of certain teaching strategies, it was vital to 'teach the student you have, rather than to any "method" as one size never fits all' (T25) and to develop the ability 'to acknowledge and validate that they do feel certain things about their playing (even if I disagree)' (T6). Teacher 10 described how their approach had changed with experience: previously they had explained, demonstrated, 'then simply insist[ed] they do it "correctly", i.e. my way'; now they treat resistance to change more empathetically, considering potential physical discomfort and neurodiversity issues, alternative approaches to explanation or ways of amalgamating the previous teacher's method with their own.

One respondent referred to their own unhappy childhood experience of transferring to a new teacher with a very different approach that was not explained or discussed and which 'impacted my practising enthusiasm and slowed the pace of my progress' (T1). After their parents noticed, they returned to the previous teacher, although in hindsight recognizing that they might have benefited by persevering with the new teacher. The concept of having the right teacher at the right time was highlighted by several respondents, one commenting that their transfer at postgraduate level was 'probably only suitable because I was old enough' (T6).

Transfer between Different Music Education Cultures

It was observed by many respondents that initial challenges for both teacher and student may be greater when the student transfers from a different music education culture, especially between one that values imitation and preservation of a traditional master-apprentice approach and one that encourages exploration and independence of thought. Whichever way the transfer is made, this could lead to discomfort as the student faces different expectations of personal responsibility, and possibly to feelings of unexpected inadequacy, especially if the longer-term benefits are not explained and too much is demanded of the student in the transition period. Teacher 4 recalled a transfer student who had 'learnt by rote to about Grade 5 level' without reading music. When asked by their school to play in a prestigious concert, they were unable to learn the music in time, and the opportunity was withdrawn, with 'devastating effects to the student's self-esteem'. Other teachers referred to 'students who have been taught "parrot fashion", playing hugely complex music at a young age with very little understanding or technical fluency' (T26) and those who 'see the difficulty of the piece as the definition of their standard' (T6). In this case it was suggested that 'to preserve their psychology you can give them challenging material … alongside more manageable material where there is space to work on various generic skills' (T6). Also mentioned were students who had not previously been 'taught to think about their playing or to question what they do … I do my utmost to give them permission to question and think by asking them questions and getting them to ask me too' (T25).

The survey responses frequently demonstrated teachers' resourcefulness and willingness to meet transfer students halfway or to find common ground. Several teachers had taught children who spoke no English when they first transferred, which one considered 'an interesting challenge but not a problem' (T13) while another had made use of increased demonstration, facial expression and praise (T32). Many teachers had responded flexibly by using both sol-fa and note names, or American and English rhythm terminology, in parallel. Some went much further: a clarinet teacher learnt fingerings for the German system clarinet to support a student who had moved from Germany (T11); another learnt music braille notation after a blind student transferred to them, commenting that 'I let them take the lead with this as they were far more expert … they relished demonstrating their knowledge and this made us both feel more comfortable' (T23); a third, with a student struggling to read notation rather than relying on imitation (after transfer from the Suzuki method), 'responded by researching and observing Suzuki techniques and adopting a multi-sensory approach to learning' (T24).

Longer-Term Challenges

Longer-term challenges may arise if the new teacher is less knowledgeable or thorough than the old teacher or if their approach is actually damaging. Several teachers had experienced this themselves as students: one bravely asked to change from their allocated teacher at conservatoire, as 'I knew that I needed more technical input to progress' (T17), adding that they now encourage their own students to talk confidently to new teachers about their progress. Unfortunately, one respondent's attempts to do this as a student were unsuccessful: 'Despite voicing my frustration, concerns and struggles … they were not validated, addressed or resolved' (T20). Another transferred to a recommended vocal coach who 'did a lot of damage, mentally and physically, by suggesting incorrect repertoire' (T27). Teacher 26 vividly remembered moving from childhood teachers who 'set me up for a love of music which has lasted a lifetime' to university teachers who were 'downright horrible' including one who 'completely broke my heart and my self-belief'. However, determined that something beneficial should emerge from such negativity, they stated: 'I want to make students feel good about the positive things they achieve … I don't want my students to feel as poorly about themselves as I have been made to feel', a purpose echoed by Teacher 32, who had 'become a string teacher as a way of undoing all the wrongs in my own learning and making sure each pupil I have under my care never has the same experience I had'.

Transfer Away from the Teacher

Respondents' experiences of students transferring away from them varied, although most agreed that a lack of communication was discourteous and that they understood and empathized more if consulted by students or parents in advance. Many felt sad at the time of transfer, but those who received clear communication, or for whom the change came at a time of natural progression for the student, seemed to find the transfer easier. Negative emotions were exacerbated if the teacher 'felt some poaching had occurred' (T21), if students gave up soon after leaving or when parents initiated a transfer to a teacher who was willing to enter the student for exams the respondent considered inappropriate (T26).

Several teachers, recognizing their own limitations, themselves suggested transfers at a certain point, aware from experience that 'different teachers suit different people' (T19). Many emphasized the importance of focusing on the student's best interests and that older students in particular 'must be free to make their own decisions and judgements … and all courtesy and care extended in making the transfer as happy an experience as possible' (T9).

If aware in advance, several respondents endeavoured to investigate potential new teachers' approaches: Teacher 4, whose own transfer experience as a student was 'devastating', looked for new teachers who would 'encourage and nurture' their students. Many prepared for the change through discussion with both the student and the new teacher, and some mentioned providing notes on students' progress for the next teacher. Other strategies included '[preparing] particular pieces to play in the first lesson' (T18); making the student aware that 'different teachers use different language' (T17); 'a fun, last lesson and a conversation about keeping in mind their aims and ambitions to pass on to their next teacher' (T2); or simply 'speaking positively of the change and the new teacher' (T16).

Implications for Practice and Suggestions for Further Research

We initially expected that responses to our survey would focus primarily on the practicalities of managing the transfer of students between teachers by considering the benefits, the challenges involved and effective strategies in responding to them. However, responses also revealed the range and depth of feelings experienced by both students and teachers, how this might affect the process of transfer and, for teachers, how their understanding of transfer may develop during their career.

The wide range of emotions described demonstrates how influential the teaching relationship can be in areas such as personal development, confidence and enjoyment, as well as in more practical areas of instrumental or vocal proficiency. However, potentially difficult feelings such as sadness and frustration felt during the transfer process were not exclusively negative. Sometimes discomfort seemed to be transformative, leading to personal growth for student and teacher and in some cases inspiring the respondent's own future work. This propels reflection on how much our own experiences of transfer affect the ways that we handle it in our teaching, and suggests that it could be helpful for us to interrogate these experiences. Focus on an area that caused us significant personal distress, for example, could inform the way we support our students but also has the potential to distract us from exploring other relevant areas. In addition, it raises the question of whether we might be less aware of potential issues if our own experiences of transfer have been positive and well-managed.

Teachers who have experienced more students transferring to and away from them may find it easier to be pragmatic about transfer, including being able to recognize that a student might thrive more with another teacher at a particular point. Awareness of this could help a less experienced teacher who might otherwise doubt themselves. Seeing transfer as a normal, regular occurrence might also allow teachers to enjoy more reciprocal benefits such as the opportunity to explore different strategies they observe from other teachers, and to reflect on why they consider something to be a priority if a previous teacher did not. Many survey respondents clearly regarded challenges as a spur to continued professional development, leading to enrichment of their teaching.

Communication seemed to be universally helpful between all parties in the transfer process. This enabled the sharing of practical information about what had happened pre-changeover and allowed individuals to discuss their aims and thoughts about progress. Normalizing communication about transfer could increase the benefits to both students and teachers by sharing approaches and ideas.

When invited to comment further, many survey respondents expressed a keen interest in this research, one mentioning the lack of 'concrete support out there for those preparing to receive or hand over students' (T7). Another highlighted the challenge posed by instrumental tuition being an unregulated profession with no prerequisites for becoming a teacher, observing that 'I see too many transfer students who have wasted lots of time and money receiving poor guidance' (T26), a statement supported by the experiences of several respondents quoted earlier. In addition, a number of areas for future research were suggested, including the experience of teaching transfer students with additional needs and consideration of whether it is beneficial or healthy for a student to stay with one teacher for a long time and *not* transfer. Two respondents suggested looking further at situations where a student transfers from, and then returns to, their original teacher. This could be through student choice, because of planned absence by the original teacher, due to attendance at masterclasses and summer schools (Mio and Brenner 2023) or having multiple teachers concurrently (Haddon 2011).

This chapter has focused on teachers' experiences of transfer and has relied on their personal reflection for the students' point of view. It would now be valuable to undertake a complementary study of current students' experiences of transfer. This would serve not only to expand teachers' understanding but also, in encouraging students to reflect on their personal experience, give them greater insight if they become teachers themselves.

Notes

1. Survey responses were anonymous. A teacher (T) number has been allocated to each respondent.

References

Boyle, K., and D. Widdison (2021), *The Essential Handbook for Musicians Who Teach: A Practical Guide for Instrumental and Singing Teachers*, London: Faber Music.

Burwell, K., G. Carey and D. Bennett (2019), 'Isolation in Studio Music Teaching: The Secret Garden', *Arts and Humanities in Higher Education*, 18 (4): 372–94.

Denenburg, M. (2018), 'A Fresh Look into the Transfer Student Process', *American Music Teacher*, 67 (6): 18–21.

Haddon, E. (2011), 'Multiple Teachers: Multiple Gains?', *British Journal of Music Education*, 28 (1): 69–85.

Harris, P. (2008), *Improve Your Teaching! Teaching Beginners: A New Approach for Instrumental and Singing Teachers*, London: Faber Music.

Harris, P. (2014), *Simultaneous Learning: The Definitive Guide*, London: Faber Music.

Mio, V. (2018), 'An Investigation of Postsecondary Violin Instructors' Remedial Pedagogy: A Case Study', *International Journal of Music Education*, 36 (2): 297–308.

Mio, V. (2019), 'The Need for Remedial Pedagogy in Undergraduate Violin Instruction: A Case Study of Postsecondary Instructors' Perceptions', *Update: Applications of Research in Music Education*, 37 (3): 36–45.

Mio, V., and B. Brenner (2023), '"Unlearning and Relearning": Adolescent Students' Perspectives on Transitioning to a New Teacher and Environment', *Update: Applications of Research in Music Education*, 42 (1): 72–80.

Watkins, C., and L. Scott (2012), *From the Stage to the Studio: How Fine Musicians Become Great Teachers*, New York: Oxford University Press.

Williamon, A., J. Ginsborg, R. Perkins and G. Waddell (2021), *Performing Music Research*, Oxford: Oxford University Press.

16

Examining a Tradition: Teachers' Views on the Content, Accessibility and Use of Graded Performance Examinations

Caroline Owen, Rosemary Lynch, Kristl Kirk and Helen Madden

Introduction

Graded music performance examinations have long been valued in many countries, and UK exam boards offer qualifications across the globe. However, in the UK, the number of candidates entering exams of the Associated Board of the Royal Schools of Music (ABRSM), Trinity College London and Rockschool has decreased year on year since 2012, mirroring declining numbers of pupils studying music as a curriculum subject in UK state schools (Daubney, Spruce and Annetts 2019). In recent years, the authors of this chapter have perceived changes in their pupils' attitudes towards graded exams. To investigate whether such changes are part of a widespread trend, UK instrumental teachers were asked about their motivations for using graded music exams; their views on examination requirements, repertoire, marking and accessibility; possible implications of examination-led teaching and alternatives to examinations for motivating focused practice. Beginning with a brief history of music performance examinations in the UK, we consider the appeal, advantages and potential limitations of the options currently available to exam candidates with reference to relevant literature, as well as the views of teachers and their pupils.

The Music Performance Exam Tradition: History and Evolution

Graded music examinations were introduced in the United Kingdom by Trinity College of Music (1886), London College of Music (1887), the Associated Board of the Royal Schools of Music (1889) and the Guildhall School of Music and Drama (1912) (Salaman 1994). Originally conceived to assess conservatoire applicants' playing, these exams have become a marker of progress in instrumental playing and singing for learners of all ages, and examination syllabi provide a standardized core repertoire – one which may serve as a guide for some teachers and learners and may even form an entire curriculum for others (Bath et al. 2020). Salaman (1994) asked whether the use of such examinations – originally designed for the benefit of colleges, not pupils – encourages a narrow musical education and an assessment-led curriculum. He suggested that some teachers, perhaps owing to pressure from schools or parents to offer evidence of their pupils' progress, may rely heavily on the exam syllabus to the potential detriment of their pupils' holistic musical development. Salaman proposed a more holistic approach to assessment (and by extension to teaching and learning) whereby candidates could demonstrate technical fluency through study pieces rather than scales and arpeggios and aural skills through a viva voce discussion of the exam repertoire they have performed. Additionally, aspects of musicianship traditionally not assessed in exams, such as ensemble skills, could be added.

Decades later, Barton (2020: 201) surveyed nearly five hundred private music teachers and found 'either an overreliance on exam syllabi to form the basis of curricula, or [that] teachers feel compelled to follow such syllabi due to its embeddedness in the system', aligning with a view of the examination system as rooted in historical values and therefore perpetuating tropes of a specific musical canon and concurrent elitism (Johnson-Williams 2024). Critical of the examination system as a 'hegemonic culture' and 'unsuitable and inaccessible to children learning to play musical instruments in a group learning context', Bonfield-Brown (2018: 3) called for significant changes to the way musical performance is assessed to address the needs of contemporary learners.

Recent decades have seen the emergence of new examination boards such as Rockschool (RSL) and the Music Teachers' Board (MTB), growth in the range of qualifications on offer and changes to methods of assessment. An increasing variety of optional supporting tests includes studies or orchestral extracts (Trinity College London 2025a), improvisation (Trinity College London 2022) and duets (MTB Exams 2024a) as additions or alternatives to the traditional scales, arpeggios, sight-reading and aural tests. The opportunity to demonstrate ensemble musicianship is now possible through initiatives such as the ABRSM Music Medals (ABRSM 2022) and ensemble certificates at various levels (ABRSM, 2025; Trinity College London 2025b). Some boards additionally offer qualifications based on a recital performance without supporting tests, given 'live' at an examination centre or recorded on video. The evolution of digital exams, pioneered by the Music Teachers' Board (MTB), proved timely as the outbreak of the Covid-19 pandemic in 2020 called to a halt all face-to-face musical encounters. All UK exam boards have since embraced the flexibility offered by digital examinations. Global crisis notwithstanding, the digitization of exam submission and marking and the broadening of exam curricula reflect wider societal changes, both within and outside education.

Examination boards may have adapted their offerings to some extent in response to busier lifestyles. Often, music may have to compete with other activities pursued by learners, and it may be difficult for some pupils to understand the need for time and sustained effort to progress their performance skills. This chapter's authors have encountered teachers who believe that only the traditional exam structure with scales, sight-reading and aural tests provides the 'gold standard' test of musical development, along with concern that a broader choice of supporting tests makes exams offered by some boards 'easier' to pass than others. Likewise, specific changes to exam requirements (e.g. the option to select preferred supporting tests) may be perceived as a way to attract candidates who might struggle to devote regular time to technical practice. Critics of some aspects of more recently added supporting tests include Olsen (2019), who argued that the assessment criteria for improvisation was not sufficiently defined by Trinity College London or the ABRSM. Teachers and their pupils interviewed by Olsen 'cast doubt on the ecological validity of the assessments because the improvisation tests were not perceived as assessing real-life contexts of improvisation' (Olsen 2019: 184); moreover, 'it was not clear to [Olsen's] participants what exactly was being examined' (Olsen 2019: 182).

So, what do, or what should music performance exams assess? Boyle (2021) notes that the exams originally designed by the aforementioned UK conservatoires were founded on testing the technical and musical skills those institutions sought to develop to the highest level. As such, even now, 'the attainment of advanced or master status through the development of practical skills represents the most common way in which musical understanding can be measured or assessed' (Boyle 2021: 10). Again concerning skills, the Cambridge Dictionary (2023) defines musicianship as 'a person's skill in playing a musical instrument or singing'. But what qualifies 'skill' in playing or singing, and how reliably can musicianship and technical skills be assessed? According to Williamon (2012: 61–2), 'Typical forms of music assessment seek either to determine the ranking of a performance in comparison with others (norm referenced), or how well a performance satisfies predetermined examination criteria (criterion based).' Williamon cautions, however, that while markers may think they are assessing 'musical value', the human, subjective aspects of their judgements may inevitably lead to some degree of inconsistency or 'measurement error' (2012: 65). On the other hand, if exams can only measure a musician's ability to decode a printed score, or 'correspondence to pre-given stimuli', as van der Schyff and Schiavio (2017: 12) put it, rather than their artistry or creativity, is that too narrow a view of 'musical value'?

Granted, the skills under scrutiny in traditional graded 'practical' exams are important if a learner hopes to have a good experience playing in an ensemble requiring music to be interpreted at sight. The Western tradition of preserving and conveying intended musical sounds through written notation, with its roots in ecclesiastical uniformity and governance (Bent et al. 2001), allows quick transmission of new repertoire to musicians who can decode a score. However, does the examination system promote notation-led teaching at the expense of developing the creative aspects of musicianship?[1] As Salaman (1994) noted, many of the world's most revered musicians have never learned to read notation, and 'there is little evidence to suggest that the processes of learning to read music will automatically promote musicianship. Indeed, the struggle to convert notation into sound accurately often serves as a barrier to expressive playing and singing' (213). Arguably, an exam candidate might legitimately learn repertoire by ear and perform it from memory.

Three decades on, have Salaman's concerns been addressed? What is the value placed by contemporary teachers and learners on the UK-graded music exam system? How well do the exam boards' current offerings serve learners with diverse needs? What are teachers' perceptions of the relevance of exams for those wishing to develop their musicianship and performing skills? To address these questions, we collected UK teachers' views about the wide range of options now available within the graded music performance exam system, from the variety of options within each syllabus to digital access and adaptations to accommodate specific needs, and about their own and their pupils' choices and the motivations behind these.

Research Design

In order to gain data from a potentially wide range of instrumental teachers, the authors created an online survey. Ethical approval was granted by the University of York, and the survey was promoted via email and social media and published online between July and September 2023. After providing informed consent, participants responded anonymously to open questions regarding their experience of music performance exams in the UK, their choice of exam boards and components and the motivations behind their choices, as well as their views on the importance and pedagogical relevance of exams and their perceptions of the viewpoints of pupils, their parents and schools. The authors took a deductive approach, analysing the data at the semantic level (Braun and Clarke 2006), to compare current views with those of Salaman (1994). Given significant adaptations by exam providers in recent years, no doubt accelerated by the Covid-19 pandemic, to what extent have views of and approaches to exams changed, if at all? Applying researcher reflexivity, it is acknowledged that the authors' own experiences as teachers and examiners may to some extent guide the interpretation of the data.

Participants

Fifty teachers responded: a modest sample, perhaps in part owing to the timing of the survey coinciding with the UK summer holiday period, but geographically diverse and representative of most instrumental disciplines and teaching contexts. The majority of respondents were based in southeast England, the Home Counties and northeast England. Six had additionally taught outside the UK (in Switzerland, Italy, Greece, Hong Kong and Australia).

All instrumental families except brass were represented: respondents had taught violin, viola, cello, double bass; classical, acoustic and electric guitar, bass guitar, ukulele; recorder, flute, oboe, clarinet, saxophone, bassoon; piano, keyboard, orchestral percussion and drum kit; all voice ranges, as well as composition and theory. Teachers had between 0 and 320 pupils at the time of responding, and the majority had been teaching between eleven and fifty years, with one under five years and one more than fifty years. Their collective experience included work in state, independent and specialist music schools; twenty-eight had worked in a music hub, five in a conservatoire and fifteen in a university or other higher education institution. Almost all had taught privately, and thirty-five had taught online. All respondents had taught pupils in one-to-one lessons, thirty-six in small-group lessons and just over half had taught whole-class 'First Access' lessons. Their pupils' ages ranged from under five years to adult; all respondents had taught eleven- to eighteen-year-olds. Lesson duration ranged from ten minutes to two or more hours, the most common being thirty or sixty minutes.

Despite the huge range of teaching experience, there were no discernible differences in the nature of teachers' responses based on either the number of years they had been teaching, the geographical regions they were based in or the instruments they taught. The results from this small sample may not be generalizable; however, further research could establish any patterns in responses relevant to teaching experience, location or instrumental specialism.

Teachers reported on the exam boards and assessment methods they had used: thirty-six had used recorded or digital exams, twenty-four used ABRSM, fourteen Trinity College London, eight MTB, six London College of Music Exams (LCME), two Rockschool, one RSL[2] and two did not specify. Teachers' estimations of the proportion of their pupils who had taken exams in the past year ranged from none to 80 per cent, with a mean of around 30 per cent. Teachers were asked to comment on how they and their pupils felt about exams; their pupils', parents' and their own motivations for taking exams or encouraging exam-taking; and their choice of exam board and preference for digital or face-to-face exams.

Teachers' and Learners' Views

Exams, Boards and Syllabi

Teachers generally felt quite positive about exams, many mentioning that they could be a source of motivation and give pupils a 'yardstick' for marking their achievement. Although twenty-five participants reported that their teaching largely revolved around preparing exam repertoire, the majority (forty-four) prioritized their pupils' interests or goals. Twenty-three respondents said they consider exams important, while a similar number felt pressured into using exams by parents or schools. Teachers recognized that pupils had differing motivations for taking exams including parental or school pressure, competition with other pupils and a sense of personal achievement. Parents and pupils were reportedly often influenced by a desire to gain UCAS[3] points to support applications to higher education courses.

Teachers expressed an overall preference for the Associated Board of the Royal Schools of Music (ABRSM) exams; however, many teachers varied their choice to suit pupils' preferences, strengths, needs and past experiences with exams. ABRSM exams were often the first choice of parents and pupils, but some teachers also noted a preference for these because of personal familiarity, having taken them as learners themselves. Trinity College London exams were the second-most preferred, notably for the range of options for supporting tests and repertoire. Some teachers praised the Music Teachers' Board's (MTB) flexibility with repertoire choice, consistency of marking and ease of uploading recorded submissions. London College of Music Examinations' (LCME) musical theatre exams were lauded. Some teachers felt that Rockschool offered the most suitable repertoire for certain pupils. Ease of booking or taking exams was also a factor in teachers' choice of board.

The overall preference for ABRSM and Trinity College London is perhaps unsurprising given their well-established reputation. Nonetheless, most teachers used a combination of exam boards, and many sought an ideal combination of elements to allow pupils to perform to their individual strengths. Meanwhile, in promoting greater choice and encouraging candidates to seek out bespoke products, the exam boards' increasing diversity of offerings is perhaps also reflective of the general cultural climate concerning digital access and broader inclusivity in music education (Fautley and Daubney 2018).

Challenges Associated with Exam-Taking and Preparation

Exams were evidently a source of stress and anxiety for some pupils and teachers. One teacher commented that examiners could be 'stern'. The periodic updating of exam syllabi requires teachers' ongoing learning of the material, and pupils who might underestimate the amount of work needed were recognized as potential sources of stress. Teachers noted that not all pupils wanted to take exams, and adult pupils rarely did; however, many acknowledged the tremendous sense of pride that parents and pupils gained in achieving an exam pass.

Particular challenges associated with preparing and taking exams were mentioned, such as memorizing scales and managing practice time. Exam preparation might be particularly challenging in group lessons where pupils have diverse strengths and needs or if time is limited: the shortest lesson duration reported in the survey was just ten minutes per week. In such cases, exam preparation might necessitate focus on a limited repertoire over an extended period, potentially causing pupils to become bored or to lose interest in practising. Some teachers explained that a lack of lesson time available to cover all the exam requirements sometimes meant that pupils entered exams unprepared for some tests, sharing a concern that pedagogical focus should not become blurred by the lure of an exam certificate. But what scope is there within the exam system to measure progress and reward musical achievement when lessons are shared or lesson time is limited? Some boards now provide qualifications specifically aimed at those learning in groups, recognizing that these allow the development of certain skills – such as ensemble musicianship – that may not be as easily learned in one-to-one lessons. ABRSM Music Medals allow players of different levels of experience to play ensemble pieces together; some boards offer graded assessments specifically for ensemble musicianship.

Alternatives to Exams

When asked whether they would consider not using exams at all, teachers' responses were varied. Many felt that pupils needed deadlines or goals to work towards and that exams provided these. Teachers who would consider *not* using exams cited pupil choice and the need to mitigate stress. Some teachers asserted that musical development is not dependent on exams and that, in some cases, the exam might dampen a pupil's enjoyment of music. Suggested alternatives to exams for measuring pupils' progress included the use of increasingly challenging repertoire, along with worksheets, and teacher-led and pupil-led evaluation. One teacher described keeping 'a type of "curriculum" in mind, which follows the basic ABRSM exam'. Some teachers prioritized musical or instrument-specific goals such as developing tone quality and technical facility. One highlighted the importance of involving the pupil in their own learning plan and of having clear objectives. Another found allowing pupils to choose their own repertoire effective in motivating them to practise. As a means to mark achievement, many teachers mentioned encouraging their pupils to perform in concerts, festivals or to peers in school. Several offered 'mock' exams, which could be rewarded by a written report of achievement and a certificate created by the teacher – an option which may gain appeal in the light of the recent decision by some exam boards to charge for a printed certificate. Furthermore, some pupils might prefer to receive written comments from a teacher who knows them well rather than from an examiner who sees only one performance where not everything a candidate has prepared might come together successfully in the moment.

Views on Exam Reports and Marks

Teachers expressed conflicting views of exam marking, particularly with reference to the ABRSM. Two teachers felt that ABRSM exam reports could be unpredictable or harsh and described their negative effect on pupils. Despite these comments, it was clear that many teachers, as well as parents and schools, still view the ABRSM as the 'gold standard'. Several teachers praised both Trinity College London and MTB for the clarity and consistency of their marking – perhaps unsurprising given the very specific criteria examiners must follow when marking for these two boards (MTB Exams 2024b). Most boards require examiners to attend training at least annually, which includes standardization exercises to ensure consistency in marks and written reports (e.g. Trinity College London 2024). MTB additionally promises that exams are marked only by specialists on the instrument being examined (MTB Exams 2024c).

Views on Accessibility

In recent years, examination providers have worked to update their offer in relation to access and equality. The Equality Act of 2010 made it a legal requirement for awarding bodies to make reasonable adjustments where a person with a disability would be at a substantial disadvantage in completing the examination. Despite this legislation, barriers for those with disabilities may still exist if teachers are not aware of what is classified as reasonable adjustments or lack an understanding of how to prepare pupils for the exam. A number of other challenges, including finding information about reasonable adjustments on exam board websites, determining eligibility of those who require reasonable adjustments and practical application of these adjustments have been identified (British Dyslexia Association 2020).

Most of the survey respondents said they were aware of reasonable adjustments for pupils with specific needs. Some teachers felt that exams were very accessible or improving in accessibility with the advent of recorded exams and the choice of a variety of exam boards. Others expressed concern that despite the flexibility offered by certain exam boards regarding accommodations for pupils with specific learning needs, some candidates with additional needs might require further support from teachers who might not always be willing or able to take on the extra work required.

About half of the respondents had made use of reasonable adjustments, describing mainly positive experiences, with one reporting that their pupils had been 'exceptionally well catered for on all occasions'. Another cited proactive engagement by some examiners in checking whether 'there are any pupils [with additional needs] they need to be aware of'. Conversely, one found that 'you usually have to remind the examiner – they are rarely properly informed by the exam board'. While many referred specifically to available adjustments that were helpful to their pupils, such as extra time, the use of coloured filters and enlarged print for sight-reading tests, two also highlighted the ease of the application process.

The respondents mentioned using reasonable adjustments for pupils with dyslexia, dyspraxia and visual impairment. One vocal teacher based their choice of exam board on the adjustments available: 'I changed to Trinity so that those with anxiety can use music [scores] to perform.' Another mentioned 'an increased number of pupils who require extra time for whatever reason', suggesting that either awareness of conditions is now better understood and diagnosed or that there is an increase in pupils presenting with issues that require reasonable adjustments – something a UK Research and Innovation study led by the University of Exeter plans to investigate (UKRI 2024). Equally, if provision is signposted and encouraged so that more pupils can feel confident to take exams and their teachers understand how to apply for the necessary adjustments, this might be a positive indicator of growing inclusivity in the examination industry.

One respondent raised the point that some pupils with dyslexia 'were embarrassed to be labelled' and chose not to seek reasonable adjustments. Another commented that 'the autistic children I teach have said they do not want the exam board to know'. Despite an awareness of the facility, here is evidence of a disinclination to make use of it. Self-exclusion may be an important consideration for future research.

Another notable issue concerned obtaining the necessary evidence to apply for reasonable adjustments, as summarized by one teacher: 'Some dyslexic pupils can't get an official diagnosis without paying for it privately so aren't able to have the accommodations.' The cost of private assessment, prolonged waiting times for Education and Health Care (EHC) plans and a lack of knowledge regarding which accommodations might be available or appropriate may also be barriers. According to Harding et al. (2023: 11), 'Parents identified significant school-based barriers to diagnosis including funding for an assessment, their child's age combined with the use of a "wait and see" approach, and lack of knowledge around dyslexia.' Educational and physical needs notwithstanding, cost appeared to be a significant barrier for many respondents, as well as transport to exams and the need for additional parental and teacher support.

Views on Digital and Live Exams

Despite growing numbers of pupils taking digital exams, survey responses indicated a general preference for the 'live' exam experience. Although some teachers viewed digital access as essential, many considered recorded exams as a fall-back option or a means to avoid traditional supporting tests, such as scales, sight-reading and aural tests. Some found the option to restart an exam recording valuable for pupils experiencing performance anxiety; however, others felt this less helpful for those with perfectionist tendencies with multiple takes actually adding to pupil anxiety and requiring additional (possibly unpaid) teacher time. Clearly, pupils' individual needs are a dominant factor in teachers' choice of exam syllabus and format.

Where Are We Now?

The findings from this small sample of respondents reveal generally positive views of music performance examinations. Exams remain strongly valued as defining markers of achievement and goal-related progress. Choice appears ever more important: candidates are taking advantage of an increasing variety of possible boards and more inclusive syllabi to achieve graded recognition of their progress, which may in turn put pressure on exam boards to further broaden and enrich their offerings to attract a clientele with diverse needs and preferences.

Group learning and lesson duration are factors influencing choice of board or syllabus, as well as the option to choose exam elements to play to learners' strengths. Although some still view the traditional 'practical' exam with scales, sight-reading and aural tests as the 'gold standard', many teachers recognize the value of alternative supporting tests or 'performance' exams where stagecraft and presentation (rather than additional instrument-specific skills) form supporting evidence of the candidate's developing musicianship.

With increasing awareness of specific needs, examinations are becoming more widely accessible, although not all applicants are knowledgeable about available adjustments or wish to take advantage of these. Teachers are sensitive to pupils who choose not to take exams, and many have a repertoire of resources and strategies to ensure pupils understand how they are progressing and to reward their achievements. In terms of further enhancing accessibility, exam duration could be reviewed: could musical excellence be demonstrated through a shorter programme if this might benefit some candidates? Future research exploring the views of both pupils and parents on music examinations would provide valuable insights here, particularly as this study focused on the views of teachers and therefore could not impartially indicate the needs and perspectives of other stakeholders.

Further research could determine whether the views of these fifty survey respondents are representative of the numerous teachers and learners across the world who use exams provided by UK boards. As to the question of what is being examined, the current syllabi offer a much broader range of options than the original tests set by conservatoires auditioning pupils for performance training, and perhaps some now come closer to inspiring what Salaman (1994: 221) termed a 'truly musical education'. Musicianship can be demonstrated via composition, improvisation, performing by ear or from a printed page, as a soloist or in an ensemble. In a society where the need to demonstrate and measure one's learning is emphasized in order to reach a higher level of education or even gainful employment, music exams are an ongoing source of evidence and seem likely to continue to evolve as an important part of our musical and educational culture.

Notes

1. See individual exam boards' websites for detailed information on their weighting of assessed elements.
2. One respondent referred to RSL, which the authors have taken to mean 'RSL classical suite' exams; RSL offers a popular music syllabus and also classical music exams (currently for violin, piano and guitar). https://www.rslawards.com/graded-music-exams/.
3. The UK's Universities and Colleges Admissions Service: https://www.ucas.com/.

References

ABRSM (2022), 'What Are Music Medals?' Available online: https://www.abrsm.org/en-gb/other-assessments/music-medals (accessed 29 June 2024).

ABRSM (2025), 'Ensembles'. Available online: https://www.abrsm.org/en-gb/other-assessments/group-exams/ensembles#:~:text=Our%20Ensemble%20exams%20are%20open,of%20around%20Grade%208%20standard (accessed 14 May 2025).

Barton, D. C. M. (2020), 'The Autonomy of Private Instrumental Teachers: Its Effect on Valid Knowledge Construction, Curriculum Design, and Quality of Teaching and Learning', PhD diss., Royal College of Music, London.

Bath, N., A. Daubney, D. Mackrill and G. Spruce (2020), 'The Declining Place of Music Education in Schools in England', *Children and Society*, 34: 443–57.

Bent, I. D., D. W. Hughes, R. C. Provine, R. Rastall, A. Kilmer, D. Hiley, J. Szendrei, T. B. Payne, M. Bent and G. Chew (2001), 'Notation', Grove Music Online. Available online: https://doi.org/10.1093/gmo/9781561592630.article.20114 (accessed 14 May 2025).

Bonfield-Brown, J. (2018), 'The Assessment of Musical Attainment: Acquiring Cultural Capital and Building Learning Power in Instrumental Music Tuition', PhD diss., Nottingham Trent University.

Boyle, K. (2021), *The Instrumental Music Teacher: Autonomy, Identity and the Portfolio Career in Music*, Abingdon: Routledge.

Braun, V., and V. Clarke (2006), 'Using Thematic Analysis in Psychology', *Qualitative Research in Psychology*, 3 (2): 77–101.

British Dyslexia Association (2020), 'Music and Dyslexia'. Available online: https://cdn.bdadyslexia.org.uk/uploads/documents/000-BOOKLET-Dyslexia-music.pdf?v=1614338349 (accessed 29 June 2024).

Cambridge Dictionary (2023), 'Musicianship'. Available online: https://dictionary.cambridge.org/dictionary/english/musicianship (accessed 29 June 2024).

Daubney, A., G. Spruce and D. Annetts (2019), 'Music Education: State of the Nation', *Report by the All-Party Parliamentary Group for Music Education, the Incorporated Society of Musicians and the University of Sussex*. Available online: https://www.ism.org/images/images/State-of-the-Nation-Music-Education-WEB.pdf (accessed 29 June 2024).

Equality Act 2010 (2010), See Section 20: 'Duty to Make Adjustments'. Available online: https://www.legislation.gov.uk/ukpga/2010/15/section/20 (accessed 29 June 2024).

Fautley, M., and A. Daubney (2018), 'Inclusion, Music Education, and What It Might Mean', *British Journal of Music Education*, 35 (3): 219–21.

Harding, S., M. Chauhan-Sims, E. Oxley and H. M. Nash (2023), 'A Delphi Study Exploring the Barriers to Dyslexia Diagnosis and Support: A Parent's Perspective', *Dyslexia*, 29 (3): 162–78.

Johnson-Williams, E. (2024), 'The Historical Context of Instrumental Teaching', in N. Beach and G. Spruce (eds), *Instrumental Music Teaching: Perspectives and Challenges*, 15–27, London: Trinity College London Press.

MTB Exams (2024a), 'Syllabus Guidance and Updates'. Available online: https://www.mtbexams.com/syllabuses/syllabus-guidance-updates/ (accessed 29 June 2024).

MTB Exams (2024b), 'Marking Criteria'. Available online: https://www.mtbexams.com/how-it-works/marking-criteria/ (accessed 29 June 2024).

MTB Exams (2024c), 'Specialist Examiners'. Available online: https://www.mtbexams.com/how-it-works/about/ (accessed 29 June 2024).

Olsen, P. G. (2019), 'Assessing Improvisation in Graded Music Examinations: Conflicting Practices and Perceptions', PhD diss., University of Cambridge.

Salaman, W. (1994), 'The Role of Graded Examinations in Music', *British Journal of Music Education*, 11 (3): 209–21.

Trinity College London (2022), 'Supporting Tests/Trinity College'. Available online: https://www.trinitycollege.com/qualifications/music/grade-exams/about/supporting-tests (accessed 29 June 2024).

Trinity College London (2024), 'Standards and Regulation'. Available online: https://www.trinitycollege.com/about-us/standards-and-regulation (accessed 29 June 2024).

Trinity College London (2025a), 'About our Graded Exams'. Available online: https://www.trinitycollege.com/qualifications/music/grade-exams/about (accessed 14 May 2025).

Trinity College London (2025b), 'Group Certificates'. Available online: https://www.trinitycollege.com/qualifications/music/music-certificate-exams/groups (accessed 14 May 2025).

UKRI (2024), 'Increased Diagnosis of Developmental Disorders: Are There Really More Children with Autism, Dyslexia, or ADHD?' University of Exeter Department of Child Health. Available online: https://gtr.ukri.org/projects?ref=ES%2FK003356%2F1 (accessed 29 June 2024).

van der Schyff, D., and A. Schiavio (2017), 'Evolutionary Musicology Meets Embodied Cognition: Biocultural Coevolution and the Enactive Origins of Human Musicality', *Frontiers in Neuroscience*, 11 (519): 1–18.

Williamon, A. (2012), 'Measuring Performance Enhancement in Music', in A. Williamon (ed.), *Musical Excellence: Strategies and Techniques to Enhance Performance*, 61–82, Oxford: Oxford University Press.

17

The Language of Tuition Books

*Richard Powell, Elizabeth Haddon,
Polly Sharpe, Federico Pendenza and
Sara Norouzi Iranzad*

Introduction

This chapter takes as its inspiration Tommy Igoe's *Groove Essentials: The Play-Along* for drummers (Igoe 2005). Igoe's book is designed to be used by musicians from beginner to professional level, who can work through it alongside an accompanying DVD demonstrating the forty-seven grooves detailed in the notated examples with supporting text; backing tracks are provided, and various styles – rock, funk, jazz, world, R&B and Hip-Hop – are included. The book appears to be addressed to the learner rather than to a teacher, perhaps implicitly acknowledging the self-taught or informal learning context of many drummers (Dylan Smith 2013). Potentially, the book could be used alongside Igoe's other output, which guides drummers through technique, warm-ups and various rudiments; therefore, its focus appears to prioritize the exploration of groove structures, pattern or drum kit instrument choices, 'feel', listening and confidence.

Two of the chapter authors encountered this book when one of their students chose to use material from it as part of a one-to-one lesson assessment for our MA Music Education: Instrumental and Vocal Teaching course at the University of York, UK. Igoe's book made a strong impression on us; we discussed the contrast between the immediacy, warmth and personality exuding from Igoe's written text with the somewhat drier, depersonalized and formal writing style presented in many of the materials we were using in our work as violin and piano teachers and in tutor and technique books that we had experienced within our own instrumental learning. We wondered whether and how the writing style in pedagogical texts might influence an instrumental teacher's thinking; how it might subsequently influence teacher-student dialogue within instrumental lessons; and how consciously aware teachers might be of this influence. We also wondered in a somewhat speculative manner whether writing style could contribute to potential positionalities and stereotypes of instrumentalists aligning with certain characteristics (e.g. 'violinists are serious'; 'drummers are laid back') and whether these could then act as self-perpetuating and influential 'labels'. We thought about what it might have meant for us, as learners, to have encountered a violin tutor book written in the style of Igoe's book and what the implications might be for us now as teachers, for example, concerning our verbal teaching language and how this might influence our students, particularly relating to their self-view and relation to others as musicians, and what this might mean for our mindsets in instrumental pedagogy: our openness, playfulness and creativity.

Our collaborative exploration of Igoe's text involved discussing the material, reflecting on our responses to it and – as non-drummers – considering how we might relate to the material as learners (either as novice drummers or applying some of the ideas within our learning of other instruments), aligning with a 'real-world' orientation (Robson and McCartan 2016). One of the chapter authors had access to a drum kit and explored the book practically as a novice drummer, sharing reflections on this process with the other collaborating authors. In addition, we reflected on the potential of Igoe's communicative style to suit learners across different ages and levels, especially in the context of adult education – known as andragogy (Pike 2022). Adult learners are likely to take initiative over their own learning and 'can be highly self-directed' (Pike 2022: 8). On a preliminary examination, Igoe's writing style seemed to promote a self-guided approach to musical learning; this prompted us to consider the potential ways in which the nuances of his writing style might help in fostering learner autonomy and agency, though we do not view this as exclusively the domain of adult learners.

We conducted a systematic process of thematic text analysis (Braun and Clarke 2022), dividing the book into sections, working through these individually to manually code the text and cross-checking our coding of certain passages collaboratively to support the validity of the coding. Many themes emerged from this process; our overarching themes, discussed in this chapter, are empathy, mindset and trust. The characteristics and qualities discussed within these thematic areas contribute to the more holistic 'stance' of Igoe's text as invitational: to learning, to dialogue, to musicianship, to exploration. Our collaborative examination of the publication has not only enriched our considerations of the pedagogical materials we draw upon but has more broadly informed our ever-developing conceptions of student-centred approaches to teaching.

Empathy

Recent shifts in pedagogical theory and practice have resulted in a turn away from 'master–apprentice' teaching relationships and the more didactic modes of delivery they often entail. Approaches instead seek to empathize with the learner and to anticipate, comprehend and foreground their needs. Accordingly, teaching roles continue to be re-conceived and expanded in various ways to allow for greater adaptation; notions such as educator as 'fellow adventurer' (Allsup 2016) align with understandings of learning that place emphasis on knowledge as being collaboratively constructed rather than simply transmitted. Such changes may also invite evaluation of the extent to which publications used to supplement teaching help in facilitating this more dynamic and democratic approach to pedagogy. This has particular implications for tutor books designed to scaffold technical development. Previous authors of such volumes, in seeking to emulate and encapsulate predominant teaching styles, may have felt under pressure to invoke through their written style the textual equivalent of 'the master positioned as representative of the practice' (Burwell 2013: 287): static points of reference, impersonal and infallible, performing a function comparable to that of an instruction manual of the instrument. (The notion of such a text – and the written tone that inevitably accompanies it – may bring to mind for readers memories of encounters with particular materials in their experiences as learners.)

Departures from more prescriptive approaches to teaching might be viewed as presenting something of a challenge to contemporary authors: how might a tuition book – an essentially 'fixed' component of learning and teaching contexts – supplement development in a flexible, dynamic and learner-centred manner? Such a brief might easily – logically, even – result in a 'neutralized' publication, objective and dispassionate to allow space for learner preference and growth. In *Groove Essentials*, however, Igoe resists temptation to de-personalize the material, instead ensuring that his 'character' remains central to his articulation of knowledge and the scaffolding of learner development. Rather than unfolding in the manner of a monologue, the writing is notably sensitive to the learner – its tone dialogic, immediate, even conversational. The broader consequence of Igoe's relational approach for the 'atmosphere' of the book is one of empathy, a striking textual embodiment of the connection Bowman (2022) draws between the construction of teaching persona and intended learning environment.

Embedded within Igoe's writing, and contributing to its mentor-like quality, is an implicit understanding or anticipation of how a reader may feel at stages in their learning, often accompanied by a reassuring underlining of shared experience: 'We're all in this together' (2005: 17). This is used reflexively to ensure that the authorial voice is that of a musician who may have achieved the status of 'expert' but is nevertheless able to recall the challenges and felt experience of acquiring that expertise in the first place. The potential for specialist areas of knowledge to be perceived as inaccessible or even gate-kept is frequently offset. This proves notable in Igoe's introduction to jazz grooves:

> I'm sure there are many drummers who arrive at the jazz section of any book, including *Groove Essentials*, with a sense of insecurity and dread … I've seen lists of recordings in books, but I know if *I* listened to them straight away with no jazz experience I'd be more than a little confused. Jazz has a vocabulary that can be very advanced and implied, unlike most rock music that is more obvious and clear. (Igoe 2005: 59, emphasis in original)

Igoe is quick to acknowledge the palpable alienation that learners may feel in moving from one genre to another: 'Playing the hi-hat like we do in this groove is mysterious for many drummers, particularly those of you coming from rock backgrounds. It's so different from everything else you've done before, and it's going to feel bizarre in the beginning' (2005: 75). More broadly, he frequently moves to demystify and occasionally deprecate specialist terminology where it carries the potential to intimidate ('ostinato' is explained as 'fancy Italian for a continuously repeating figure' (2005: 50)) or to overwhelm ('All the terminology for shuffles can get confusing, so in keeping with my keep-it-simple approach, when you hear the term "shuffle", simply think: swing with some kind of backbeat' (2005: 72)).

The empathic framing Igoe provides also carries practical value, helping the learner to anticipate how they may feel at critical musical junctures, for example, when playing along with the backing tracks:

> When the [backing track] percussion drops out the last time through, you may feel as if your friend, who you were so nicely locking up with, suddenly abandoned you. Repeat after me: 'Thou shall not drift when the percussion stops.' No, when the percussion stops, you must dig in to the time even *deeper*. Drive that bus, baby. (Igoe 2005: 20, emphasis in original)

This passage is redolent of the playful, self-deprecating humour that pervades the book, but it also exemplifies the recurrent emphasis that Igoe places upon musical 'feel' as aural intuition and sensitivity in combination with developing technical skill, a holistic encapsulation of the qualities he promotes in relation to each groove. The risk of this coming across as some kind of nebulous conception of innate – and thus inaccessible – 'musicality' is sidestepped by Igoe's portrayal of 'feel' as attainable through strategic perseverance. 'Feel' is itself groove-like in character: understood and experienced as a musical perspective and role within a texture, acquired through developing relationships with surrounding components and the musicians controlling them. An empathic approach to the honing of this reflexive musical skill is maintained through consideration of learner experience: requisite tenacity is encouraged, but the negative feelings (frustration, disappointment, despondency) that so often go hand in hand with this process are acknowledged rather than denied:

> For some reason, this simple-looking groove is a coordination killer. It's funny how you can't tell what will throw a student a curve-ball, but for some reason, this groove makes most drummers very uncomfortable with the coordination. If it stinks today, work it into submission tomorrow. It still stinks? There's always the day after that. Don't give up! (Igoe 2005: 37)

The disruptions of 'feel' that may emerge as learners encounter new musical contexts are also anticipated. While this assists in normalizing potentially unsettling sensations, Igoe's enthusiastic embrace of novelty (sonic or social: 'You'll encounter different things happening (good and bad) to yourself and the other musicians' (2005: 21)) also aids in the development of positive resilience and welcoming of challenge ('It can feel funny to go so long without playing your kick, but it's a great sound' (2005: 50)). This construction of empathy may support the motivation of the learner, as well as potentially influence the language that they use to talk to themselves while learning: a kind of self-empathy may therefore emerge through the embedding of the language used by Igoe in the mindset of the learner.

Mindset

Throughout his book, Igoe embraces a compassionate and communicative approach encouraging learners to acknowledge the challenges inherent in the musical journey while also celebrating their progress and success along the way. Various strategies stem from this implicit philosophy, assisting learners in their musical learning and skill development. By orienting a mindset towards learning grounded in realistic expectations, Igoe recognizes occasional dissatisfaction as a natural part of the learning process, thereby alleviating pressure to achieve immediate results: 'If you don't like the variations or how you are playing them, set them aside for another day' (Igoe 2005: 20). The importance of self-monitoring, pacing oneself and not rushing learning is further acknowledged, with Igoe reinforcing his supportive approach: 'As always, feel no pressure to play it today if it doesn't yet feel right' (2005: 39).

Igoe places emphasis on empowering learners to navigate challenges at their own pace, recognizing the complexity involved in skill acquisition, as well as the patience and perseverance it requires: 'It's a tough one for co-ordination so take your time' (2005: 52). Assertive yet sensible remarks like 'Don't hurt yourself' (2005: 52) suggest that progress takes time and that the learner's health should be prioritized. Further practical suggestions are provided, and when describing issues encountered in playing passages in '2-feel', Igoe's emphasis on enjoyment and exploration within learning permeates his use of language: 'However, I recommend in the beginning, that you just enjoy playing your tin hat and manipulating it with your hand, stick and foot' (2005: 74).

This positive and exploratory approach to learning is evident in the overt normalization of mistakes, which are embraced as a vital part of the learning process.

As Igoe highlights early in the book, 'While honing your musical instincts, you can make mistakes' (2005: 11). This idea is reinforced later on: 'Making mistakes is important, because if you don't make mistakes, you don't grow' (2005: 12). A growth mindset (Dweck 2006) is promoted, freeing learners from perfectionist attitudes towards their learning. Expertise is framed as an iterative trial-and-error journey in which practice, again, is the optimal place for experimentation and exploration:

> You can try mixing and matching different grooves from different chapters to experiment with what fits and what doesn't. Remember, it's okay to make mistakes now; we're practicing! I know a few professional chefs, and they all say they had to ruin many soufflés before becoming masters of their art. (Igoe 2005: 32)

A similar open-ended approach to learning is advocated through various holistic examples that Igoe puts forward in different sections of the book. Learners are encouraged to explore beyond the realm of music notation and to interpret its broader meanings subjectively: 'All the notation markings in the world won't help, so experiment and enjoy' (2005: 29). This subjectivity extends to musical interpretation, which is viewed as an individual and fluid experience, in which 'tempos, as with all things musical, are subject to interpretation' (2005: 77). Explanations such as 'A study of jazz is also a study of American history: a story of people, passion and life' (2005: 59) give this exercise a sense of importance and relevance, inviting learners to explore the human element of music beyond its immediate application. This fosters a creative approach to learning within which 'drum charts aren't supposed to be answer books. They are wide-area maps that tell you the basic stuff about a song, so that you can make smart drumming decisions' (2005: 12). All of these examples appear indicative of a broader aim to foster a sense of learner's agency from the outset of their musical learning rather than focusing on an initial idea of ability or knowledge.

Learner agency is also fostered through an emphasis on continuous honing of craft and quality. This is communicated through practical suggestions developing technical and analytical skills, whereby learners are encouraged to aim for a deliberate rather than rushed approach to learning: 'If the sixteenths aren't perfect, regardless of accents, then stop, slow it down, figure it out, and only when it's fixed try to play it at your tempo goal. No rush – enjoy the journey' (2005: 54). While here Igoe's communicative style demonstrates his recurrent focus on enjoyment, in other instances the idea of craft is interspersed with frequent use of humour. This enlivens the learning experience, making the musical material relatable and encouraging learners to engage with it in a relaxed and enjoyable manner: 'Listen closely: If you play the tango like a dead fish, some crazed Argentinean will find you and set fire to your drumset. Don't laugh, I've heard stories' (2005: 110). This may sound prescriptive, but learners are encouraged to take an active role in their learning, which could yield interesting and surprising musical outcomes: 'And please, don't forget to turn off your snares! If you don't, you'll sound like a marching band instead of a Caribbean rhythm section – hey, maybe that would sound cool, though' (2005: 89). Challenge is acknowledged but often also cast as a springboard to learning opportunities, where humorous language again adds flavour to the underlying message of craft and continuous learning development:

> There is an ensemble figure in this chart that happens again and again in this tune. Take a look at it now; it's right there in the very first bar. See it? Be afraid. Be very afraid. It looks so cute and innocent, doesn't it? Well it's not. It's an evil little rhythm. I don't know what it is, but it's tricky to get everyone to play this figure the same way. Fortunately, since the band on the [backing] track is tight, you'll get to see if you have command of that figure. Here's a hint: Don't rush the last note. (Igoe 2005: 103)

Ultimately, the joy of music-making is not just encouraged but celebrated. As Igoe remarks: 'Tell me, did you have fun? I hope so because like I've always said, if you can't have fun playing the drums, then … well, I don't know, but you should definitely have fun playing the drums, don't you think?' (2005: 124). The sensory focus of much of the language used and the open acknowledgement of positive feelings encourage an embrace of the joy of music-making, perhaps implicitly inviting the learner, too, to revel in the sense of discovery that permeates the learning process: 'Playing the hi-hat part with one hand, instead of two, gives the entire groove a different packet. I find it fascinating that such a simple thing can change everything about a groove' (2005: 50). This transformative nature of exploration is promoted, along with a sense of camaraderie and connection between the tutor and the learner. The learning process is thus a journey characterized by challenge and craft but also by enjoyment and fun, underpinned by the understanding of mistakes as part and parcel of the learning process, linked to exploration and experimentation, and nurtured and sustained by a growth mindset.

Trust

Groove Essentials is aimed at 'all levels of drummers' (Igoe 2005: 6), and students are encouraged to take responsibility for judging their own level and rate of progress. Igoe treats the student more like an embryonic expert than a beginner with minimal skills:

> This book is designed for you to fail the first time you try … I'm throwing you into a very professional situation with no rehearsal and expecting you to sink or swim. So, perhaps you'll sink. So what? Sink a little less the next time, and the next, and next. (Igoe 2005: 114)

Igoe includes material that may be outside a beginner's capabilities but which they will be able to play in due course and with practice ('You should feel absolutely no pressure to play these grooves if it isn't quite time yet. [They will still be there] … when your skill level rises' (2005: 9)). A sense of trust that the learner will achieve this competency is achieved through language that positions the student as on the way to mastery; this may affect the way they understand themselves and their musical journey, which may in turn positively affect the way they work and progress.

Igoe enables learners to build awareness of process and skill development, recognizing the need for ongoing effort: 'You must do the hard work to understand and execute what you need to play' (2005: 114) but with a foundational element of the learner developing trust in themselves. He uses informal language to encourage this, such as in the development of an internal sense of pulse by minimizing reliance on the use of metronomic clicks on the accompanying backing track: 'I've put a click in for you the first time through the form … After that, you will be expected to keep time by yourself' (2005: 78), and 'You are generously provided a click the first time through, but that's it, amigo. After that, you are on your own' (2005: 38). Frequent reminders to learners to record themselves for self-evaluation and self-analysis are often accompanied by playful self-awareness: 'Hey, it's been over 30 seconds since I've asked if you are recording yourself. Are you?' (2005: 35), and 'I'm asking you to record yourself (Hey! It's been too long …) and listen impartially to your performance. It's hard to do, but it's great for your playing' (2005: 103). Igoe's written text also enables the learner to trust their own decisions about their playing: 'Read these descriptions carefully for all the charts. They will help you make smart musical choices' (2005: 20).

When offering tips and advice, Igoe encourages the learner to trust their own judgement, both musically and technically, such as when describing crossing hands to play a floor tom: 'This is comfortable for me, but for many drummers it's not; so if you are one who gets stuck in the choreography of the crossing motion, then simply play the tom part on the upper toms. It works just fine there too' (2005: 108). Implicitly, this conveys an orientation towards inclusivity: achieving the end goal by varied means to suit different individuals is not only acceptable but can be a normalized part of collaborative practice. This may work to support ongoing positive views of future ensemble colleagues, students or other performers who adopt different approaches. Igoe sometimes gives general suggestions – 'Have a nice musical conversation with [the piano player]' (2005: 61) – and sometimes more specific ones – 'Instead of beat variations, in Variations A and B, I give you some slick reggae fills to play at the ends of phrases or whenever a fill/solo seems appropriate' (2005: 87), leaving space for the learner's own interpretation. The learner is also encouraged to explore and embody musical styles, such as when discussing samba: 'Listen to the authentic music of the country and copy the feel of the masters. Then, see how you can apply their feel to your drumming' (2005: 92). Igoe trusts that the learner will use their own initiative in understanding some of his descriptions, such as when he suggests making one groove 'a little bit syncopated' (2005: 75), while another has 'a triplet that should be light and flow forward' (2005: 75). This extends to the assumption that the learner will develop a creative individual style, such as when talking about choosing grooves: 'Make up a few grooves of your own and ask yourself the question: "Is this groove serving the song?"' (2005: 21). The emphasis on inspiration rather than didacticism raises helpful questions about how much beginners can be encouraged to take ownership of their own development and musical journey while also supporting the development of the learner's trust in their skills, musical discernment and decision-making and creativity. Again, the varied outcomes of the open processes may support the learner's awareness of alternatives in performance approaches, giving positive foundations for collaborative inclusivity in ensemble contexts, as well as ongoing curiosity and excitement in exploring further possibilities in their own playing.

Open Ends: Implications for Learning and Teaching

A pervasive strength of *Groove Essentials* identified during the course of our analyses and reflections on the book was the way in which we seemingly gained a sense of Igoe himself. This may not come as a surprise. As with any tuition book that explicitly presents its author as the 'tutor' (and, indeed, as a key selling point of the publication), prospective readers may expect or even desire that the content will in some ways typify aspects of that individual's personality, hoping to benefit from kernels of their expertise translated into a pedagogical method. A notable achievement here is that rather than the content translating simply into a form of self-promotion, or there being a sense of the author striving for objectivity (and, by implication, authority), Igoe positions himself in relation to the material in a manner that ultimately proves personable and relatable rather than sage-like or egotistical. In doing so, he offers a thought-provoking model for how tuition books might be positioned, demonstrating routes by which they might epitomize characteristics of their author while simultaneously creating space for the personality, autonomy and growth of the reader-learner.

These considerations of Igoe's presence in his pedagogical writing prompted us as educators to reflect on our own selection and use of tuition books and materials in our teaching. Issues of language and tone in particular served to illuminate dimensions of these publications that, on reflection, we felt we had either been less conscious of or deemed a lower priority than the focus of the musical and technical content itself. More broadly, we found ourselves evaluating the extent to which resources we used in our own teaching represented the wider pedagogical values and qualities that we want to nurture in our students and the relationships we established with these publications. The influential power of these publications to help shape the experiential undercurrent of our students' learning – mindset, motivation, the degree to which they themselves feel included, understood and supported – was evident, as was the way in which the materials might be reinforcing, contradicting or even conditioning aspects of our teaching approach and style. In turn, we were struck by the potential this offered for future tuition book publications in terms of the capacity they may have through their language to shape the *experience*, as well as the focus and content, of learning.

Furthermore, we were inspired by a range of broader pedagogical implications of Igoe's writing and its modelling of an engagingly personal teaching approach. It proved particularly encouraging that an idiomatic style could actively serve to create space for students to develop as individuals: that there is potential for a student-centred approach to be enriched (rather than stifled) by expression of teacher personality and character, providing it is sensitively and strategically articulated. This safeguarding of autonomy and independence reinforces the open-ended understanding of musicianship cumulatively promoted over the course of the book, one in which both pupil and teacher perspectives are assimilated alongside a professional outlook in a manner comparable to the socially engaged 'lifelong learner' outlined by Shieh and Allsup (2016): 'Fostering musical independence means that we aim for something unexpected, something teachers can't always predict, measure, or compare against others' (2016: 35).

The implicit call of *Groove Essentials* is for outward-looking musicians: responsive, flexible and open to the opportunities that group music-making offers and ready to forge empathetic and supportive collaborations with fellow practitioners. It is an inclusive, explorative ethos that gently dismantles more conventional, competitive notions of excellence; musical skill is, here, more holistic, embracing creativity, play, feel, patience and joy-taking. Just as this philosophy offers much to learners seeking to forge individualized paths in their musical development, the range of ways in which Igoe articulates and embodies it through the language he uses can offer much to teachers seeking to cultivate a supportive and empowering learning environment for their students.

References

Allsup, R. E. (2016), *Remixing the Classroom: Towards an Open Philosophy of Music Education*, Bloomington: Indiana University Press.
Bowman, J. (2022), *The Music Professor Online*, New York: Oxford University Press.
Braun, V., and V. Clarke (2022), *Thematic Analysis: A Practical Guide*, London: Sage.
Burwell, K. (2013), 'Apprenticeship in Music: A Contextual Study for Instrumental Teaching and Learning', *International Journal of Music Education*, 31 (3): 276–91.
Dweck, C. S. (2006), *Mindset: The New Psychology of Success*, New York: Random House.
Dylan Smith, G. (2013), *I Drum, Therefore I Am*, Abingdon: Routledge.
Igoe, T. (2005), *Groove Essentials, the Play-Along 1.0: The Groove Encyclopedia for the 21st-Century Drummer*, New Jersey: Hudson Music.

Pike, P. D. (2022), *The Adult Music Student: Making Music Throughout the Lifespan*, Abingdon: Routledge.
Robson, C., and K. McCartan (2016), *Real World Research*, 2nd edn, Chichester: John Wiley.
Shieh, E., and R. E. Allsup (2016), 'Fostering Musical Independence', *Music Educators Journal*, 102 (4): 30–5.

18

Teachers as Creators of Educational Materials for Music Learners

Federico Pendenza, Elizabeth Haddon, Helen Madden and Marianna Cortesi

Introduction

In creating educational material, it is recognized that experienced composers may find the process challenging, requiring good understanding of the instrument(s) and technical level of the intended players and commitment to producing quality output (Duncan and Andrews 2015). While instrumental teachers may work in contexts where they could create material for their own pupils, various factors may influence their confidence. Initially, limited or no training as composers or as creators of educational material may impact the extent to which instrumental teachers might include compositional activities within their portfolio of work (Stijnen, Nijs and Van Petegem 2023); this may influence the confidence of subsequent educators to create material for their learners when pupils in turn become teachers. Limited resources for teachers may also influence their understanding of educational approaches to composition (Andrews and Giesbrecht 2013). While material could be created by teachers and students within lessons as well as outside them, pedagogical priorities such as the building of technique and expressive skills (Beach 2012) may preclude a focus on creative and compositional activities within the limited lesson time available (Stijnen, Nijs and Van Petegem 2023). However, creative activities can develop awareness of the potential of the instrument and its player(s), and support musical understanding through their close relationship to analysis, harmony, thematic motif-building and development (Verney 1991). At the early stages of instrumental learning, tailored compositional activities can reinforce familiarity with notation, as well as help the teacher assess whether concepts have been understood (Harris and Crozier 2000). Utilizing starting points of improvisation and associated notation could build skills and confidence both for students and teachers in creating new material.

This chapter explores the creation of material in the one-to-one context, either as a 'one-off' activity or as a process with the potential to result in a more extended resource. The authors also explore aspects relating to group and ensemble teaching, which may require the teacher to arrange existing repertoire for the particular needs of the group, therefore including consideration of instrumentation, pupil levels and number of players of each instrument. The implications for teachers who may be expected to deliver newly created material for no extra remuneration are indicated, as well as questions of perceived legitimacy in the role of creator-educator.

What motivates educators to create educational materials for music learners? What challenges do they encounter along the way? How do they navigate these challenges? What support might they need? In our conversations as educators, we wondered about these questions and the potential implications for instrumental teachers working with students of different ages and levels. This chapter explores the real-life experiences of three of the co-authors – Helen, Federico and Marianna, uncovering their approaches to creating educational materials for their students. Helen, an experienced piano teacher and composer, recalls her experiences of creating educational materials to support the development of improvisation and composition skills with one adult learner. Federico considers his journey as a guitar ensemble leader arranging materials for a group of young students of diverse backgrounds and levels, and Marianna shares her experiences as a piano teacher adapting existing materials to overcome technical challenges. These reflections will unfold as a continuous thread of events, culminating in a discussion section that draws together the themes identified in the three case studies. To protect the identity of the students, pseudonyms are used throughout the educators' narratives.

Helen's Case Study

Jean, a mature learner seeking to incorporate improvisation and composition into her piano lessons, had limited knowledge of chords and scale theory beyond the requirements of the Associated Board of the Royal Schools of Music (ABRSM) Grade 5 theory exam taken recently. Despite her lack of confidence in playing from a melody and chord sheet, I encouraged her to try this new skill while recognizing her initial hesitance. Adopting a person-centred approach, I met Jean at her starting point and provided theoretical materials aimed at bolstering her self-assurance and developing the foundational skills required for improvisation. Jean exhibited considerable uncertainty when attempting anything beyond rudimentary rhythms, struggling to maintain a consistent and steady pulse even in those instances. Much focus was therefore dedicated to reinforcing her confidence in counting and sustaining rhythmic continuity, as this is an essential foundational skill in improvisation, which relies on the musician's adeptness in assuming control over not only the rhythmic elements but also the selection of harmonies, construction of chords and on-the-spot melodic development and composition. Taking a step-by-step approach, I separated the rhythmic focus from teaching chords with their various extensions, ensuring that I stayed within her Zone of Proximal Development (Vygotsky 1978).[1] Resulting from a previous conversation about the parallels between learning improvisation and beginning to learn the piano from scratch, we understood that Jean would need to adopt a distinct approach to learning and practising, with the integral development of a strong foundation in chord knowledge. However, acquiring this proficiency would require time and dedication. Progressing on a weekly basis, we delved into the fundamentals of chord construction, and I presented Jean with two distinct approaches for determining chords: using the 3rd, 5th and 7th notes of the corresponding scale or, alternatively, deciphering the chord structure based on intervals. Jean exhibited greater proficiency when deducing chordal structures through interval analysis, for example, combining a major 3rd with a minor 3rd to form a major chord. Our journey commenced with triads, then progressed to exploring 7th chords, followed by incorporating extensions such as 9ths, flat 9ths and sharp 13ths. We also explored the II-V-I progression in every key, and this was incorporated into Jean's practice schedule in all inversions.

To monitor Jean's development and gauge her response to the material, I maintained personal written reflections; these served as a valuable feedback mechanism. We discussed potential resources for shaping future lesson plans and her feelings regarding her progress. Whenever Jean expressed uncertainty related to a practice or theory area, I provided supplementary resources to aid her understanding. For example, during one session, Jean expressed difficulty in navigating half-diminished chords, prompting us to dedicate time to exploring these in various keys and inversions. I further supported her by crafting a worksheet for notating the chords on paper, and I composed a short musical passage for her to practise, thereby exemplifying how the half-diminished chord could be incorporated within a musical context.

We also explored melodic development as a separate element. We began by embellishing a given melody, leading to the creation of a new melodic line. We slowed down the process, exploring this as a composition exercise: I provided the left-hand voicings (with chord symbols) and asked Jean to compose and notate a variation on the original melody and then create a new one. This gave time to think deeply and carefully about the sounds that she wanted to create. Improvising is a complex, multifaceted activity; during times of low confidence, I explored easier material with Jean, reminding her of the progress she had already made. I maintained transparency about the Zone of Proximal Development approach and encouraged her to share her feelings during lessons. We initiated our journey by tackling straightforward pieces consisting of only three chords; within a year, she progressed to playing jazz standards incorporating chords with extensions. We also used duets and practised vamping chords together to build confidence. The journey continues as we begin to look at re-harmonization and composing a piece of music from scratch.

Federico's Case Study

I started working for a music centre in the UK in 2017. At that time, I was a young guitar player with a few years of teaching experience in one-to-one and one-to-two contexts but without any experience in larger ensemble settings. Additionally, my music performance degrees had not equipped me with pedagogical skills. I was, nonetheless, extremely passionate about pursuing a teaching career and came to the UK to acquire a music teaching qualification while developing my pedagogical skills in a real-life setting.

Music centres and hubs in the UK provide learners with the possibility to attend junior, intermediate and senior ensembles. Despite not having any group or ensemble teaching experience, I was entrusted with leading a guitar ensemble of pupils of different ages (eight to fourteen years old) and levels. Many of these pupils possessed limited knowledge of reading musical notation or lacked fluency in it; additionally, many of them were not taking any one-to-one or group guitar lessons alongside these ensemble sessions, and thus they frequently relied on previous knowledge acquired through unsystematic music training. However, there were a few students with reasonable reading fluency. These diverse musical levels posed challenges related to the pace of the session and learners' engagement with the ensemble experience: those with limited reading skills were holding back the more advanced learners who, for obvious reasons connected with their age and personalities, lacked the patience to accommodate their peers at their current level. One solution would have been to divide the ensemble into two groups of learners of different levels; however, at the time, numbers were low, and it would not have been financially or logistically feasible to implement this solution.

The available published materials for guitar ensembles had limitations in terms of adaptability and applicability to this context: parts were often too difficult for many of the pupils, and I perceived an incongruence in the level indicators among publishers in different educational contexts and countries. For example, the publisher Les Productions D'Oz (2024) – a specialist publisher for guitar or classical guitar – classified some repertoire as suitable for beginners, but many of the pupils in my ensemble would struggle to play these pieces. While there was free online material provided by other guitar teachers, finding pieces that would be playable by everyone in my ensemble was challenging, if not impossible. Furthermore, I felt pressure to ensure that pupils were satisfied; this linked to expectations for the group to perform at the end of each term.

I therefore decided to adapt existing resources to cater to the diverse needs of the learners, aiming to promote participation and a sense of progress. Composing from scratch would have been unrealistic for me: I lacked the confidence and the skills needed to compose a new piece for ensemble, and it would have been time-consuming and challenging due to my other commitments and the limited financial remuneration. Having experience of arranging for classical guitar and voice, including music by Monteverdi, Ravel and Tosti, I felt confident to arrange and simplify existing music for guitar ensemble.

To develop a deeper understanding of the available materials and find appealing resources, I searched online guitar sheet music catalogues containing scores for beginner-intermediate level guitar ensembles or guitar trios and quartets. These catalogues ranged from popular music companies (e.g. Hal Leonard) to independent guitar teachers promoting and selling their own compositions or arrangements. When I found a potentially interesting piece of music, I reviewed the preview score to get a first impression of the material and then searched for an audio or video recording of the piece to evaluate its suitability and, therefore, meet pupils' interests. Indeed, during the guitar ensemble sessions, I would often try to find out what kind of music pupils would like to play to enhance their motivation and boost their engagement with the guitar ensemble.

After finding potentially interesting music, I would purchase the score and familiarize myself with the material by playing it through on my own. This enabled me to understand the interplay among the guitar parts, anticipate the technical challenges that pupils might face and, consequently, offer preliminary insights into ways in which I could address difficulties inherent in the pieces. For example, common challenges revolved around note values and rhythmic patterns requiring agility (e.g. quavers at a fast tempo; use of semiquavers), syncopation, leaps across multiple strings, notes in high position along the fretboard (e.g. beyond the fifth fret) and figurations involving sequential or simultaneous movements by the thumb and fingers of the plucking hand. I usually arranged pieces using the music notation software Sibelius provided by the university in which I was studying – if I had not had this opportunity, I would have probably used free software alternatives, such as MuseScore.

My first step was to notate the bass and soprano parts as closely as possible to the original version of a piece (with regard to ensemble pieces, these were usually Guitar 1 and Guitar 4 parts). In general, I aimed to simplify the material, considering the common challenges highlighted above; for example, when encountering problematic passages relating to notes in high position, I would transpose these segments an octave lower, making sure to maintain phrase consistency. I often reduced quavers and semiquavers to crotchets to simplify passages requiring agility; however, I ensured that this modification did not significantly impact the harmony, especially for appoggiaturas and passing notes – I wanted to respect the original material and composer's ideas as much as possible.

The second step was to arrange the other parts (i.e. Guitar 2 and 3), usually following the process described above. At this stage, however, the general structure of the pieces started to take shape, and I began to consider in more depth the individual player(s) to whom I would assign the different parts. I would usually adapt some parts to individual players and often notated additional versions, such as Guitar 3a and Guitar 3b. This enabled pupils to play similar parts with their neighbours in the ensemble and fostered a sense of group solidarity. It was apparent that for beginners, it was difficult to sit next to players who played a radically different part from their own; therefore, providing similar parts could focus and boost their confidence.

Having arranged the whole piece, I would print it and distribute the individual parts to the players during the first rehearsal. I would usually approach the first rehearsal in a 'trial and error' mode, giving pupils time to try out the different parts, both individually and as a group, and providing opportunities for voicing any challenges. I also ensured to note any changes needed in the score and thus enhance its playability in the future. Unfortunately, in a few instances, I had to discard pieces because I had set unrealistic goals, but I was able to use them years later when the group had progressed.

Although there were some ups and downs, this was a valuable learning experience, both for me and the group. I developed more confidence as an ensemble leader, the group grew, and, in a few years, we built up an hour's worth of repertoire. Considering that in many instances I had arranged subversions of the main parts, pupils had the opportunity to recycle favourite pieces but could move on to a more challenging version of their initial guitar part, which fostered a sense of progress and enhanced their motivation. While this experience has been invaluable in supporting learning, it also resulted in a sense of inspiration because pupils started to see the possibilities that arranging for ensembles could offer. In fact, in the last year of my service, one of the most advanced pupils wanted to arrange a piece and asked for advice on how to undertake this. It was surprising to realize that I had not anticipated this as a potential outcome of what was originally a 'sink or swim' situation!

Marianna's Case Study

I gave Paul piano lessons for three years. Paul was a sixty-year-old man who had no formal music training prior to our lessons; he was keen on learning the basics to be able to play some simple pop piano pieces on his own. During these years he learned how to read music, basic time and key signatures, the most common rhythmic patterns and major scales, as well as playing a melody with chordal accompaniment. As a piano teacher, I quickly discovered that pupils learn in different ways: while some may excel in one area, others show strengths in different aspects of their musical learning. Paul internalized the principles of music reading in the treble and bass clefs relatively quickly; nonetheless, as things got more complicated – for example, when he started learning chords – he struggled to develop fluency in reading and, crucially, putting the reading into practice on the keyboard by executing the relevant motor actions. Despite these difficulties, he was keen on learning music through reading rather than playing music without a score.

When we started to work on chordal accompaniment for a melody at the end of our second year of collaboration, Paul's pace of progress slowed down suddenly, and he started feeling that he was not progressing at all. This had a negative impact on his self-efficacy (on more than one occasion, he claimed to feel he would not be able to master a particular piece we were working on) as well as on his motivation. I feel that this situation led him to end his piano lessons after three years, and having spent a considerable amount of time reflecting on what did not work for him, I believe there were a number of strategies that I could have implemented more effectively to facilitate his learning. One of these relates to music arrangement.

At one point, Paul decided that he wanted to learn the UK national anthem. I chose the simplest arrangement that I could find, with very basic chords in the left hand accompanying the melody played by the right hand. It became clear that the chord progression was quite tricky for Paul to master, especially given some mobility issues affecting his hands, and, therefore, I decided to simplify the music to make it more suitable for him. I encouraged Paul to remove the octaves in the left-hand chords and play only the notes that facilitated smoother hand movements. This small action improved Paul's ability to play, but he still struggled to manage the left-hand movements. Therefore, he tried playing only the lowest left-hand bass note in each chord instead of the full chordal accompaniment. I then notated the resulting arrangement on manuscript paper, and, with these adjustments, Paul managed to successfully play our bespoke version of the full piece. However, I felt that this experience had a negative impact on him: when I initially presented him with the score, I believed he could manage it, but the adjustments we had to make to match his skill level may have left him feeling inadequate. In addition, he might have perceived my expectations as really high and felt he had disappointed me. Upon reflection, I feel this experience was somewhat dispiriting for him, and I could have made things easier by selecting the repertoire more carefully, approaching any necessary arrangements with greater consideration to avoid the need for frequent adjustments to match his abilities.

Strategies and Challenges in the Creation of Educational Materials

The narratives presented above exemplify Helen, Federico and Marianna's approaches to the creation of educational materials and the challenges they experienced in their work as instrumental teachers. These accounts provide insights into the strategies they deployed to navigate the barriers they faced regarding learners' engagement, progress and development, which led them to create tailored educational materials to support students' learning trajectories. The act of creation took many forms, from the creation of bespoke theoretical resources to the arrangement of existing materials, showing examples of the varied situations in which instrumental teachers may find themselves when working with different students across varied learning contexts (one-to-one, group and musical ensemble). Despite the differences in the final products, the three educators demonstrated similar approaches to the creation of educational materials, with their accounts displaying a number of shared goals aimed at supporting learners' progress, empowerment and growth.

Helen, Federico and Marianna approached the creation of music materials from a student-centred perspective, arranging and creating material to suit learners' needs. This provided a means through which individual learning goals could be achieved, regardless of the limitations of the available resources or the learning context. As evidenced in the accounts above, published materials may not always be suitable for addressing individual challenges, despite grade indicators provided to aid understanding of the difficulty (Giesbrecht and Andrews 2021). These resources may need to be altered or integrated with bespoke materials to support pupil's learning, and, therefore, instrumental teachers need to be able to achieve this with confidence and competence. Additionally, in a group setting the needs of the collective may be at the expense of those of the individual, especially if there is an imbalance in students' levels. However, the creation of specific educational materials seemed to *entirely* foster a learning process centred around the learners' individual aims, allowing individual challenges to be addressed as needed. This was evident from the strategies that the three educators adopted to overcome these.

Helen and Federico highlighted an approach to the creation of educational materials geared towards learners' skill development, while Marianna's approach connected to the aspirational motivations of the learner, facilitating realization of his ambitions. The three educators also engaged in evaluation processes of their resources through a reflective diary (Helen) and a dialogic approach to teaching (Helen, Federico and Marianna), prompting monitoring and feedback. This connects with previous studies highlighting the importance of close contact with students, composers and teachers for the creation of effective educational compositions addressing pupil's technical abilities (Giesbrecht and Andrews 2021). Instrumental teachers appear uniquely placed to support learners and tailor their learning experience given their direct and frequent interaction with them, with composers finding feedback and input from teachers helpful (Wendzich and Andrews 2022). The sense of progression and increased engagement resulting from the approaches displayed in Helen, Federico and Marianna's accounts thus highlights the importance of creating *adaptable* and *adaptive* resources aimed at building learners' individual skills and tailored to their *evolving* needs. These strategies, with learners at the centre of the process, appear to promote accessible and inclusive learning environments, both in one-to-one and group contexts where dedicated resources can support wider participation. The pedagogical modelling of the process of arrangement may also motivate learners to undertake their own musical arrangements. This could have implications for school curricula, such as GCSE level in the UK, where students engage with music composition tasks and could be inspired by teachers providing bespoke educational resources.

While arranging and simplifying existing materials may benefit student development, it is not exempt from limitations. Marianna simplified one of Paul's favourite pieces to help Paul achieve his personal goals. As Pike (2022: 82) suggests, 'If students want to play a challenging piece of music, creating an easier appropriately leveled arrangement of the work or finding an easier piece in a similar style can be both motivational and develop necessary technical skills.' This also aligns with strategies to accommodate adult learners' characteristics related to 'normal aging' and 'possible age-related concerns' (Pike 2022: 45). However, Paul's potential feeling of inadequacy suggests that the act of arrangement could be perceived as a process that brings individual limitations to the surface. This might undermine students' self-esteem, echoing Pike (2022: 85), who states that 'perfectionism can be a concern with some of our adult music students' who may feel inadequate if they do not achieve the same result as professional performers. Therefore, Marianna's experience raises questions about the reception of arrangements among students with different personalities, aims and ambitions. This concerns not only adult learners but also younger ones who may find less ambitious material tedious and uninspiring (Andrews 2009). Nevertheless, it also triggers reflection on the extent to which a more collaborative approach to arrangement, whereby learners actively contribute to the creative process rather than acting as passive recipients, might mitigate the challenges highlighted above.

These narratives also pose questions about the confidence of educators in approaching this task. While Helen seemed confident about creating materials given her background as a composer, Federico was hesitant to create music from scratch but, due to his previous experience of arranging for classical guitar, felt empowered to arrange pre-existing music to navigate the challenges encountered. Divergent levels of confidence might emerge across instrumental teachers who may come from diverse educational backgrounds with varied interests and experiences (e.g. in composition). In addition, there may be self-limiting beliefs among educators regarding the act of composition as a skill reserved only for those formally trained as composers (Winters 2012), fuelling a sense of inadequacy that may hinder their engagement with the creation of educational materials. This resonates with research among Canadian composers, which showed the challenges in composing educational materials attributed to a perceived lack of training (Duncan and Andrews 2015). It is also worth noting that creating materials for music learners could be time-consuming for instrumental teachers, with questions about remuneration both in an institutional and private setting. Nonetheless, the experiences of Helen, Federico and Marianna serve to potentially debunk unhelpful perceptions about the act of composition for educational purposes, acknowledging a need for professional development and training to equip teachers with the skills needed to create and adapt materials to support a diverse student population. For example, Wendzich and Andrews (2022) showed how collaboration with composers could provide teachers with an understanding of compositional processes. Similarly, while Federico felt confident in using musical notation software, other teachers may perceive it as a barrier to engagement with arrangement or creation processes. This poses questions about the availability of user-friendly and cost-effective programs among teachers, with implications for teacher training in the use of digital tools, the provision of music notation programmes in institutional or private studio settings and the development of music resources (e.g. textbooks) supporting educators in developing expertise in creating music materials for their pupils.

Further Considerations

This chapter offers insights into educational material creation, analysing three co-authors' experiences as creators of educational resources for music learners. Their accounts highlight their approaches to supporting students' learning through the creation of ad-hoc materials in one-to-one and ensemble contexts. Educational resources took the form of exercises, worksheets and simplified arrangements. Despite student-centred intentions, the creation of resources has been shown to present some challenges in terms of student motivation and self-esteem. However, to what extent could these be mitigated or resolved? Could alternative notation methods be considered, such as graphic scores, rather than traditional representations of pitches and rhythm? How might the use of different notation methods affect the perception of notation as an 'aide memoire' versus its role in preserving all the elements of a composition? Would a process of co-creation be more effective than teacher-creation of materials? If so, what might be the implications for learner motivation and progress within the inevitable restrictions of time in the one-to-one or group lesson? Currently, there is scope to develop empirical evidence providing a thorough understanding of the extent to which the experiences of the three educators are shared by a wider population of instrumental teachers. This could stimulate discussions about the interface between concerns of pedagogy, musical material, learner aspirations and abilities across different educational and cultural contexts, with implications for professional development courses equipping instrumental teachers with the skills necessary to provide them with the confidence and a sense of legitimacy to create resources that support students in varied contexts.

Notes

1. This concept was developed by psychologist Lev Vygotsky, referring to the gap between a learner's current level of ability and their potential level of development with guidance and support from a more knowledgeable individual.

References

Andrews, B. W. (2009), 'Secrets of the Pied Piper: Strategies for Composing Music for Young Musicians', *Research Perspectives in Music Education*, 13 (1): 6–14.

Andrews, B. W., and M. Giesbrecht (2013), 'Composer Perspectives on Creating Educational Music for Winds', *International Journal of Arts & Sciences*, 6 (2): 455–68.

Beach, N. (2012), 'Instrumental Teachers and Their Students: Who's in the Driver's Seat?', in G. E. McPherson and G. F. Welch (eds), *The Oxford Companion to Music Education*, vol. 2, 597–600, New York: Oxford University Press.

Duncan, A., and B. W. Andrews (2015), 'Composers' Personal Learning Composing Canadian Music for Strings', *Canadian Music Educator*, 54 (6): 26–9.

Giesbrecht, M., and B. W. Andrews (2021), 'Hidden Ground: Exploring an Approach to Educational Music for Strings', *String Research Journal*, 11 (1): 39–50.

Harris, P., and R. Crozier (2000), *The Music Teacher's Companion*, London: ABRSM.

Les Productions d'Oz (2024), 'Les Productions d'Oz'. Available online: https://productionsdoz.com/ (accessed 11 July 2024).

Pike, P. D. (2022), *The Adult Music Student: Making Music Throughout the Lifespan*, Abingdon: Routledge.

Stijnen, J., L. Nijs and P. Van Petegem (2023), 'Instrument Teachers' Practices, Beliefs, and Barriers Regarding Musical Creativity: Exploring the Creative Process of Interpretation', *International Journal of Music Education*, 42 (3): 425–41.

Verney, J. (1991), 'The Integrated Instrumental Teacher: Learning to Play through Performance, Listening and Composition', *British Journal of Music Education*, 8 (3): 245–69.

Vygotsky, L. S. (1978), *Mind in Society*, Cambridge, MA: MIT Press.

Wendzich, T., and B. W. Andrews (2022), 'Through the Looking Glass: A Researcher's Perspectives on a Collaborative Music Composition Project', *International Journal of Music Education*, 40 (1): 66–77.

Winters, M. (2012), 'The Challenges of Teaching Composing', *British Journal of Music Education*, 29 (1): 19–24.

19

Resilience, Autonomy and Well-being in Instrumental Teaching and Learning

Penny Talbot, Edwina Smith, Rosemary Lynch, Bella Powell and Jennifer Cohen

Introduction

In this chapter the authors reflect on their own experiences across a broad range of face-to-face and online teaching settings, with particular reference to developing and maintaining resilience, autonomy and well-being. We suggest practical strategies that support these for both teacher and student and also consider how flexibility in teaching formats allows for greater equality, diversity and inclusion within instrumental teaching. The opportunities for teachers to recognize students' well-being issues at an early stage are noted, but so too are the limitations of teachers' suitability to provide professional well-being support, with some suggestions of where to access additional help and resources when or if required.

Resilience

Ledesma (2014: 1) defines resilience as 'the ability to bounce back from adversity, frustration, and misfortune', while George (2023) suggests that it is the ability to react in a healthy way to life's ups and downs, whether major events or general daily stresses, adapting to challenges without long-term difficulties and feeling more in control. Recognizing that not everyone has the same natural levels of resilience or equal starting points in life, Pooley and Cohen (2010: 34) describe it as 'the potential to exhibit resourcefulness by using available internal and external recourses in response to different contextual and developmental challenges'. Not only does this *resourced* resilience describe what many instrumental teachers aspire to promote within the learning environment, it is also vital to our own sense of well-being. We consider resilience here from both perspectives.

Student Resilience

At any time, each of our students may be facing a range of life challenges, perhaps coming to their lesson in a state of emotional upheaval. As instrumental teachers, we are in the privileged position of spending time on a regular basis with a student, often in a one-to-one setting, and may sometimes need to provide opportunities for them to discuss external issues if lessons are to be successful. But how can a teacher help students to build longer-term resilience in a short instrumental lesson? Petty (2014) suggests a range of child-centred strategies to encourage general resilience-building, focusing on actively listening and acknowledging the importance of each child's ideas, helping them to learn from past experiences, plan positively for the future and not to fear mistakes. In addition, teachers are encouraged to provide opportunities and guidance to help children develop personal responsibility and empathy. Edgar, Ireland D'Ambrosio and Hackl-Blumstein (2023: 192) consider that music lessons provide 'fertile ground' for helping young people develop a range of social and emotional skills, leading to a positive sense of identity, belonging and agency, all important factors in strengthening personal resilience. Informed by these authors, and through discussion of our own teaching, we offer here various resilience-building strategies that might be explored in instrumental lessons with students of any age:

1. Take time to listen carefully to what a student says, demonstrating respect for their ideas to help them gain confidence. Strategies might include guiding the student to indicate what they want from music lessons, listening to their likes and dislikes, having non-judgemental discussions and reminding them to ask about anything they do not understand.
2. Encourage the student to develop autonomy through setting their own goals and taking ownership of their musical aims and by guiding them to make their own musical or technical decisions, such as developing their own interpretation or practice methods. Make sure they encounter and celebrate success, and praise specific achievements to bolster self-confidence and feelings of competence.
3. Use any setbacks as a learning experience, to help develop a growth mindset (Davis 2017), acknowledging low spirits and possible causes of low

motivation but then looking forward and finding ways to build more positive connections to the student's goals.

4. Teach mindful playing and practice: Tanner's *The Mindful Pianist* (2016) gives useful advice and ideas. Encourage the student to think carefully about decisions and to process negative thoughts in a questioning way.
5. Provide the space for students to experiment, seeing mistakes 'not as an enemy to be vanquished but as a friend with much to teach us' (Davis 2017: 11) and using these to learn patience, analytical skills, problem-solving and perseverance.
6. Explore improvisation: even from the earliest stages a learner can choose pitches, rhythms, differing articulation and dynamics to demonstrate how they are feeling or to depict various scenarios. An imaginative story-telling situation may even develop into a solution or acceptance, a letting go and moving on.
7. Inspire students to be aware of connecting with others – respecting others' needs may help them to move out of their comfort zone and learn new life skills. This can be done in a gradual manner, such as volunteering to perform for residents in care homes or recording performances to send to a relative or friend who lives at a distance or is feeling lonely.
8. Arrange duet or small group playing, to bolster interpersonal skills, or an informal concert with students not only performing but also helping with the practical arrangements.
9. Encourage the student to recognize that it is possible to learn new ways of coping and changing behaviour. If they are upset about making mistakes or not doing well in a performance or exam, for instance, aim to guide the student away from self-recrimination to reflect on how to approach similar situations in the future. This could include discussing practice strategies or ways of managing performance anxiety while also emphasizing that the student is learning and growing positively through the setbacks.
10. Perhaps model coping strategies by deliberately making a mistake when demonstrating or by relaying real-life scenarios. By sharing some personal challenges in our own instrumental practice, we may create a space where honest and pragmatic conversation can develop trust and an atmosphere of creativity and collaborative enquiry so that both student and teacher can flourish. Indeed, as Straka (2018) suggests, teachers 'construct resilience' through exploring their vulnerability in their teaching.

Even if a teacher senses that the student's engagement is being affected by issues that they are unwilling to discuss (and it is important to recognize that sometimes the teacher's involvement is not appropriate: they are not a therapist or counsellor), using some of the strategies above may have a positive effect in the lesson and help to build longer-term resilience. In our experience, students in this situation become visibly calmer when focusing on setting a goal or on choosing what to engage with in the lesson, giving them back a sense of control when they might have felt powerless in the setting(s) they were in beforehand.

Many teachers will recognize the strategies listed above as already being part of their usual practice: it is empowering to appreciate that in addition to teaching music effectively we are also helping our students to develop valuable life skills.

Teacher Resilience

Research indicates that teaching in general is a demanding and stressful profession (Agyapong et al. 2022; McCarthy, Lineback and Reiser 2014). Instrumental teachers can also find themselves juggling a portfolio career, which, although it may give flexibility and variety, can be personally and financially challenging (Coulson 2012). Many work long, often unsocial, hours, and in private studio contexts there may be the additional challenge of isolation (Burwell, Carey and Bennett 2019).

Although there is little resilience-focused research specifically relating to instrumental teaching, Bakker's study (2005) of instrumental lessons in Dutch music schools indicated that 'a combination of autonomy, performance feedback, social support from colleagues and supervisory coaching' were important predictors of teachers achieving 'flow'. Flow, defined as 'a short-term peak experience that is characterized by absorption, work enjoyment, and intrinsic work motivation' (Bakker 2005: 37), has itself been found to contribute to resilience and well-being (Mao et al. 2024). These benefits were also found to be contagious: 'The more flow experiences music teachers reported, the higher the frequency of comparable experiences among their students' (Bakker 2005: 38).

Similar predictors have been found to support resilience in classroom teachers, and many successful strategies in that setting are applicable to instrumental teaching. Ainsworth and Oldfield (2019: 123) suggest that, in addition to personal characteristics such as health awareness and having 'emotional intelligence', external influences such as supportive and positive colleagues are especially beneficial to building and maintaining a teacher's resilience. Munroe's study (2022), comparing the resilience of an early-career teacher and an experienced class music teacher in schools where many students had suffered trauma, highlighted similar themes. The experienced teacher had developed ways of coping, partly through encountering life events which fostered empathy but also by having supportive colleagues, whereas the early-career teacher felt unsupported. The experienced teacher also employed calming techniques such as yoga with their students, celebrated students' and their own successes and was proactive in researching their students' challenges and attending relevant courses. Their positive attitude was influenced by the Orff Schulwerk approach – 'a pedagogy based on the unity of music, movement, and speech' (Beegle and Bond 2016: 27) – and confidence also grew from helping and advising trainee teachers. A study of novice classroom teachers by Chen (2022: 7) found that resilience increased through 'self-compassion', turning a negative mindset to a more positive one, again drawing upon support from people around them, and consciously permitting themselves to have a better work-life balance.

Many instrumental teachers, however, work solely in their own home or studio or travel to students' homes, having no contact with schools or community settings. In this situation, the teacher may experience a sense of isolation, possibly leading to a longer-term lack of motivation, stimulation or awareness of current teaching practices (Bautista, Stanley and Candusso 2021; Burwell, Carey and Bennett 2019). To pre-empt or alleviate this, the authors of this chapter have found it helpful to develop their own networks of colleagues by attending courses, joining professional organizations or simply enjoying informal discussion groups where challenges can be shared and successes celebrated. Some of us have approached a more experienced teacher for support, who guided us in considering our work-life balance, and some have explored self-help methods such as Alexander Technique (Kleinman and Buckoke 2013), yoga (Butzer, Ahmed and Khalsa 2016) and mindfulness (Holmes 2019). In addition, if teachers are not already performing as part of a portfolio career, seeking out opportunities for performance (formal or informal), or even learning a new instrument, can help maintain motivation to practise, explore new repertoire and styles of playing and collaborate with fellow musicians. All these can inform and refresh our teaching as well as supporting our sense of well-being as a musician.

Autonomy

Supporting Student Autonomy

Bonneville-Roussy, Hruska and Trower (2020: 99) describe autonomy-supportive teachers as those who 'consider students as self-determined individuals who are capable of mastering their own learning, of making choices, and who are aware of their own needs'. Encouraging students to take responsibility for their own ideas and development, rather than to rely solely on teacher-delivered instructions, is a step towards them becoming independent learners (Reeve 2016) and promoters of their own well-being and resilience. Through dialogic teaching methods, where the teacher guides the student to reflect on their own playing through questions and discussion, students can be given greater responsibility and encouragement to assess their playing while teachers gain clearer feedback on the student's understanding (Meissner and Timmers 2020). This autonomy-supportive style of teaching is not, though, to be mistaken for a 'laissez-faire or hands-off' approach, instead providing 'both choice and structure' (Bonneville-Roussy, Hruska and Trower 2020: 99). Although students sometimes need time and encouragement to adjust to a dialogic, autonomy-supportive teaching style if moving from a more teacher-directed environment, there are long-term benefits for their overall well-being: Bonneville-Roussy and colleagues (2020: 97–8) found that 'teachers' transmission of passion for music and autonomy-supportive behaviors were related to students' well-being, whereas controlling behaviors hindered well-being'.

Online teaching provides opportunities to promote even greater student autonomy: de Bruin (2021) found that instrumental teachers observed their online school-aged pupils during the Covid-19 pandemic to be articulate about their progress, learning needs and processes, demonstrating critical thinking and responding to the new format in ways which enabled a greater sense of student-teacher equality and increased dialogic teaching. To compensate for the vagaries of Wi-Fi, the limited scope of tonal and dynamic contrast and the lack of clarity of detail in many online settings, students can be encouraged to act as the teacher's 'ears' by assessing, for example, the effectiveness of their own dynamic range, tonal variety and clarity of articulation. In the authors' experience, students respond with enthusiasm once they become aware of how valuable their self-assessment is to their teacher. This understanding accelerates their development as an independent learner and objective assessor of their own playing.

Encouraging students to record aspects of their own practice and performance is another autonomy-supportive strategy: through listening to and reflecting on their recordings, students develop greater independence and autonomy in deciding how to improve. Self-recording can also provide valuable performance experience: our students frequently comment that playing for a recording generates a sense of performance, even when alone. Increased opportunities to submit recorded performances for graded exams are another reason to encourage the practice, as well as these providing greater choice of exam format and improved accessibility to students who might not previously have been able to take them.

Teacher Autonomy and Online Teaching

According to Boyle (2021: 80), teacher autonomy and job satisfaction in the instrumental teaching sector are high, as teachers are 'able to determine the amount, context and curriculum of their teaching'. Where teacher autonomy is high, burnout is diminished (Skaalvik and Skaalvik 2014), aligning with the positive effects of building resilience and well-being strategies into our working environment.

Those who teach in students' homes, however, often face the challenge of frequent travel between workplaces or limited access to transport. The increased acceptance of online teaching may potentially offer these teachers, and those with caring commitments, a greater sense of autonomy, with the option of teaching online from home even if they do not have an appropriate space for face-to-face lessons. This has the immediate benefit of decreased travel costs, increased time available for additional teaching or other activities and the potential to extend the teacher's market both nationally and internationally. It might also allow new parents to return more gradually to teaching or those with increasing caring responsibilities to continue their teaching practice, thus maintaining vital connections with the outside world and their professional identity.

Well-being

A sense of well-being is another important factor in developing and maintaining resilience for both teacher and student. As George (2023) highlights, well-being does not mean a state of constant happiness, rather a 'state of positive feelings and meeting full potential in the world' (Simons and Baldwin 2021: 990). To sustain a teaching career, it is important to consider our own sense of well-being, but also, as Norton's research (2016: 190) indicates, many instrumental teachers hold 'a fundamental belief that teachers have a responsibility to safeguard, and preferably enhance, their pupils' health and well-being'. We discuss below how we can support the well-being of our students and ourselves in relation to physical and mental health, age-related considerations and online teaching, finishing with examples from the authors' experience of small changes providing long-term benefits.

Caring for Our Students and Ourselves

Learning to sing or play an instrument can be physically and mentally demanding (Kenny and Ackermann 2016). We can help our students by teaching good body use and healthy playing and practice techniques, having positive discussions about performance and any related anxieties and encouraging care of hearing and eyesight; also important is helping students to learn when and how to say 'No', to avoid overwork and burnout (Hamann and Gordon 2000). Modelling healthy behaviours in lessons helps address this responsibility, benefiting both ourselves and our students, while creating an open and accepting atmosphere may help students feel comfortable to discuss physical and mental challenges that might be hindering their progress.

As suggested above in relation to resilience, instrumental teachers may sometimes recognize issues affecting students' health and well-being at an early stage: research by Williamon and Thompson (2006: 411) found that conservatoire students 'showed a significant inclination to go first to their instrumental teacher for advice about health and psychological problems, before appropriate medical practitioners'. This may enable us to offer advice and support, but unless we have training in, for example, mental health support, it is vital (both for ourselves and for our students) that we recognize our limitations and have a clear idea of when, and where, to guide students to seek other support. For younger students this might be within their family or educational institution (Boyle and Widdison 2021), but for ourselves and our adult students, invaluable practical help and advice are available from a range of organizations including the British Association for Performing Arts Medicine (BAPAM),[1] the British Voice Association (including the Voice Care Network),[2] Musicians' Hearing Services,[3] the Healthy Conservatoires Network[4] and ArtsMinds.[5] In addition to online resources, books such as *The Musician's Body* (Rosset i Llobet and Odam 2007), *Performance Anxiety: A Practical Guide for Music Teachers* (Daubney and Daubney 2017) and *The Essential Handbook for Musicians Who Teach* (Boyle and Widdison 2021) give detailed, accessible and practical advice on specific areas of well-being in music teaching, learning and performance.

Age-Related Considerations

Over the course of a teaching career, we may teach students of all ages. It is important, therefore, that we are aware of age-related aspects of well-being, teaching in a way that is safe and appropriate for the age of each individual student, whatever stage of technique they have reached or repertoire they wish to learn (Phillips, Williams and Edwin 2018; Sataloff and Davidson 2018; Upjohn 2019). When teaching older students (particularly singers) we may also need to be prepared for an 'overwhelming loss of confidence and defensive aggressiveness' (Sataloff and Davidson 2018: 67) due to age-related changes in ability. In this situation, responding with respect and sensitivity and employing tailored physical and psychological strategies may enable the student to move forwards with positivity. To maintain a long career ourselves, this understanding of how our own body and mind may change at various stages of our life is also vital for a positive and healthy approach. Just as for our students, these changes may be challenging to our personal (and professional) pride and sense of self. With them, however, come experience, wisdom and empathy, which can contribute much more to our teaching than the ability to demonstrate a particular technique that has become less comfortable with age.

Online Teaching and Well-being

In addition to the autonomy-related benefits of online teaching mentioned above, this format may present well-being benefits. Practically speaking, teaching online alleviates the challenges of carrying teaching material and valuable, sometimes bulky, instruments from place to place and reduces the likelihood of issues with unsuitable seating, lighting and temperature in the teaching room. When online, the teacher can have their own instrument, seating and some control of the environment while avoiding illnesses passed on by students and their families, together with allergy or asthma triggers from pets, perfumes and flowers.

The wide acceptance of online instrumental teaching has also brought benefits to many teachers and students with physical disabilities, allowing equality of access in professional music teaching or learning without the frustration of navigating buildings poorly equipped to accommodate them. Also, some teachers and students challenged by mental health issues, or other people's acceptance of their neurodiversity, may have a preference for teaching and learning from the security and familiarity of their own home, enabling participation and inclusion in music-making on their own terms.

As previously mentioned, teaching and learning online do have their own challenges relating to sound quality, unstable connections and the difficulty of incorporating certain valuable teaching strategies. In addition, some institutions may insist on face-to-face tuition, there may be significant practical challenges in teaching very young beginners online and some students (and teachers) may simply prefer face-to-face tuition. There are also potential negative effects on well-being to guard against: long periods of headphone use may pose dangers to hearing health; teaching online for long hours without breaks can lead to mental exhaustion and eye strain; and students and parents may consider that, as teachers are online, they are permanently 'on call' which might necessitate boundary-setting around availability to teach or respond to queries. However, an increasing number of music-specific online teaching platforms are now available, reducing the need to rely on those primarily intended for speech-based video conferencing. Even if we do not choose to embrace online teaching as our main format, its availability is a worthwhile contribution to our sense of well-being and autonomy.

Small Changes with Long-Term Benefits

In addition to discovering the benefits of online teaching during the Covid-19 pandemic of the early 2020s, some of the authors found that necessary safety adaptations made when returning to face-to-face teaching benefited long-term well-being while also having positive implications for the development of student and teacher autonomy. Even simple health recommendations, such as opening windows, have led to more understanding in institutions of the need for fresh air in the teaching room, while teachers can request clean hands when playing shared instruments without appearing over-fussy. Using a clear screen between teacher and student, originally intended as protection from airborne viruses, also provides a minor acoustic shield, helping to protect the teacher's hearing. If space and resources allow, using separate music stands for teacher and student delivers numerous benefits: in instrumental teaching, the distance between student and teacher might be based on the teacher's preferred personal space requirements, which may cause discomfort for the student if they have a psychological need for something different. Teacher and student can have their stands at different heights to comfortably accommodate their potential height variations; using separate stands may also convey a greater sense of equality, leading to more comfortable discussion. As a pedagogical aid, it may also encourage students to project their sound and musical ideas with a greater sense of performance if the teacher is further away. Even small changes like this can have a major effect on the sense of well-being, autonomy and ultimately the resilience of both students and teachers.

Concluding Thoughts

Connections between resilience, autonomy and well-being have appeared throughout this chapter. Through autonomy-supportive teaching and attention to our students' well-being we can assist them in developing resilience, not just in the lesson but in their wider life and learning. To enable us to do this, it is equally important to focus on our own well-being, perhaps learning from strategies employed by classroom teachers to maintain resilience and by being proactive in making changes that will give us more autonomy and support our personal needs. The wealth of available resources includes opportunities to maintain connections with the music teaching community for discussion, friendship, knowledge-sharing and giving or receiving advice. By engaging with these, we can help both ourselves and others. In 2019, staff and postgraduate students at the University of York initiated a Music Education Forum for this purpose. It continues to provide an invaluable pedagogical, intellectual and social community for ourselves, alumni and international colleagues and has resulted in the creation of this book.

Notes

1. British Association for Performing Arts Medicine (BAPAM): https://www.bapam.org.uk.
2. British Voice Association: https://britishvoiceassociation.org.uk.
3. Musicians' Hearing Services: https://www.musicianshearingservices.co.uk.
4. Healthy Conservatoires Network: https://healthyconservatoires.org/network.
5. ArtsMinds: https://www.artsminds.co.uk.

References

Agyapong, B., G. Obuobi-Donkor, L. Burback and Y. Wei (2022), 'Stress, Burnout, Anxiety and Depression among Teachers: A Scoping Review', *International Journal of Environmental Research and Public Health*, 19 (17): 10706, doi.org/10.3390/ijerph191710706.

Ainsworth, S., and J. Oldfield (2019), 'Quantifying Teacher Resilience: Context Matters', *Teaching and Teacher Education*, 82: 117–28.

Bakker, A. B. (2005), 'Flow among Music Teachers and Their Students: The Crossover of Peak Experiences', *Journal of Vocational Behavior*, 66 (1): 26–44.

Bautista, A., A. M. Stanley and F. Candusso (2021), 'Policy Strategies to Remedy Isolation of Specialist Arts and Music Teachers', *Arts Education Policy Review*, 122 (1): 42–53.

Beegle, A., and J. Bond (2016), 'Orff Schulwerk: Releasing and Developing the Musical Imagination', in C. R. Abril and B. M. Gault (eds), *Teaching General Music: Approaches, Issues, and Viewpoints*, 25–48, New York: Oxford University Press.

Bonneville-Roussy, A., E. Hruska and H. Trower (2020), 'Teaching Music to Support Students: How Autonomy-Supportive Music Teachers Increase Students' Well-Being', *Journal of Research in Music Education*, 68 (1): 97–119.

Boyle, K. (2021), *The Instrumental Music Teacher: Autonomy, Identity and the Portfolio Career in Music*, Abingdon: Routledge.

Boyle, K., and D. Widdison (2021), *The Essential Handbook for Musicians Who Teach: A Practical Guide for Instrumental and Singing Teachers*, London: Faber Music.

Burwell, K., G. Carey and D. Bennett (2019), 'Isolation in Studio Music Teaching: The Secret Garden', *Arts and Humanities in Higher Education*, 18 (4): 372–94.

Butzer, B., K. Ahmed and S. B. S. Khalsa (2016), 'Yoga Enhances Positive Psychological States in Young Adult Musicians', *Applied Psychophysiology and Biofeedback*, 41 (2): 191–202.

Chen, J. J. (2022), 'Self-Compassion as Key to Stress Resilience among First-Year Early Childhood Teachers during COVID-19: An Interpretative Phenomenological Analysis', *Teaching and Teacher Education*, 111, https://doi.org/10.1016/j.tate.2021.103627.

Coulson, S. (2012), 'Collaborating in a Competitive World: Musicians' Working Lives and Understandings of Entrepreneurship', *Work, Employment and Society*, 26 (2): 246–61.

Daubney, G., and A. Daubney (2017), *Performance Anxiety: A Practical Guide for Music Teachers*, London: Incorporated Society of Musicians Trust.

Davis, V. W. (2017), 'Error Reflection: Embracing Growth Mindset in the General Music Classroom', *General Music Today*, 30 (2): 11–17.

de Bruin, L. R. (2021), 'Instrumental Music Educators in a COVID Landscape: A Reassertion of Relationality and Connection in Teaching Practice', *Frontiers in Psychology*, doi: 10.3389/fpsyg.2020.624717.

Edgar, S. N., K. Ireland D'Ambrosio and E. Hackl-Blumstein (2023), 'Compassion and Care through Musical Social Emotional Learning', in K. S. Hendricks (ed.), *The Oxford Handbook of Care in Music Education*, 192–204, New York: Oxford University Press.

George, K. (2023), 'Responding to Stress with Resilience' [video], YouTube online talk, 17 May, https://www.youtube.com/watch?v=SnRsrxaUZWY (accessed 2 August 2024).

Hamann, D., and D. Gordon (2000), 'Burnout an Occupational Hazard: Many Elements of a Music Teacher's Life Can Contribute to Stress and Burnout', *National Association for Music Education*, 87 (3): 34–9.

Holmes, K. (2019), 'Neuroscience, Mindfulness and Holistic Wellness: Reflections on Interconnectivity in Teaching and Learning', *Interchange*, 50: 445–60.

Kenny, D. T., and B. J. Ackermann (2016), 'Optimizing Physical and Psychological Health in Performing Musicians', in S. Hallam, I. Cross and M. H. Thaut (eds), *The Oxford Handbook of Music Psychology*, 2nd edn, 633–48, Oxford: Oxford University Press.

Kleinman, J., and P. Buckoke (2013), *The Alexander Technique for Musicians*, London: Bloomsbury.

Ledesma, J. (2014), 'Conceptual Frameworks and Research Models on Resilience in Leadership', *Sage Open*, 4 (3), doi.org/10.1177/2158244014545464.

Mao, Y., X. Luo, S. Wang, Z. Mao, M. Xie and M. Bonaiuto (2024), 'Flow Experience Fosters University Students' Well-Being through Psychological Resilience: A Longitudinal Design with Cross-Lagged Analysis', *British Journal of Educational Psychology*, 94 (2): 518–38.

McCarthy, C., S. Lineback and J. Reiser (2014), 'Teacher Stress, Emotion and Classroom Management', in E. Emmer and E. J. Sabornie (eds), *Handbook of Classroom Management*, 2nd edn, 301–21, New York: Routledge.

Meissner, H., and R. Timmers (2020), 'Young Musicians' Learning of Expressive Performance: The Importance of Dialogic Teaching and Modeling', *Frontiers in Education*, 5: 1–21.

Munroe, A. M. (2022), 'Novice and Experienced Music Teacher Resilience: A Comparative Case Study', *Research Studies in Music Education*, 44 (1): 99–109.

Norton, N. (2016), 'Health Promotion in Instrumental and Vocal Music Lessons: The Teacher's Perspective', PhD diss., Royal Northern College of Music and Manchester Metropolitan University.

Petty, K. (2014), 'Ten Ways to Foster Resilience in Young Children – Teaching Kids to "Bounce Back"', *Dimensions of Early Childhood*, 42 (3): 35–9.

Phillips, K. H., J. Williams and R. Edwin (2018), 'The Young Singer', in G. McPherson and G. Welch (eds), *Vocal, Instrumental, and Ensemble Learning and Teaching: An Oxford Handbook of Music Education*, Vol. 3, 44–59, New York: Oxford University Press.

Pooley, J. A., and L. Cohen (2010), 'Resilience: A Definition in Context', *Australian Community Psychologist*, 22 (1): 30–7.

Reeve, J. (2016), 'Autonomy-Supportive Teaching: What It Is, How to Do It', in W. C. Liu, J. C. K. Wang and R. M. Ryan (eds), *Building Autonomous Learners: Perspectives from Research and Practice using Self-Determination Theory*, 2nd edn, 129–52, Singapore: Springer.

Rosset i Llobet, J., and G. Odam (2007), *The Musician's Body: A Maintenance Manual for Peak Performance*, Aldershot: Ashgate.

Sataloff, R. T., and J. W. Davidson (2018), 'The Older Singer', in G. McPherson and G. Welch (eds), *Vocal, Instrumental, and Ensemble Learning and Teaching: An Oxford Handbook of Music Education, Vol. 3*, 60–75, New York: Oxford University Press.

Simons, G., and D. S. Baldwin (2021), 'A Critical Review of the Definition of "Wellbeing" for Doctors and Their Patients in a Post Covid-19 Era', *International Journal of Social Psychiatry*, 67 (8): 984–91.

Skaalvik, E. M., and S. Skaalvik (2014), 'Teacher Self-Efficacy and Perceived Autonomy: Relations with Teacher Engagement, Job Satisfaction, and Emotional Exhaustion', *Psychological Reports*, 114 (1): 68–77.

Straka, A. L. (2018), 'Perception, Permission and Purpose: Portraits of Vulnerability and Resilience in Teaching', PhD diss., University of Cincinnati.

Tanner, M. (2016), *The Mindful Pianist: Focus, Practise, Perform, Engage*, London: Faber Music.

Upjohn, S. (2019), 'Play Well: Educating for the Prevention of Playing-Related Musculoskeletal Injuries at a Specialist Music School in the UK. A Physiotherapist-Led Action Research Project', EdD diss., University of Cambridge.

Williamon, A., and S. Thompson (2006), 'Awareness and Incidence of Health Problems among Conservatoire Students', *Psychology of Music*, 34 (4): 411–30.

Index

adult learners 18–19, 223, 232, 248–9, 251, 262
Alexander Technique 169, 259
andragogy 232
assessment
   measurement error 220
   norm referenced or criterion based 219
   performance assessment and graded examinations 33–4, 81, 82, 83–4, 135, 153, 169, 210, 211, 214, 217–27
   accessibility and reasonable adjustments 224–6, 260
   certificates 224
   formats 219, 226, 260
   history of graded performance examinations 218–19
   marking of examinations 224
   mock examinations 224
   supporting tests 153, 218, 219, 222, 226
   theory assessment and graded examinations 152, 153–4
Associated Board of the Royal Schools of Music (ABRSM) 2, 57, 125, 135, 152, 153, 154, 159 n.2, 217, 218, 219, 221, 222, 223, 224, 244
aural training 151, 152, 164, 180
authenticity
   in Chinese music education 93
   of teacher's persona 26, 27, 34

banking model of education 16, 17
body mapping 169

Cartesian dualism 165
Central Conservatory of Music, Beijing, China 56
Certificate for Music Educators (CME) 57
China – as context for instrumental teaching 51–2, 55, 56–7, 58, 59, 91–101, 105–15

Chinese traditional instruments
   semi-improvisation 93
   teaching of 91–101
   values 93, 98, 100
Chinese National Academy of Arts (CNAA) 56
chords 138, 140, 153–4, 155, 157, 244, 245, 246, 249
cognitive biases 13, 18–19
cognitive load 168, 197, 200 n.4
collaborative writing 4
collective ownership 16
communities of practice 3, 8
competition 41, 115, 222, 240
composition 84, 85, 243–53
conceptual metaphors 163–4
confirmation bias 15, 19
Confucianism 107
constructivism 14, 15
convergent thinking 100
Covid-19 pandemic 5, 7, 8, 45, 69, 73, 152, 182, 219, 221, 260, 263
critical incidents 1, 4, 13–14, 15–18, 19–21
critical thinking 19, 20, 58, 260
cross-cultural teaching 59, 91–101, 105–15, 119–29, 212–13
   cultural competence 21
   cultural intelligence theory ('CQ') 6, 91–2
   cultural norms 29, 34, 107
cultural supremacy 151

Dalcroze 164, 169, 197
doctoral students' anxiety and isolation 3
duets 218, 246, 257

effective pedagogy 16, 111, 115, 211
embodiment 12–13, 163–72, 197
   embodied cognition 165, 175, 176

embodied simulation 166
emotional intelligence 258
enculturation 28–31
English as an additional language (EAL) 6, 99, 100, 114, 115, 119–29
    BICS (Basic Interpersonal Communication Skills) 121, 124
    CALP (Cognitive Academic Language Proficiency) 121, 124
    strategies to support EAL learners 119–29
English Baccalaureate (EBacc) 151
ensemble participation 85, 141, 181, 182, 218, 219, 220, 223, 238, 239, 246–8, 257
epistemology 14, 15, 95
Equality Act 2010 (UK) 224
experimentation 4, 21, 139, 164, 182, 236, 237

facilitation 16, 106, 111, 113
'flow' 164, 258
formal and informal learning 83, 87, 154, 157, 158, 159, 231, 232, 257, 259
Fryderyk Chopin University of Music, Poland 122

game-based learning 137–9, 144, 164, 180–1, 198, 210
GCSE music examination 70, 84, 150, 251
growth mindset 236, 237, 256
Guildhall School of Music and Drama, London 57, 218

health – physical 261, 263
health and safety 69, 70
higher music education 41, 42, 44–5, 54, 55, 56, 58, 106, 151–2

Igoe, *Groove Essentials* 231–40
image schemata 165, 168, 169
improvisation 6, 55, 85, 135–45, 157, 172, 182, 219, 227, 244–5, 257
    Baroque 136–9
    'freestyle playing' 182
    games 137–9
    jazz 139–42, 143
        call-and-response 141
        'enclosures' 143, 145, n.1
        'trading fours' 142

rock and pop 142–4
'semi-improvisation' in Chinese music 93
Style Scrapbooks 137–9
transcribing 144
Independent Society of Musicians (ISM) (UK) 54, 57, 59
infants 163, 164, 167, 171
instrumental learners
    access and inclusion 152, 183, 191–200, 224–6, 260, 263
    adjustment to new teacher 206–16, 260
    agency in learning 86, 96, 105, 106, 155, 169, 199, 232, 236, 255–64
    aims (*see also* goals) 31, 112–13, 214, 215, 250, 251, 256
    autonomy (*see also* independence) 83, 86, 93, 96, 100, 139, 169, 170, 196, 232, 240, 256, 259–60
    beginners (*see also* novice learners) 18, 31, 35, 110, 112, 136, 143, 169, 178, 181, 182, 237, 239
    behavioural issues 34, 70, 72, 97, 112, 198, 199
    challenges in understanding verbal discourse (EAL students) 119–29, 212–13
    confidence 127, 139, 140, 144, 199, 244, 245, 246, 249, 256
    curiosity 239
    discomfort 180, 212, 214–15, 263
    discovery in learning 17, 210, 237
    dissatisfaction 235
    effort 83, 199, 219, 238
    emotional attachment to teacher 209–10
    engagement in lessons and learning 20, 83, 100, 106, 107, 111, 120, 126, 142, 155, 196, 198–9, 246–7, 250, 257, 259
    enjoyment (*see also* fun) 32, 83, 112, 113, 139, 182, 184, 210, 214, 223, 235, 236, 237, 240
    frustration 199, 208, 209, 210, 234, 246, 255
    fun (*see also* enjoyment) 43, 139, 141, 180, 181, 214, 237
    goals (*see also* aims) 53, 81, 83, 87, 152, 178, 179, 183, 196, 210, 222, 223, 236, 238, 251, 256, 257, 258
    identity 38, 54–5, 198, 256

inclusion 7, 222, 224–6, 238, 246, 251, 255–64
independence (*see also* autonomy) 17, 20, 53, 59, 83, 86, 96, 98, 99, 100, 106, 111, 114, 169, 198, 207, 209, 210, 212, 240, 259–60
injury 171
isolation 177, 178, 182, 184
kinesthetic awareness 171, 197
'learned helplessness' 198
learning difficulties 30, 196
lifelong learner 58, 184, 240
mental health 70, 199, 261–62, 263
metacognition 94, 111, 196, 212
mindset 58, 97, 100, 232, 235–7, 238–9, 256
motivation 70, 83, 86, 92, 94, 112, 177, 179, 180, 182, 194, 198, 199, 206, 208, 210, 222, 224, 235, 239, 247, 248, 249, 250, 251, 252, 253, 257
neurodiversity 212, 263
novice learners (*see also* beginners) 168, 248, 249, 263
ownership (*see also* responsibility) 16, 34, 83, 107, 155, 175, 180, 181, 182, 239, 256
peer learning 85, 182–3, 246
perfectionism 30, 34, 178, 181, 226, 236, 251
repertoire choices 81, 84, 151, 213, 224, 249
resilience 199, 235, 255–8, 261
responsibility (*see also* ownership) 34, 83, 170, 212, 237, 239, 256, 259–60
risk-taking 137, 210
self-concept and self-view 198, 232
self-efficacy 94, 96, 249
self-empathy 235
self-esteem 212, 251, 252
self-evaluation 238, 260
self-paced learning 235
self-presentation 33, 34, 114, 225
self-regulation 93, 99, 100, 175, 176, 178, 180, 182, 184
SEN (Special Educational Needs) 72, 191–200
  autism 199, 225
  barriers to learning and progression 191, 192–5, 225

braille score 197, 213
communication between stakeholders (learner, parents and schools) 193, 194, 195–6
data protection 193
D/deaf learners 194, 197, 198, 199, 200 n.3
diagnosis 225
disclosure 193, 195, 225
dyslexia 194, 195, 197, 225
dyspraxia 193, 200 n.1, 225
education and healthcare (EHC) plans 225
goal-setting 196
inclusive teaching approaches 191–200
instrument adaptations 197
models of disability 191–2
multisensory instructional strategies 197, 213
non-visible disabilities 193
organizational support 198
progress 196
safeguarding 193
social attitudes 191
Sounds of Intent framework 196
stigma 193
Universal Design for Learning 196, 197
visual impairment 191, 225
stress and anxiety 84, 96, 111, 140, 141, 181, 195, 199, 208, 209, 212, 213, 223, 225, 226, 234, 255, 261
technique 139, 169, 171, 208, 211, 236
trauma 258
trust 142, 208–9, 210, 237–9, 257
well-being 92, 97, 100, 180, 199, 208–16, 235, 256–8, 259, 260, 261
instrumental practising 7, 18, 20, 31, 32, 40, 41, 75, 83, 96, 109, 112, 114, 167–8, 171, 175–85, 197, 219, 223, 236, 256, 257
acronyms 180, 181, 183–4
  'LEST' (Listen Empathetically, Strategize Together) 183
  'MITs' (Most Important Things) 183
  'PRACTICE' (Practice of Relevant Activities Causes Technical Improvement, and, Correct Execution) 183

chunking 180, 181–2, 197
cognitive barriers 177, 178, 184 n.2
'concentration hat' 181
EDI (Equality, Diversity and Inclusion) barriers 177
environmental barriers 176–8
gamified practice 180–1, 198
influence of geopolitical climates 177–8
practice apps 177, 179, 180, 197, 198
recording and evaluating 180, 238, 260
strategies for effective practice 179–84
instrumental stereotypes 232
instrumental teacher
　adaptability (*see also* flexibility) 27, 31, 45, 68–9, 114, 210, 211
　administrative roles 51, 54, 66
　agency and autonomy 18, 45, 66, 260–4
　assumptions 13, 20, 21, 33, 192
　authority 92, 93, 96
　awareness of self 22
　'becoming' 21, 22
　boundary-setting 263
　burnout 260, 261
　communication with pupils' parents 31, 33, 66, 111, 114, 177, 179, 193–6, 197, 210, 211, 214, 215, 218, 222, 263
　compassionate teaching practices 3, 4, 192
　confidence 42, 46, 55, 80, 109, 110, 111, 115, 127, 135–6, 141, 200, 215, 243, 247, 250, 251–2, 259, 262
　conscious and subconscious decisions and influences 13, 15, 16, 17, 19, 21, 26, 27, 28, 30, 31, 32–4, 42, 121, 126, 166, 168, 232, 239, 259
　conscientiousness 34
　cross-cultural teaching (China and Western) 5–6, 59, 91–101, 105–15, 119–29
　curriculum 59, 154, 218, 223, 260
　demonstration (*see also* modelling) 53, 98, 106, 109–10, 141, 157, 167, 171, 212, 213, 251, 257, 262
　dialogue and discourse in teaching 17–18, 19–20, 83, 97, 106, 138, 149, 155, 158, 208, 232, 250, 256, 257, 259–60
　　questioning 17, 19–20, 83, 96, 98, 110–12, 113, 114, 115, 120, 124, 125, 126, 154–5, 157, 158, 170, 179, 212, 259

　　Socratic questions 20, 110–12
　efficiency 17, 94, 157, 181
　emotions 195, 212, 213, 214–15
　empathy 27, 53, 112, 128, 171, 177, 179, 184, 192, 199, 207, 208, 209, 214, 233–5, 258, 262
　employment 54, 66, 69, 71, 74, 92
　expert 233
　expertise 51, 53, 233–4
　'failed performer' 42
　　'thwarted performer' 44
　'fellow adventurer' 233
　feedback to learner 109, 196
　flexibility (*see also* adaptability) 22, 28, 32, 34, 40, 68–9, 73, 74, 82, 112, 115, 157, 207, 210, 211, 233
　humour 28, 68, 234, 236
　identities 4, 17, 22, 29, 37–46, 54, 55, 91–2, 100, 261
　influences on teaching 13–23, 26, 27, 28, 29, 30–1, 32, 38, 43–4, 54–5, 97, 107, 109, 113–14, 232, 235, 243, 258
　isolation 1, 3, 59, 78, 80, 207, 258, 259
　job satisfaction 260
　learning from students 207
　lesson time constraints 78, 81, 82, 85, 98, 176, 211, 223
　lesson timetabling 66, 68, 69, 70, 73, 75 n.3, 78, 86, 223
　limitations 16, 214, 255, 262
　listening 3, 177, 179–180, 184, 198, 256
　　'Listen Empathetically, Strategize Together' (LEST) 7, 183
　master-apprentice mode 2, 17, 18, 53, 55, 58, 59, 105, 107, 108, 112, 115, 212, 233
　mentor-friend mode 2, 98, 105, 106, 108, 109, 113, 114, 115
　mindset 17, 58, 92, 114, 232, 235–7, 259
　mirroring learner 167
　modelling (*see also* demonstration) 141, 179–80, 181, 251, 161
　motivation 46, 70, 82, 100, 259
　multiple modalities 121
　novice, early-career and trainee teachers 2, 21, 32, 41, 46, 53, 57, 58, 68, 74, 258, 259

openness 22, 114, 153, 195, 232
outsider 20, 74, 193
peer learning 17–18, 22, 215, 259
perfectionism 30
performer (*see also* teacher-performer or performer-teacher) 29, 33, 37–46, 51, 52, 54, 55, 58, 93, 163, 170–1, 259
peripatetic teaching 65–75, 77–87
persona and personality 25–35, 233
planning 82, 157, 193, 196, 210, 245
praising pupils 31, 96, 125, 137, 199, 207, 208, 213, 220, 256
pressure 40, 85, 86, 107, 218, 222, 247
professional competence 110, 114, 114, 127
professional development (*see also* training) 1–4, 44, 51–9, 97, 195, 207, 215, 252, 253
professional regulation 52, 55, 59, 152, 215
professional relationships with school whole class teachers 65–75, 77–87
providing piano accompaniment in vocal lessons 110
pupils' parents' expectations 33, 70, 71, 74, 99, 111, 112, 114, 152, 177, 179, 193–4, 214, 218, 222, 263
reflection 1–3, 15, 17, 20, 21, 22, 26–8, 29, 30, 32, 34, 35, 97, 100, 108, 112, 113, 114, 115, 179, 192, 196, 215
resilience 31, 255–64
resource creation 243–53
respect for 41, 53, 82, 93, 105–6
roles 37–8, 39, 40, 41, 43, 44, 45, 51, 52, 53–5, 66, 78, 80, 81, 82, 92, 107, 108, 194, 197, 233, 244
scaffolding learning 142, 167, 198, 233
self-awareness 22, 28, 32, 34, 121, 262
self-compassion 259
specialist or non-specialist instrumental teacher 208
status of teacher 37–43, 66, 72
strategies for supporting learner motivation 9, 83, 179, 180, 182, 198, 210, 222, 234, 235, 247, 248, 251, 252–3, 256–7
stress 40–1, 223, 258
student-centred teaching 2, 17, 30, 31, 53, 55, 82, 93–4, 96, 97, 98–100, 105–15, 137–45, 175–6, 179, 193, 196–9, 208–14, 226, 233, 240, 244–53, 256–62
student-teacher relationship modes 2, 17, 29, 31, 53, 55, 59, 93, 96, 97, 98, 99, 105–15, 207, 208, 210, 233, 260
teacher-performer or performer-teacher (*see also* performer) 37–46, 54–5
training (*see also* professional development) 1–2, 22, 29, 30, 31, 33, 41, 42, 44–5, 51–9, 91–101, 105–15, 194, 195, 200, 206, 207, 243, 252–3, 261–2
unseen influences 14–23
values 16, 23, 29, 32, 40–41, 42, 43, 68, 82–5, 91–3, 106, 107, 115, 208, 234, 239
views on group and one-to-one lessons 84–5, 223, 246–8
vulnerability 257
well-being 45, 70, 92, 100, 255–64
instrumental technique 31, 83, 85, 96, 98, 109–10, 139, 165, 168, 169, 171, 180, 207, 208, 210, 211, 232, 213, 218, 219, 224, 233, 234, 236, 238, 239, 243, 247, 251, 256, 262
international master's students
cross-cultural adaptation 91–101, 105–15
instrumental teaching 96–101
language challenges 94, 119–29
motivation 94
returnee teachers 17, 107
self-presentation 114
value of qualification 107

jazz 139–42, 143, 234, 236

Kahneman (Systems 1 and 2) 19
Kindermusik 169, 172 n.1
knowledge (explicit and tacit) 167–8, 171
  collaboratively constructed 3, 233
  embodied 165, 166
Kodály 169

logical fallacies 13, 18–19
London College of Music 57, 135, 218, 221

Manchester Metropolitan University 57
mindfulness 169, 257, 259
mirror neurons 166

mistakes in learning 42, 96, 141, 209, 235–6, 237, 256, 257
music hubs 7, 40, 41, 52, 59 n.1, 75 n.1, n.2, 195, 200, 208, 246
music literacy skills 54, 151, 152
Music Mark (UK) 57, 58, 59
music notation 54, 93, 142, 151, 152, 154, 157, 164, 169, 197, 213, 220, 236, 244, 246, 249, 252
music performance anxiety 40, 42, 81, 96, 170, 226, 257, 262
music stands 177, 263–4
music subject terminology 119–29, 155, 213, 234
   pronunciation 121, 124, 125, 127
Music Teachers' Board (MTB) 153, 154, 218, 219, 221, 222, 224
music theory 54, 122, 124, 128, 136, 143, 149–59, 164
   compartmentalization of theory and practice 149
   role of piano in music theory 154
   theory examinations 152–4
musical analysis 84, 85, 144, 155, 157–8
musical arrangement 244–52
musical canon 149, 218
musical creativity 106, 110, 139, 140, 152, 164, 167, 169, 171, 209, 220, 232, 239, 240, 243–53, 257
musical diversity 105
musical expression 15, 18, 144, 164, 165, 167
   expressive movements 170
   imagery 170
   use of persona for expressive communication 170–1
musical 'feel' 142, 144, 157, 165, 167, 168, 231, 234, 235, 238, 240
Musical Futures (UK) 78
musical intervals 155, 157, 245
musical ornamentation 136, 138
musical performance 26, 33, 40–2, 45, 53, 55, 57, 81, 82, 83, 84, 85, 86, 136, 153, 163–5, 168, 170–1, 257, 259, 260, 264 (*see also* assessment – performance assessment and graded examinations)
musical understanding 155, 164, 169, 219, 243
Musicians' Union (MU) (UK) 57, 59, 66, 74

musicianship 153, 159, 210, 218, 219, 220, 226, 227, 240
'musicking' 163, 164, 166, 168, 169

National Curriculum for Music (UK) 78, 150, 151, 152
National Plan for Music Education (UK) 52, 199, 220

Ofsted (Office for Standards in Education, Children's Services and Skills) (UK) 75 n.1, 77–8, 87 n.1
online teaching 260–1, 262–3
ontology and ontological beliefs 14, 15
Orff 169, 258

pedagogical language 232–40
pedagogical resources 149, 177, 208, 262
   adaptable and adaptive resources 251
   creating material 243–53
   graphic scores 252
   using software 198, 247, 252
pedagogy
   dichotomising tendencies 17
   diverse approaches 105, 113–14, 150, 246, 147, 252
   pace of teaching 20, 98, 111, 137, 246
   pedagogy of correction (accuracy) 137, 139, 141
   risk 157
   safe space 171
philosophy 14–23
portfolio career 39–41, 44, 45, 46, 54, 66, 258, 259
Positivism 14, 17
Pragmatism 15
public liability insurance 58, 71

qualitative and quantitative – definitions 14

'real-world' research and orientation 3, 4, 232
reflection 21, 22, 29, 32, 34, 97, 100, 108, 110, 112, 113, 114–15, 179, 192, 196, 209, 215, 245, 249
   of learners 18, 83, 128, 140, 154, 169, 176, 196, 257, 260
research design and methods

non-participant observations 123
participant recruitment 67, 78, 108, 206, 220
questionnaire 78-9, 123
semi-structured interviews 67, 95, 108-9, 123, 139
survey 39, 205-6, 220-1
thematic text analysis 95, 108-9, 123, 232
written reflections 26, 244-9
researcher
  bias 108
  insider-outsider 108
  reflexivity 192
rock music 142-4, 154, 234
Rockschool 57, 154, 217, 218, 221, 222
Royal Birmingham Conservatoire, UK 55
Royal College of Music, UK 56, 57
Royal Northern College of Music, UK 57

safeguarding 69, 70, 193, 261
samba 238
school classroom music teachers 65-75, 77-87, 258-9, 264
social constructivism 108
socialization 38
spaces for teaching 68, 69-70, 71, 72, 73, 74, 260-1
  room hire charges 71, 73, 74
Suzuki 169, 172 n.1, 213

'teleomusical acts' 164
thematic analysis 26, 79, 95, 109, 123, 220-1, 232
  MAXQDA software 95, 109
Tianjin Juilliard School 56, 57
transfer students 7, 205-16

Trinity College London 57, 78, 125, 135, 153, 154, 155, 217, 218, 219, 221, 222, 224, 225
Trinity Laban Conservatoire, UK 56, 57
truth 17, 18
tuition books 231-40
  author positionality 239
  empathy with learner 233-5
  Igoe, *Groove Essentials* 231-40
  influence on learner mindset 235-7, 239-40
  teacher reflections on potential influence of tuition books 231-40
  writing style 232-9

universal reality 15
University of Exeter, UK 225
University of Sheffield, UK 151
University of West London 56, 57
University of York, UK
  MA Music Education: Group Teaching and Leadership 2
  MA Music Education: Instrumental and Vocal Teaching 2, 4, 6, 17, 20, 56, 108, 122-9, 231
    Talking About Music (TAM) 122-9
  MA Music Education with Performance 2
  Music Education Forum (MEF) 1, 3, 4, 38-9, 41, 264

workshops 16

Yandell, Naomi – *Fun Fair Blues* 155-7
yoga 258, 259

Zone of Proximal Development (Vygotsky) 245, 246